First published 1987
by Collins Publishers
100 Lesmill Road, Don Mills, Ontario

Canadian Cataloguing in Publication Data
Gabereau, Vicki.
This won't hurt a bit!
Includes index.
ISBN 0-00-217753-6
1. Interviews. 2. Biography – 20th century.
I. Gabereau (Radio program). II. Title.
CT120.G33 1987   920'.009'04   C87-094392-8

Printed and bound in Canada by John Deyell Company

Contents

For my mother
Veryl Filion

Acknowledgements

It is a certainty that I would not have dared to write a book were it not for Denise Bukowski, ace agent. She talked me into it and she nagged me on with it. There were at least thirty or forty occasions when I lost my nerve and seriously considered giving back the advance money, except that I had spent most of it the minute I got it. But in the end, I'm glad I persevered.

My family, who put up with papers all over the kitchen table for the past year, is glad too. Eve, my daughter, felt slightly neglected throughout the ordeal, but she did get to use my car a lot. My son, Morgan, cleverly placed himself in Ottawa and provided his advice long distance. Tom Rowe, with whom I live and who, at the very least, is a saint, was not so lucky. I am forever in his debt.

I am grateful to the CBC, and especially Radio Archives, for their co-operation and assistance. My thanks to Anne Elvidge for transcribing the tapes and to Elizabeth Wilson for helping me sort through the many transcripts.

It has been my great fortune to have worked with and for many talented people: in Toronto—Judy Brake, Kim Orchard, John Disney, Matt Blajer, Janice Parker, Tom Shipton, Kathryn O'Hara, March Thompson, Brian Dawes, Keith Duncan, Mark Lee, Ira Basin, and Ron Solloway; in Vancouver—Susan Englebert, Rosemary Allenbach, Elizabeth Wilson, Chuck Davis, Margie Taylor, Rochelle Collins, David Wisdom, Connie Smith, Doug I. Jones, Tod Elvidge, Gary Heald, John Wade, Brooke Forbes, Anne Elvidge, Don Hardisty, Rick Staehling, and J. B. Shayne; in London—Trudie Richards, Sue Western, Anne Koch, and Barbara Duncan; in New York—Linda Perry and Susan Farkas; in Los Angeles—Ken Zelig and Ralph Hart. There isn't one to whom I don't owe lunch. (What am I saying?)

Special thanks go to Alex Barris, who had a nightly spot on "Variety Tonight" featuring the music of the big-band era. He had an enormous following, as did Bob Pye, whose specialty was anything pre–big-band. I owe them more than lunch.

I loved working with editor Mary Adachi, who generally works with real writers. I thank her for making an exception.

At first I had no idea what to call this book, but I finally settled on *This Won't Hurt a Bit!* because apparently I say that to most guests. Now I say it to you and hope for the best.

ONE

Vaccinated with a Phonograph Needle

Radio grabbed me and hasn't let go yet. I'd say my obsession began as a kid when I won—well, sort of won—my very own radio in a contest. Always on the lookout for a little excitement, my best friend, Valerie Deyman, and I were delighted to learn that a new car dealership was to open up in Kerrisdale, the relentlessly middle-class neighbourhood in Vancouver where I grew up. Saturday was the day for the unveiling of the show-room, and hot dogs and other free stuff were to be offered, but only to children accompanied by adults. We lurked around until a suitable-looking couple appeared and then marched along with the unsuspecting souls until we had inhaled quite a few treats.

Naturally, the dealership ran a contest, and we filled out at least twenty-five forms before a salesman approached "our mother." Would she please tell her little darlings that that really was enough? By the time she finished explaining that we were strangers to her, we had fled across the street, howling.

That night the dealership called my house to say that I was the lucky winner of a radio, no less. Good God, my very own radio. You may not think, in a day when most people had television, that a radio was a big deal, but it was pink and would take batteries, which made it portable and too good to be true. I instantly called my pal to tell her of my good fortune. Somehow she did not see it quite that way. Wasn't it *our* radio? Didn't *we* enter the contest? The fact that the first name on the stub was mine, not hers, and that I, not she, had received the phone call didn't cut any ice with her. Flustered, I suggested that we share it. I never did and she never let me forget it.

How I loved that radio; I slept with it for years. It was on most of the time, especially at night, really late, when radio signals are crystal clear. San Francisco broadcaster Ira Blue, from the night spot the Hungry I, rattled on under my pillow with the likes of Lenny Bruce and assorted arty weirdos and musical madmen. A show from Salt Lake City gave me my first inkling of what a phone-in programme could accomplish.

And then came Webster—Jack that is. When, at the age of fourteen, I found Webster on the dial, he had been blasting for seven years with a variety of commentaries and a daily on-air explosion known as City Mike. The sound of his voice and his relentless approach made me wild with excitement. No one ever got off the hook, and to this day those who fall under his scrutiny quake, afraid to appear on his show but more afraid *not* to.

I went to school with Jack's daughter Jenny, a fair-faced and sane young woman, but I never had the nerve to ask her if I might watch her father in action. My father, for some years a press photographer, knew Webster from the *Vancouver Sun*, a newspaper that was staffed by journalists of considerable bravado. I would have asked for an introduction, but my father so loathed anything smacking of nepotism that that route was out. However, within the decade I was to meet Jack at a party. I happened to mention a passing interest in radio and he invited me to his studio.

Poor man, I followed him around for years; I drove him crazy. I'd go to his studio two or three times a week and watch everything. He has since announced over national airwaves on *my* radio show that when I was a kid I was "the most aggressive, tough, roustabout young woman I ever knew in my life." My poor beleaguered parents, who suffered a reign of terror from my earliest years, agreed. Very often, and I mean often, when it appeared that the jig was well and truly up, I would lock myself in the bathroom, seeking asylum from Mama, whose name is Veryl. I was too stupid to realize that the pins in the door hinges were on the outside and she knew how to pry them out.

In the fifties Kerrisdale closely resembled a small town, with an active main street and the regular assortment of shops. My father, a photographer, had a portrait studio, and my friend Valerie's mother operated a gift shop that sold cards for all occasions, and china and silver items. I especially coveted the porcelain budgies, which came in three colours—blue, green and yellow (what else)—and were very big sellers. All Valerie's friends received one at Christmas and birthdays. Young girls made a habit of collecting such things then.

Valerie and I knew every merchant within a six-block radius, and we made it our life's work to inspect all their stock. We must have been a constant source of irritation. We once harassed a local lawyer for weeks on end, insisting that we were fascinated by the law, and would he please be so kind as to show us how it all worked? This patient man dragged us to court rooms and let us play with the typewriter and generally upset the daily workings of his office until, finally, he called our mothers and begged for release from this commitment. He had thought we'd go away sooner rather than later; he was wrong, we were steadfast. We were nine years old and momentarily crushed at our dismissal.

Unlike now, I was then a joiner. When I was twelve I taught Sunday school and had in my charge, for one hour a week, a rather dandy little troupe of six- to eight-year-olds. They were a well-behaved lot, and we produced more than our required number of paintings and drawings of a Biblical nature. I delighted in telling them the tales set out in the Sunday School Teachers' Primer. However, when the minister discovered that his flock was being tutored by someone who had not even been christened or trained in any way, he dumped me.

I fared better as a Brownie, although I am still the only person I know who failed in her first attempt to secure her Golden Hand, a badge awarded for mastery of a number of tasks, like the tying of knots, the knitting of a six-inch square, and the making of fruit blancmange, all fields in which I achieved little expertise. My second try, you'll be relieved to know, was successful and I was able to receive my badge with all my Brownie buddies in the ceremony known as Flying Up to Guides.

As it happens, that spring the one and only Lady Baden-

Powell, widow of the founder of the Scouting movement, was in Vancouver and participated in the award-giving. The Brownies stood in a line forming a coil, and each girl in her turn delivered the Brownie salute to the by-then-aged Lady and proudly took her badge. As I reached the inner part of the coiled line, my anticipation was so great that at the precise moment of meeting I laughed. Loudly. I don't remember if Lady Baden-Powell said something funny or if I just panicked, but my mother, sitting in the audience, was quite stunned. Why had her darling child been the only one to utter a sound? Everyone else had been so dignified and silent. But she still took me to the White Spot for a chicken burger to celebrate.

Dogs have always been my favourite creatures, and until recently I have always owned one. My father, also a dog nut, and I used to spend hours poring over magazines and books dedicated to the canine, and he collected specialty journals from all over the world. He would stop and talk to any dog on the street; they all fell for him and never showed any aggression. Huge bloodhounds were known to sit on his lap and cuddle and mostly howl. My father was a large man and yet he was particularly fond of small breeds—dachshunds and Pekes. He had had them as a child, and I don't think you ever lose that allegiance to a breed.

I have owned four dachshunds: Lorelei, Ambrose, Fenwick, and Prince; one bull-terrier, Hilda, and a black Lab, Wayne. Lorelei was my first pet, save for the odd stray cat, and she and I muddled about together from the time I was eight until she died when I was fifteen. My father was so distraught at her death that he punched the wall in his darkroom. I loved him for that.

We were the best of pals, Lorelei and I, and she must have been a dog of great tolerance because she never seemed to object to the un-doglike situations into which she was delivered. She loved to go for walks and I would take her on any errand, but the problem lay in the routing to the store. She would not pass on the same side of the street as the offices of Doctors Powell, a wife-and-husband team of veterinarians whom I worshipped but whom she hated. I would try to trick her, by talking or distracting her by throwing a ball or promising a cookie. Nothing ever worked. She pulled and strained and sat down and exhibited mule-like stubbornness, and I never won the battle.

There were, of course, times when she just had to be taken to the vet for shots or whatever, and while she wouldn't walk past the office, she would happily ride. I had an old doll carriage and would put her in it. She could then be wheeled right into the office before she knew she was trapped. Perhaps it was the scent of the plastic buggy that confused her sense of smell until it was too late.

I once took her skating, but only once. My friend and I both had Barbara Ann Scott dolls (please tell me you remember the 1948 Olympic Gold Medal figure skater), hence two pairs of dolly skates. They fitted little Lorelei to a T. Over to the rink we trekked. I strapped the pink skates on the unsuspecting dachshund and put her on the ice. She wobbled a bit and the skates fell off, but then she zoomed around with great relish until I was afraid her unprotected paws would freeze. Eventually she was captured and taken home. I think I got into trouble. I usually did.

For as many years as I can remember (now quite a few), I have had a conqueror's attitude to getting as many jobs in quick succession as possible. The veterinarians Powell were the first to employ me. Each day after school I would walk a number of dogs up and down the lane behind their office. They paid me twenty-five cents. I would have done it for free and forever, but unfortunately the doctors moved their operation to Vancouver Island.

I would not, however, have been too thrilled to do my next job for free. I only mention it because I have never since known such specialization in the workplace. In the days when men's trousers had cuffs, it was essential for dry cleaners to brush out the lint, otherwise the process of dry cleaning would cause the fuzz to solidify and remain for all time. Armed with a small brush, I sat on a stool designed for an elf, which I was not, with a pile of trousers in front of me until the day's orders were ready for the machine. I knew dry cleaning was not to be my chosen field.

An insurance company that employed me briefly was horrified to discover that I had cost them three hundred and fifty dollars over and above the handsome one dollar per hour they paid me in wages. Before hiring me they had given me an aptitude test, which I had apparently passed; it was one of the few tests I had passed in many years. It asked, in a multiple-choice format, "What is the Muslim Book of Prayer?" I knew that one. "Where would one find the taiga?" I knew that one, too. The insurance company thought I was a genius, but then so did I.

They took me on as a typist, but it was painfully obvious within the first five minutes on the job that I was no good. My task was to type, with no corrections, life-insurance policies. In eight hours at my desk I produced not one perfect document. All my desk drawers, my purse, the garbage can, and even the pail belonging to the efficient girl next to me (she didn't know about the taiga but she typed as if possessed) were filled to bubbling over with scores of two-ply, very expensive, $25-a-form insurance policies. I quit the job seconds before being fired.

My next job was with a local private nursing home as a nurse's aide. A dollar an hour and all the bedpans I could wield. Frankly, I was a natural. The hours stank but the uniforms were cute. I worked nights, 11:00 P.M. to 7:00 A.M. There was a registered nurse in charge of a battery of four or five aides, some of whom had trained as registered nurses, mostly abroad, and had been unable to take the time to retrain or upgrade in Canada. These women knew their business, but I was basically a domestic.

Geriatric medicine has its superb moments. Contrary to what many think about the aged, old people are not dead people, nor are they wrinkled children. Many happy and hilarious hours were spent listening to tales of the Boer War, told by a pair of craggy veterans who acted as if they had seen it all. Maybe they had. These two buddies always had a stash of brandy and often had to be routed out of the reception area when they became too animated.

This was not a chronic-care facility, so most of the residents were in relatively good shape, certainly in good enough condition to be found in each other's company at what might be considered a disreputable hour. There were several occasions when a particularly affectionate couple, she at least eighty and he nearer ninety, were suspected of advancing their relationship beyond the hand-holding stage.

Although this hospital was not designed for the very sick, there were a few exceptions. One woman of whom I was fond could never have known my feelings towards her. I had been attending to this woman, on and off, for nearly a year and she had hardly moved and never spoken a word. She had not had one visitor. We knew almost nothing about her save her name and age and that she might have been a teacher. She weighed at most eighty pounds. She was suffering with what we now call Alzheimer's Disease and was in a permanent fetal position. Or so it was thought. One night, close to 3:00 A.M., I found her sitting completely upright and engaged in a desperate attempt to get out of bed. The sight of this frail soul struggling sent me flying to find the head nurse. Within minutes every nurse on the floor came to witness this bizarre sight. She was encouraged to lie down; she refused. She asked to get up but was told it would be too dangerous for her. She was lifted into a wheelchair and for fifteen minutes I wheeled her up and down the hallway. She whispered that it was enough; she had just wanted to know where she was. On her return to her room she drank a cup of tea from a spouted cup. In response to my questions she confirmed what we had suspected. Yes, she had been an elementary-school teacher—for fifty years. She had never married, and she had no family. By the end of the shift she died in her sleep.

In a hospital of approximately seventy-five patients of a certain vintage, there is an expected loss of two or three people a month. Yet weeks can go by uneventfully and then, curiously, many beds will empty. I never got used to it. At seventeen my sense of immortality no longer existed.

As befits that age, I was restless, reckless and disjointed, a bane to my parents, and it was becoming abundantly clear that my high-school career was close to being terminated. In other words, I quit before being fired. I often wonder what would have become of me if my father had not launched a campaign for my rehabilitation in January of 1965.

One of the great joys of my father's life was his love and affection for his best friend. They met in 1943, in the mess at the Officer's Training Centre at Gordon Head, near Victoria, only days after my father and mother had married. Unlike many wartime friendships that fade after the camaraderie of battle has passed, these two one-pip wonders remained fast and furious friends till the day my father died, forty years and six months to the day after that first meeting. Harry Francis Filion and Pierre Francis Berton laughed, screamed, and drank as much as God and nature would allow.

After the war they found themselves working in the newspaper business. My old man took the pictures and Pierre wrote the words. They must have been good words, too, because soon enough Pierre was an ace reporter. In March 1946 he married his colleague Janet Walker. My father was the best man and mother hid, not wanting her picture taken huge with child and wearing a dress she truly hated. My parents produced only me, but the Bertons went on to be responsible for considerably more—eight.

Nine, if you count me. In the spring of 1964 my panic-stricken father sent me off to Kleinburg, Ontario to live with the Bertons. He had to; I'd quit school, was driving to the States every day (some guy at a taco stand, in Bellingham I think), and I was running around in my spare time with a tugboat sailor, who by the way turned out rather well. I was shipped eastward for a course of enlightenment at the hands of the Berton Squad. My father's parting words, as he handed me an extra fifty dollars and a copy of the latest *New Yorker*, included "be polite," and "don't drink gin." Twenty minutes out of his sight I met an Australian in the train corridor and graciously accepted his offer of a drink—a Pink Lady laced with gin. At least I was polite.

Shortly after my arrival at the fabled household I discovered that I was to be put back in school, and not given a swell job in television as I had come to imagine. The Berton children (it makes me laugh to call them children, now that we are all so old, old, old) were all, unlike me, brilliant students, cooperative, helpful around the house, and hardly ever talked back to their parents. I could not believe it. Could this be an act? Twenty-odd years later I'm here to tell you that it was no act. These people were civilized, even the teenagers. For example, only once, in the six months that I lived there, did I see Penny, the oldest, get into trouble, and even then it was my fault. I had conned her into helping me paint moustaches on all the Ilya Kuryakin (David McCallum's character in "The Man from U.N.C.L.E.") pin-ups that her younger sister Patsy had lovingly pasted to her walls. The child became hysterical when she discovered our handiwork. Penny and I rolled about on the floor. Janet Berton was not a happy woman. Patsy has forgiven me, but only last week.

Life at Kleinburg was a constant source of surprise to this kid from Vancouver. All manner of famous folk graced the backyard; I nearly fainted at meeting Johnny Wayne and Frank Shuster. The now late but then very much alive cartoonist and painter George Feyer made an occasional appearance and drew caricatures on the kids' arms and legs. Harold Town made me dance at a party; he was a "free spirit" and I was not . . . yet. There were exotic Hungarian men who drank endless cups of espresso. One of them in particular raved on about older women, and I couldn't wait to be one. Now I am—what was the hurry?

Janet and Pierre dedicated themselves to a number of fund-raising events, and one project was to raise money for a halfway house for men coming out of prison. There was to be a huge party at a Toronto shopping centre, with a celebrity guest list.

One week before the gala, which featured Dunk the Actor and stuff like that, a series of publicity photographs were to be taken at the Bertons'. The European circus, which was to be the main attraction, brought along a few lions for the picture-taking. The female Bertons and I had been well warned that a really good-looking French lion trainer was to accompany the beasts. We were rather thrilled, as most of the males that we encountered were either the appalling age of thirty-five or callow youths.

The day of the photo session arrived at last and it was with great anticipation that I opened the front door. I was to find there, however, not the sturdy hulk of the lion trainer but the somewhat emaciated, long-haired vision of the magician. But he *was* French. His name was and is Michel. I married him six months later, and we had two children, Morgan (1967) and Eve (1970), and we lived together for the better part of two decades.

I suppose in the legal and Victorian sense, I was no longer the responsibility of my parents. You wouldn't have known it, given the endless harping for funds. Consistently they refused me, insisting that I was a big girl and ought to make my own way in the world. Time was limping on and it was becoming more evident daily that some career route was going to have to be established. The list of go-nowhere jobs was becoming very long indeed; sales clerk, canvas-banner salesperson, copywriter, waitress, hostess, beer slinger, receptionist, bird cage attendant, cocktail waitress, balloon salesperson, body-painting franchiser (forget that one), night-school teacher of macramé, gardener, street flower seller, cab driver, toy demonstrator, elephant transporter, two-bit actor. Let's stop here.

The Actors Theatre in Toronto offered classes in movement (that was good, because I could still do that) and drama. What could be so hard about acting, anyway? Well it turns out, almost everything. The drama was the especially hard part. I couldn't do it at all, and it became rather embarrassing. The patient souls who attempted to instruct me in the rudiments of stage acting were stumped. I must have tried the "Father died just a year ago,

... Irina" scene from *Three Sisters* thirty or forty times; each worse than the last. The people who operated the theatre were honest and begged me to take back my money. But no, I kept on and on. It wasn't that the instructors didn't like me; it was just that I was hopeless. But I was still slave to the actor notion.

In addition to the more serious side of studying, I thought I'd try my hand at a once-a-week comedy improvisation course at the Three Schools of Art in Toronto. Lorne Michaels, now the producer of "Saturday Night Live" was teaching (that might be too formal a word) a group of perspiring comics—many of whom have gone on to great fame—Dan Akroyd and writer/comedienne Valri Bromfield. When I saw the quality of the students and their skills, I knew that my options were running out.

The Actors Theatre, by then called the Toronto Centre for the Arts, headed by a very funny guy named David Dalton, allowed me back—not to act, but to make coffee and run their Sunday jazz concerts. Within two weeks I thought I was Sol Hurok.

At about the same time, I managed to secure a position with a clown troupe known as Puck-Rent-A-Fool. They had been a trio—Frazier Mohawk, Lynn Cavanagh (a.k.a. Penny Loafer, Mia Culpa and Flower Potts) and Mark Parr (a.k.a. Abrevo Khazad)—but had decided that a fourth fool was required. I became Rosie Sunrise.

Now that year, 1974, was a municipal election year in Toronto and the campaign was shaping up to be very dull. David Crombie was facing his second term as mayor and there was a possibility of acclamation. Even to my apolitical eye, this was an undesirable situation, so I casually suggested to Clown Commander Mohawk that we (remember that "we") run for mayor, just to liven things up. When he jumped at the idea, I knew I was in deep. Any campaign, even a bogus one, is an enormous undertaking. It had been my idea to run the four of us as one candidate, preferably in all different directions, but it was quickly decided that I was to run alone. "Rose Goes" was the verdict. I tried to protest that I was a reasonably respectable mother of two. . . . And what about my mother? She'll have my face on a plate. I couldn't win; they thought my face on a plate was a good promotion gimmick. Fortunately we couldn't afford it.

We couldn't afford much. Like lunch, or gas for my car. We always used my car. I was the only one who had one. It was a vintage Volkswagen van (I'll bet you guessed that) and Frazier insisted we paint likenesses of us all over the sides. Although the paint job was done by an artist and the giant signs on the doors saying ROSIE FOR MAYOR were executed beautifully, it was still rather a trial to go to the supermarket. The sight of it caused a tremendous scene, yet my kids thought it fun. This too would pass.

From the moment the Rent-A-Fool (later known as the Nuevo Clown Partie) candidate had been declared, the press covered our every move. They loved us. What a laugh, they exclaimed, at last a little fun. But then they turned on us. We were accused of nothing short of blasphemy. I suppose in the cold light of day they discovered their journalistic principles, accountability, and all. It didn't help our cause either that two other oddball candidates declared within days after us, the major contender being Rik of the Universe. Now this was a man of vision. He wanted to change the name of Toronto to Miami so that the weather would get better. Who could argue? The other fellow was less appealing—a Fascist, whose name I won't bother mentioning.

Our campaign, which lasted six weeks, cost about seven hundred dollars, forty of which was raised through donations. We were not too good at hustling money. One of our major contributors (twenty dollars) was future mayor Art Eggleton. Poor soul, I've never let him forget his former affiliation. At least he had a sense of humour. As did Morton Shulman (one-time coroner, MLA, and author) who, for some unknown reason, praised our participation in the election. I think he thought we were demented.

We worked like dogs. To get attention we staged a ribbon-cutting ceremony to open the Spadina Ditch, a hole in the ground that has never become the Spadina Expressway. The event even made the evening news and "The National." But the fact that I was on national T.V. in full clown regalia, leaping about like a lunatic, did not endear me to my mum. My father thought it hilarious and wanted to tell all their friends, especially their journalist friends, but he was forbidden to mention it on pain of death. I'm pretty sure he called Vancouver columnist Hymie Koshevoy within seconds.

By all accounts, Mayor Crombie was amused by the chaos surrounding his campaign, unlike some of his workers who were less enthusiastic. On several occasions when we showed up at his speeches, we sent shudders down the spines of the zealots.

But Crombie was more than willing to have his face in the same frame as mine, and frankly I think the whole performance showed him to be a good sport. I don't suppose he considered Rosie Sunrise to be much of a threat to his office. I did suggest that if it came down to the wire, I would be willing to let him be the mayor during the day and I would settle for being the night mayor. Fair is fair.

I am sure it was Richard Comber, a legitimate political organizer, whom we had talked into designing our campaign for no money (for the campaign or him), who came up with the idea of taking our message (message?) into the schools. It wasn't easy persuading the school board to let us perform our show, a tight little extravaganza, in elementary-school gymnasiums, but they finally decided that we were reasonably respectable and were unlikely to corrupt the children. At the end of each show we told the kiddos that I was the Clown Candidate and if elected I would push to lower the voting age to nine. After all, if you were old enough to take the street car by yourself, surely you were old enough to vote. We gave each child a sticker bearing Rosie's face and our slogan VOTE EARLY—VOTE OFTEN. Their parents must have wanted to murder us because those stickers had a glue on the back that continues to defy all solvents.

To this day people still ask about one campaign promise, that if elected (big if) we would mate the CN Tower with the Windsor Tunnel. It appeared in *Time* magazine but I never did say it, I swear. I know who did though. It was a product of the mind of our campaign manager, Gene Taylor, who worked for CITY-TV. He was the kind of guy that every big city needs, a real booster. So the credit for the remark must go to him, please.

As election day drew near, I started to worry that we would be humiliated at the polls. What gall. I think I was getting awfully close to taking it seriously. My stage name actually appeared on the ballot. Believe me, it was quite a startling sight to see it there on election day. SUNRISE, Rosie, Clown. I marked an X beside my name, as did nearly three thousand others. Peter Gzowski, in an interview, came armed with the true total, but I've never been one for specifics.

So, I didn't win. However, the publicity Puck-Rent-A-Fool garnered put us in big demand for the Christmas season, and we managed to pay our bills and buy the odd present for our confused relatives. The only leftover was the van, the one with the faces and the ROSIE FOR MAYOR sign on the doors. It was not quite as funny after the euphoria of the election faded away. My parents came from Vancouver on vacation, thinking the dust had cleared. I went to pick them up at the airport in the only vehicle I had, and they wouldn't get in the car. "Excuse me, but we don't think we know you." They took a cab. No sense of humour, these people. Days later the car died and was dragged away to the junk yard, and not a tear was shed.

The new year of 1975 presented its own set of problems, mostly financial, as business started to fall off and clown fever was ebbing. I was by now twenty-eight, with not a job prospect in sight, and even I was beginning to worry, so I was quick to jump at the offer of an appearance on an open-line show at radio station CHIC (Jack Webster liked to call it C-Hick), hosted by the now late Paul Richards. He thought that it would be amusing if I were to come and answer questions regarding the election and why in God's name anybody would do such a thing. During the interview, which lasted three hours, I asked him on the air if by any chance he needed a replacement. Although he was slightly taken aback, he said he'd ask the boss . . . the boss said maybe . . . I nagged . . . the boss said yes . . . but if I screwed up he'd kill me. It was a chance I had to take.

This radio station had a talk-all-day format, and after the initial two-week stint was up and Richards returned to his post, the guy on the afternoon shift saw his chance and took his vacation. I had a job for another two weeks. The process was repeated with the third guy, who never came back. I'd been on the air, raving on about anything, everything, for almost six weeks and there hadn't been a lawsuit, so it was decided that I could have the job permanently. What luck!

I was truly bad, completely unbridled and, except for an ability to keep the swearing under control, would say almost anything. Very often the boss, Harry Allen, was seen pressing his nose to the studio window in a desperate attempt to throttle me. I lasted just over a year and I still think it was the best job I ever had. Two hundred dollars in a bag every Friday—it was a good deal. I knew I'd found my game.

How is it that a radio station would hire a complete green-horn? It is a question I've asked myself. Was it blind faith or bald stupidity? I go for the blind-faith theory, but then, wouldn't you? I had, after all, been a student of open-line from childhood and I understood the basic principle: throw out an idea to which callers can peg their own two-cents' worth. I liked to choose the most volatile subjects, because they tended to cause the listeners irritation and almost forced them to call. Let's face it, if you don't have callers, you might as well go home. There is nothing more pathetic than an open-line host begging for calls.

I have always considered that running a show of this order is close in approach to selling a used car: don't let up. Canada has always been a hotbed of open-liners, with Vancouver being the major moving force. They were popular in that city before they caught on in Toronto, Montreal, and elsewhere. The argument against them is that people with little or no concrete information on a particular subject are allowed air-time to drone away, often feeding the misconceptions of the like-minded. Yet many open-line hosts have taken on the role of ombudsman and been of great public service.

Listeners to call-in programmes are often addicted, either to the host or to the other callers; a hot-line dose is a daily requirement. There is always a battery of regulars, those people who are guaranteed to call on any given topic. I had three regular callers. They were amusing and smart, and I was thankful for that. They appeared to know each other and occasionally seemed to be in cahoots. One fellow, from Mississauga, a self-confessed right-winger who called himself Mr X., provided a great deal of entertainment on my show. At the other end of the spectrum was a fellow who called himself Buddy: he loved to take on Mr X., and the two would publicly abuse each other. Their confrontations caused a lot of fireworks and the audience lapped it up. They were as much part of the show as I was, if not more. The third attraction was a woman. I never identified her in real life, unlike the other two who confessed their real names to me off air. She was dubbed Dearie and was, as far as I could tell, a woman of some years who was stuck at home; open-line was her form of diversion. She was English and had been well educated. Basically her role was to denounce the other two. I loved her. She would recite poetry and Shakespeare to illustrate her points. Oh Dearie, where are you now?

It is essential to keep an open-line show moving, and the temptation to keep even a good caller on the line must be resisted. Advertising revenue is directly related to the number of calls that come into the programme; more calls—more dollars, so it's not in the station's interest to let callers stay on the line for more than two or three minutes. You rarely hear heavy conversations about serious subjects on an open-line show, because even with a good guest, you might get twenty-five calls. If you bring on an astrologer, you get about two hundred. So you know what that means. If you want to keep your job, you go with the astrologer.

All open-line shows are required to be on a delay system, generally seven seconds, so it is fairly easy to spot an idiot who wants to take advantage of the situation. And believe me there *are* a lot of idiots out there.

TWO

Born Pregnant

Buddy, the frequent caller to the open-line show at CHIC, took it upon himself to contact Krista Maeots, who was then executive producer of "Morningside," to suggest that I be on the show. I was thankful that he called, and stunned when she did. (She practised something many people don't, she followed up every lead, just in case.) The interview went especially well and she invited me to do an "on-air" audition. I did. She suggested a desk job as a researcher. I took it.

When Don Harron arrived on the scene as host, in the fall of 1977, Krista gave me another chance to be on the air. This time it worked. I did a piece with Harron every Wednesday for the next four years. My focus of attention was supposed to be anything. Mostly they were stupid book reviews and profiles of oddities, people and otherwise. The preparation for these weekly spots generally took this line. A producer would call and say, "Wednesday's got a twelve-minute hole—fill it." I would then scratch around and find something about which I could blather on for the twelve minutes. But the instant I showed up at the studio, armed with my material, I would be told to edit fast—they needed only five minutes now. This situation arose because I was last item on the show, and as each guest in the third hour was given an extra minute or so, my time allotment would shrink. Most listeners and, indeed, CBC management thought I was too erratic on the air. I talked too fast and made them nervous. What they didn't know was that I was trying to get that twelve minutes of material into a five-minute spot. At least I was enthusiastic.

One particular morning I noticed that Harron was beginning to turn blue trying to get me to shut up. Finally I realized that the show was nearly over, thirty seconds to the news, to be exact. "Just one last thing," I squeezed, "do you realize that the reproductive cycle of the aphid is so rapid that the female aphid is actually born pregnant?" With hardly a hair's breadth left before the news, Harron said, "Yes sir, the title of Vicki Gabereau's latest book, *Born Pregnant*." I promised him that if I ever was foolish enough to commit to paper all this stuff that I would call it *Born Pregnant*. The combined generosity of executive producer Gary Michael Dault (who succeeded Krista Maeots) and Harron kept me on the air longer than I otherwise might have been allowed.

Bruce Steele, the producer of "Anybody Home?," a kids show that ran for several years, also gave me work. At one stage, after his host had been reassigned, he thought he might like to hire me. The verdict from management was basically, "No thank you," or a variation on the theme, "Not while there is a breath left in my body." Still, he continued to let me do small documentaries on kids in the circus and movie star kids and sick kids.

Those were heady days when CBC had some money. It was getting to be less and less money, but still enough to take a show out of the studio. Bruce wanted to take "Anybody Home?" on the road, to places like La Ronge, Saskatchewan, and tape enough material to be included in three or four programmes. He needed, in addition to his host, David Schatsky, and his associate producer, Patsy Pehleman, an extra body to prepare some research and set up guests and do a few interviews. He took me. The resulting programmes were a great success, and I like to think that the many native kids, who demonstrated their traditional ways of setting snares to trap small animals for food and skins, got a kick out of hearing themselves on the radio.

Summer 1980 was fast approaching and I had the feeling that Gary Michael Dault had yet to choose a replacement host for Harron, who was about to go on leave for the summer. (A little time off so he could write a couple of books, maybe a play or two, and do a bit of acting, paint the house, a few relaxing things like that.)

"Gary," I simpered, "what about me?"

"Not a chance," was his encouraging reply. "First of all, you'd be too expensive."

Was that all? Well, did I have a plan for him. The reason I was expensive was that I was a free-lancer and not a staff announcer. The cost of free-lancers comes directly out of the programme budget, while staff announcements are salaried personnel. With a limited summer budget, a free-lancer as host was out of the question.

"But how about my becoming a summer-relief staff announcer?" I asked.

I knew I had him . . . almost. Miraculously, for the first time in my work life, things fell into place. The man who attends to the staff announcers agreed, management didn't throw up on the rug, Harron thought it was OK, and I nearly did a back flip.

And then the fear set in. What had I done? How could I do it? It was one thing to dither around for five minutes a week with Harron holding my hand, but it was quite another to take responsibility for three hours a day of real radio—Network CBC radio, which people listened to for proper information, not madcap raving.

I am not talking about butterflies here. I'm talking face-the-firing-squad, the guillotine-or-the-noose kind of fear. In the days leading up to my first show on June 2, 1980, I was almost unable to breathe. Certainly I was unable to carry on a normal conversation with my kids and family. I was a basket case.

It didn't help a whole lot that one of my first guests was Gordon Liddy. The producer in charge of setting up that piece spent almost the entire weekend talking up the life of Liddy with me. We were more than prepared for any tack Mr Liddy might take. He had just published his autobiography, *Will,* and it was controversial, to say the least. He was to be the last guest on that first show, and when he walked into the studio (I had hoped he might have a bout of malaria and not show up) and made a small toasting gesture with his styrofoam coffee cup, I looked towards the fire escape. Only a greater fear kept me nailed to the chair.

Despite his formidable reputation, Gordon Liddy terrified me a lot less than I had figured. By the time we were into the conversation, I had calmed down a bit. I had wanted at all costs to avoid talking about whether he had really eaten a rat; everybody had asked him that and everybody already knew the answer. Yes, he had, and he hadn't eaten an entire rat, just a fragment, an exercise in overcoming his fear of the rodent. Look, some people have peculiar ways of handling things, right? I did want to know if by chance he was armed. Unlikely, I thought, because he had just crossed the border and that kind of international transportation of arms is frowned on. He did, however, respond in the most remarkable way.

"Well, Mrs Gabereau (now picking up a pencil), only that I have in my hand this object, a pencil, which I could ram in your throat, through to your brain, instantly killing you."

"But you wouldn't do that, would you Mr Liddy?"

"No, Mrs Gabereau, I would not." He then went on to explain that one can always be armed, not necessarily with a gun.

It's a wonder I got through that day. It's a wonder they kept me. My lack of confidence was reinforced by an unfortunate piece of paper referred to as the Listeners' Response Sheet. This frightening bit of business is prepared by the operators at CBC to give the crews an idea of what the listeners are saying. What they or at least one particular listener was saying was that he was not pleased at the choice of summer host and he figured it was going to be a long summer, if he could stand it at all. His words ran through my mind at every opportunity. It took six weeks before this sensation left me, and I might still be tortured by him had he not written later to say that although he was still not smitten with me, I had shaped up enough to be tolerable. Grateful . . . was I grateful. As the three months, which had seemed at the beginning of June to be an eternity, slid past, I grew to like the job. Even love it.

Two weeks before the end of the "Morningside" run I got a call from Edmonton. Their morning show, always a two-host programme, lacked one component, and would I be interested? I hesitated for what seemed like two or three seconds and said by golly, I thought I just might be. I flew to Edmonton that weekend and met Bill White, the director of radio and a man (along with his family) who has come to be my dear friend. I think Bill White must have been a champion encyclopedia salesman in a past life, because there was no escaping his offer. I finished "Morningside" a week later, on a Friday. By Sunday my car was packed and my son and daughter and I headed west. We looked like the Beverly Hillbillies, only worse.

The move to Edmonton was hardly in the mould of a regular corporate transfer. There were no days of staying in a fancy hotel while adjusting to your new city. No luncheon meetings with enthusiastic real-estate types while they find you the perfect house. I was not exactly Priority A, so I was given gas money and bit more, and that was it. I love it when people think the CBC blows money on this kind of thing. They surely didn't blow it on this occasion.

I couldn't have cared less. I had a job and that was more than I bargained on. We rented a house—actually a box—with four rooms and several motorcycling enthusiasts who lived and roared in the basement. We had no furniture except two beds I bought for the kids and a table of no aesthetic value. I rented a T.V. The house was fully carpeted, not an added bonus. The previous tenant seemed to have been impressed with rainbow shag. Each room had a different two-tone combination—green and green, red and pink, blue and blue. My kids thought it was like camping: I did not. We lasted at that address for eight nasty weeks.

But the work was good. Mind you, I didn't know much about Alberta, and it was with great relief that my co-host, Gail Hulnick (now the host of "The Early Edition" in Vancouver), was willing to do all the hard-news stories for the first few weeks. The years 1980 and 1981 were hot in Alberta and there was great wrangling with the federal government over the energy policy. I had done a few oil stories, but nothing of the depth and magnitude that was required here. Gail knew everything and kept me from looking the fool until I figured things out. All early news and information programmes are a grind, and they allow little time for other life. I was in no position to complain when you consider that Hulnick, while working a shift that would devastate an Olympian, was also engaged (that too) in studying for her second university degree, honours in business administration. She already had one in journalism. I could hardly keep up with the laundry and she was writing 5,000-word essays at night. She couldn't have slept much, but she never whined.

We were quite a good pair. She handled the hard stuff and I goofed around, but as I recall, after the initial shock the audience liked us and our ratings were more than decent. We did, at first, get some mail from listeners who said they would rather die than hear those two broads squawk at each other. We paid no attention . . . hardly. But I guess they got over it, because the complaints eventually stopped.

Gail has always taken her work more seriously than I have, but she was truly excited when I suggested that we rent a farm animal for April Fool's Day. The idea was to sneak the creature into the studio, hoping to drive the producer, Don Young, crazy. Gail and I went to the You Name It rental place, a small farm in the valley, to pick up a sheep. They informed us that the sheep had a cold (do sheep have colds?) and therefore we would have to settle for a goose. Hardly the same amusement factor. I had had fairly good results with sheep rentals before, so I was upset.

OK, OK, I'll tell you The Other Sheep Story. Shortly after the Toronto mayoralty song-and-dance was over, a friend of mine, Patricia Gruben, now a film teacher at Simon Fraser University in B.C., was working as a props person for TV Ontario, and she got me a job as a researcher on "Nightmusic." "Nightmusic" was definitely ahead of its time. The host was Reiner Schwartz, a former drummer and disc jockey of considerable merit. He was known as an extravagant broadcaster, who would say anything that came into his head. He had, and still does have, a gift for talking non-stop, without interruption, for indefinite periods of time. Reiner was also a terrific interviewer, going way past the "it must be hell on the road" kind of approach to conversing with musicians, his specialty. This was a five-night-a-week pro-gramme that varied enormously. One night would feature all music with pictures—old film stock, new stuff, funny film shorts, and electronic pieces. Yet another would feature an interview with a band or performer of some sort, and still another would be just Reiner carrying on.

One day Reiner decided that what was needed for that eve-ning's programme (always one-hour and live) was sheep. The sheep would mill around the studio while he talked and played music. Three sheep would do the trick. It was my job to secure them. And I did.

I drove out to the farm that kept animals for rental to the film and television business (not just sheep, but horses, goats, ducks). I pushed the three sheep into the back of my then still-function-ing VW van and drove back to the loading bay at TV Ontario. Sheep, in my opinion, are pretty darn dumb, and having had no experience with handling them, I had a rough time trying to con-vince these blockheads to get into the elevator. One of them had horns, so I pulled him by the head into the elevator and the other two followed.

A couple of camera operators came to my rescue and helped me put the sheep in the studio. We were about twenty minutes to air time. The sheep immediately stood in the corner and would not come out. No manner of coaxing, prodding, or tempting with food would entice these lamb chops to budge. Reiner went on the air with not a milling sheep in sight. He just carried on and made the occasional remark about the shy creatures in the corner. No one in the audience believed him, because they couldn't see them.

Finally the show was over (it was midnight by now), and it was time for me to take the sheep back into the elevator and into the truck and back out to the farm some twenty miles away. I didn't mind—it was a job in television and I still thought it too, too exciting. Once again I herded the sheep into the van. When I opened the loading bay door, there blocking the way was an expensive foreign vehicle, the owner of which was nowhere to be found. Next step was to call the sleeping sheep owner. "Never mind" said he, "bring 'em back in the morning."

Leaving my van full of sheep, I took a cab home, taking my colleague Patricia Gruben with me for a small glass of wine. Within seconds of our arrival, the phone rang. It was the studio director with some rather bad news. "It seems," he said apologetically, "that the sheep were infested with ticks." Being a hater of insects I flipped and so did my pal. It was suggested that we strip off and burn all our attire. We did as we were told, in the backyard. I hope it amused the neighbours. The next morning Mr Sheep Owner was called. He came immediately and took his sheep away. A common problem he said, but you'll have to fumigate the van. TV Ontario had had me in their employ for one week and they had to fumigate my truck and rent me a car for three days. I was almost not worth it.

In Edmonton we settled for the goose. I had to take it home: Gail's apartment building didn't allow barnyard creatures and my new landlords were in California. My kids thought I was ready for the bin, but they loved the creature. We had to go out to dinner that night and my son was worried that the goose would be lonely, so he set up the T.V. in the kitchen, where the cage was placed. When we returned a couple of hours later, all the lights in the house were off and only the hideous glare of the television illuminated the room. It was the stuff of which stupid postcards are made—the goose, in its cage, in the kitchen watching "Front Page Challenge."

The next morning at 4:30 I loaded up the car with the goose and drove off to work, leaving my children howling with laughter on the street. Gail and I met at the studio door, dragged our cargo inside and then disappeared. The half-asleep technician was the first to arrive; he hardly even noticed. I swear it took him ten minutes to come out into the hall where we lay in wait. Producer Don Young was next, and he hardly batted an eye. This stunt was not having the impact that we had intended. The show started at 6:00 A.M. without much mention of the goose. But as the interviews progressed, the subjects of our attention would ask what the odd noises were.

During the last hour (the 8:00 to 9:00 slot), we ran a taped piece that had been prepared by a free-lancer. It was a story of bird migration with sounds of real geese (Canada Geese, I think) at the top and the tail of the item. The minute the guys in the control room hit the migration tape, and our goose heard the sounds of its brothers and sisters on their way to the Caribbean, it went out of its mind, trying to tell them to wait up, I guess. The cage nearly came off the table. When the tape finished two or three minutes later, the goose was still vexed and the studio crew and assorted office workers were in an uproar. The phone was ringing off the hook with all lines lit up like a you-know-what. One of the callers was *our* Director of Radio, who always listened. "What exactly is happening on my radio station?" Luckily he was the father of three teenagers, so he knew how to put up with the antics of his professional children.

The regular radio season runs September to June (just like school and television), and as June approached I decided to return to Toronto. Gail was embarking on a marriage. Mine was falling apart.

By July I had returned to Toronto and was again in search of employment. In the days when I was doing book reviews with Harron for "Morningside," I had occasionally worked for TV Ontario, the educational network, as a researcher, associate producer, and producer, so I had some experience but probably not enough to accept a job at CFTO, the CTV affiliate in Toronto. The position was that of Associate Producer of "Thrill of a Lifetime." Somehow I had managed to fake it through the interview and was hired. It was the first season for "Thrill" and a lot of preparation had to be done, and a lot of editing of material, too. The problem was that at TV Ontario I had been used to editing video tape on antiquated equipment. The stuff at CFTO was state-of-the-art. I was in big trouble. I took aside a tape-editing technician and begged him to give me a lesson, without telling anybody. The deal was that I would take him to dinner, anywhere he wanted, as payment. We went out for the dinner first, somewhere expensive. I was to have my lesson the next day.

The moment the first lesson finished, the phone rang. It was Bruce Steele, (the old boss from "Anybody Home?") who had taken over as producer of "Variety Tonight." "Variety Tonight" had started life in April 1980, with a handsome budget, a talented staff, and a lot of brilliant ideas. Its host, David Cole, already a well-known writer, brought a heretofore unheard-of approach to radio work. It's hard not to think that the yet-to-be-assembled David Letterman staff was listening and making notes. I was terribly envious of the people working on that show. Things were changing, Bruce said; would I be interested in the job of host. I wasn't in the least blasé in my reaction. Yes I was! My boss at CFTO let me off the hook (he was much better off without me), and I went to the CBC.

Bruce had what I thought, and continue to think, a great idea for an interview programme. Granted, it was a dead steal from the BBC's "Desert Island Discs," a long-running show in Britain, but we had no shame. It was and is a successful format, the premise being that guests would be invited to choose music of their liking and to speak at some length about their choices. In addition, we would chat about their careers. The use of music within the body of the interview was, as far as I was concerned, a stroke of luck because it would provide a hook for the person being interviewed and give me time to think about where the interview might go and which route to pursue next. The "Desert Island Discs" format also allows the interviewees a chance to loosen up, thereby making them forget that they are being interviewed, which makes for the ideal situation.

Most people in my business would agree that the toughest thing about interviewing is getting the first question right. Sure, it is important to have your facts straight, your research done properly, and a general idea of what you want to accomplish, but you can blow the whole game plan if the first question fails to set the tone. It is also true that interviews, especially long ones (an hour or more), begin to take on a life of their own—a this-thing-is-bigger-than-both-of-us kind of feeling.

The trick in dealing with most interviewees is to talk about their latest work first, even if the point of the conversation is to tell a life story. If you don't talk about the latest thing first, the subject of your attention stays in a constant state of anxiety, waiting to promote the newest project, fearful that it will be neglected. Altogether, not a situation to be desired. So, I say, get it out of the way and then get them to talk about real stuff. The fact is that no matter how much you plan, an interview never ever goes the way you thought it would.

Back to the first-question theory. You might have gathered that I spend most of my working life being nervous. It is something that has really never gone away. I am, however, less nervous if my first question to be delivered is one that I think will provoke an interesting answer. It was the author Jerzy Kosinski who made me realize the importance of the first strike. You've got to keep, within reason, the upper hand, otherwise these big guns will blow you away. I knew Jerzy was a big gun. I did not want to be embarrassed on live radio by a smooth-talking New Yorker.

The story producer who prepared the Kosinski piece had provided reams of research and many clippings. I had seen the movie *Being There* and read all Kosinski's books. I was ready, but I still did not have the right beginning. How could I disarm this guy? He'd been interviewed a million times.

The evening before the interview, I saw Kosinski on the Dick Cavett show. Normally I wouldn't have watched; I like to avoid other interviewers in action until I've had my way with the subject, but this time I couldn't resist. They were really good together and it was obvious that Kosinski was a great fellow to interview, but Cavett and he knew each other, and that too makes a huge difference in approach. (I promise, I'm getting to the point.)

I noticed that Kosinski dressed rather informally on the Cavett programme, a beige cardigan with a big collar. I was reading his latest book, *Pinball*, while watching the interview, and I glanced at the author's photo on the back of the jacket. Guess what I saw? The same sweater. It occurred to me then that this man was no clothes horse, and if the gods were with me, he would show up at the studio in the same garb. And you know what? He did. I had my first question. He arrived some ten minutes before we went to air. It is always a bit awkward having the guest arrive early, because you have to make small talk and not blow your thunder and ask all the questions while the subjects drinks his or her tea. Finally, the show's theme music started. I could hardly believe my good fortune. Kosinski peered at me from time to time while I did the introduction; mostly he looked away, at the floor, at the piano, at anything. Ho hum, another interview. I was almost champing at the bit to get my question out.

> **VG** Good evening, Mr Kosinski.
>
> **JK** Good evening. (Not too exciting yet.)
>
> **VG** Say, Mr Kosinski, don't you have any clothes? (Now he was looking at me.) You seem to wear only that sweater.
>
> **JK** What do you mean, don't I have any clothes? Of course, I have clothes, I have a lot of clothes. You don't like this sweater? What is wrong with this sweater? You don't like the colour? I wear this sweater all the time; nobody complains about this sweater.

Frankly, I had expected a small, comical reaction, a little bit of a light start to an interview, but this outburst thrilled me to pieces. The interview went on and on; not an earth shaker, but it was pretty good. We played some music and it was over. I was content to a degree and that's about as much as you can hope for.

Next day, I was back in the studio putting together something for that evening, and the phone rang. Would I please come to the front desk because there was a man waiting, with some impatience, to see me. I vaulted to the reception area to find Kosinski pacing. I thought he'd forgotten something.

"I hardly recognize you," I said, in a slightly sarcastic tone. He was not wearing *the* sweater, you see.

"Look, look," said he, "I have other clothes . . . I wanted you to know that." He had returned to the CBC that day for a grilling from someone else, and had insisted that I be summoned. I laughed for weeks.

If you think interviewing complete strangers is a tough job, believe me, it's the interviewing of friends that will turn you prematurely grey. It is much easier to be natural with people you don't know than it is to turn what might have been last week's parlour chat into a useful and informative conversation. Forget funny, because things that appear funny in the kitchen sound insipid and stupid on the air. I find that it is darn near impossible to not admit that I know the person. I just can't fake it. Remember, I'm no actor. I suppose the professional approach is to appear distanced somehow, to be objective, but I'm no journalist, either. The problem with chatting up friends on the air is that you know too much. With a stranger you know too little, making you more bold and prying.

I've interviewed Pierre Berton at least ten times. The last nine times have been swell. The first time, I thought I might throw myself in front of a bus. I was living in Edmonton, working the morning show, and he was touring his War of 1812 opus. Can I tell you that Berton hates it, in a big, big way, when an interviewer has not read his book? His wrath is something I'd like to avoid, thank you. The book had arrived on my desk late, in fact the night before the interview. No problem, I thought, he'll call me when he gets into town, maybe take me out for a decent dinner, I'll confess about not having had a chance to read the book, and life will be wonderful. Well, he called, we had dinner, I confessed, and he agreed that so as to not blow a perfectly good six minutes of air time, I would ask *this* and he would answer *that* and so on. It wouldn't be award-winning but it would be fine; after all, he can liven up anything. I felt safe.

What a mistake. I should have stayed up all night and read that thing, because the next morning the beast of Berton showed up. He thought it would be a scream to give me a rough time. *Now*, it's a scream. *Then*, I thought I would.

I bubbled a cheerful, "Good morning, Mr Berton."

"Good morning, Vick," he grinned.

I confidently asked my first, pre-arranged, question. Huge silence.

"Yes," was the simple reply. I thought, what do you mean, yes, say something like we planned. I tried again.

"No," to the second question.

I tried in desperation with a third.

"You ought to know that, Vick, you've read the book." He was beaming. Very funny. My producer thought I was a bum, yet somehow he relished this performance. Finally, Berton shaped up and rattled on for the remaining minutes.

I was bathed in perspiration and exhausted from fear. I vowed never again to go into an interview ill-prepared; not out of a feeling of tremendous responsibility, but out of fear of being trapped. And this guy was a pal; you can imagine what a stranger might do. Our next encounter, which took place about a year later, was a considerable improvement. I was doing "Variety Tonight," and we had invited him to come on and play his favourite music and generally fool around. He appeared, we did the interview, he was perfect, and I was relieved. He even talked about his experiences during the Korean War, something about which he has hardly written and that is a shame, but I suppose he might yet.

Now, that was a situation where it helped to know the victim. I knew that he had been a war correspondent because, upon his return from Korea in the early fifties, my father and mother and I drove to Seattle to meet his inbound self. As he had entertained my father upon *his* return from overseas in 1944, Berton was given a hero's welcome, too. This second interview with Berton proved more relaxing. Most people would be surprised at how much he knows about music. He even did his imitation of current rock-and-roll singers. I didn't say too much.

> **VG** Let's play a piece of music. You chose Helen Humes's "These Foolish Things."
>
> **PB** I chose that because I don't think people write very good lyrics any more. I turn on the local radio stations and I get "Baba, baba, baba, baba, you and me! Baba, baba, baba, baba, baba, you and me!" That's a lyric? Some guy wrote that? When I used to listen to music, there was a word called "baby," which sometimes referred to small, cute children with lollipops in their mouths, but quite often referred to pretty girls. "These Foolish Things" is a typical thirties song; it came out in 1936, and it happens to be well written. In those days, people could write. "A cigarette that bears a lipstick's traces, an airline ticket to romantic places, still my heart has wings, these foolish things remind me of you." That's writing. To compact that feeling into four lines

takes talent and it sometimes takes genius. I would not say this is a work of genius, but it is certainly a work of talent. It's the kind of song that you don't get any more, because everybody's singing about "Baba, baba, baba!" So let's hear it.

VG Fine.

PB Notice that all the standards are from the thirties and forties?

VG Yes.

PB The sixties and seventies have produced a few standards . . . a few from musical comedies . . . and the Beatles. We'll give the Beatles credit. McCartney and Lennon were writers as well as musicians. But it's very difficult to write both the words and the music; very few have been able to do it. Berlin was an example of one who did, and Cole Porter was another. And the great lyrics, the great ballads came out in the thirties and the forties. "Dinner for one please, James, Madam will not be dining. Yes, you may bring the wine in. Love plays such funny games." There's the whole story. The guy's got it in three lines. Songs like that will be around for a long time.

VG Any particular explanation for this?

PB It was a progression of Tin Pan Alley, when songs were plugged and sold. It was before television, when radio was very big, and really before records were very big. It was also the big-band era. Bands played in the theatres and dancehalls, one-night stands all over the country. I remember when I was in Vancouver, Ellington, Phil Harris, Lionel Hampton, everybody came to town. We all went and we didn't dance very much. We listened to them. They're all coming back the big bands are coming back.

VG I know. Speaking of big bands, how about a little Artie Shaw?

PB Well, you know, I first heard Artie Shaw on the Bob Benchley program. Bob Benchley was a New York humorist and wit who had a half-hour radio comedy show in '36 or '37. In those days the comedy was interspersed with the music of the studio orchestra. I had never heard this studio orchestra before. I didn't know who it was, but when I heard that clarinet I thought, My God! What a sound! Artie Shaw wasn't known then, but within a year he'd done "Nightmare" and then went on to do "Frenesi." He also did "Stardust" and "Gloomy Sunday." Now "Gloomy Sunday" . . . I've gotta tell you this story because that's the one we're going to hear. "Gloomy Sunday" was written by a Hungarian in about 1933. It was translated and the lyrics are pretty gloomy. "Sunday is gloomy, my hours are slumberless. Dearest, the shadows I live with are numberless. Little white flowers will never awaken you, not where the dark coach of sorrow has taken you." It's about a guy about to kill himself. "Let them not weep, let them know that I'm glad to go" is one of the lines. Well, thirteen Hungarians committed suicide on hearing that song. And, when I was in Budapest, my friend George Feyer, who later also committed suicide, showed me the bridge they'd jumped from. Anyway, the story that we were told was that "Gloomy Sunday" was banned from the airwaves. But Shaw made a record of it, and managed to put into "Gloomy Sunday" that kind of verve and panache and drive that he put into all his work. It's just a great piece.

VG How about Ella?

PB What's she going to sing?

VG "All the Things You Are."

PB That's the song I chose. I didn't know Ella was going to sing it. I chose this song because this is Oscar Hammerstein II writing, and Jerome Kern with the music. This is poetry, Tin Pan Alley poetry, but it's poetry. It's great lyric writing, romantic writing of a kind that you rarely get now. It transcends the "baba, baba, baba" style.

VG You're not ever gonna get off that, are you?

PB Well, it really upsets me. As a writer, I am upset by the low quality. These kids who think they can do everything. And everybody wonders why the lyrics are no good. The reason is they haven't learned to write. They may have learned to play the guitar, but they have not learned to write. Oscar Hammerstein learned to write lyrics. He couldn't play the guitar, he didn't write the music, but he got a great musician to write the music—Jerome Kern—and this is the result.

VG Do you have no passion in your soul at all?

PB None at all.

THREE

Almost Identical to Marilyn Monroe

I left Toronto in 1982 to move back to Vancouver, after an absence of twelve years. Studio space at 354 Jarvis Street in Toronto, headquarters of CBC, was (and still is) at a premium. People produce radio programmes from closets and would even contemplate selling their first-born to get access to a studio, a technician, a desk or equipment. CBC management decided that there was no reason why "Variety Tonight" could not be produced outside of Toronto, and I volunteered to move.

The thought of returning to my home town with a real job provided me some anxiety. Would I now be socially acceptable and be invited to a huge number of swanky affairs? It took me months to stop droning on about how wonderful Toronto was, which did not provide an *entré* into Vancouver society. It didn't help that my son, age sixteen, had opted to stay in Toronto with his father. He was given the choice and choose he did. He presented his case well.

"Mama, you are a real nice girl, but your life moves too fast for me."

His sister, Eve, three years his junior, was not given such a choice. She came with me, and essentially became an only child overnight. We just pretended he was in an eastern boarding school. The phone bills were and are appalling, as is the cost of the endless plane tickets required to unite us all several times a year. It gets easier as they get older, I think.

Doing a nightly entertainment programme from Vancouver presented a few technical problems. Any way you want to look at it, Toronto is the clearing house for artistic and cultural activities in Canada. Most book tours, for instance, begin in Toronto, so trying to scoop the shows that originate there is not all that easy. Therefore if "Variety Tonight" was to be its own show and not a regurgitation of "Morningside," there would be constant battle. Obviously, some doubling up was inevitable, but in those cases a different approach was attempted for our show. Our format of having the main guest choose music helped in changing the focus.

Whereas "As it Happens" uses the telephone exclusively and "Morningside" only occasionally, it was decided that "Variety Tonight" should use it as infrequently as possible. Our interviews generally run for forty to forty-five minutes, considerably longer than those on "As It Happens," and a phone interview works best when it lasts no more than six minutes. The sound quality, voice match, and other technical considerations can become problems when the telephone is the only link to the interviewee.

The solution is the double-ender. This is how it works. A stringer (free-lancer) with a tape recorder in Los Angeles or any other studio-less city—London, Paris, New York and Washington all have CBC studios—goes to the office or household of the interviewee and sets up his or her machine. We, in Vancouver, then call the subject on the telephone. He or she and I have a conversation over the phone lines, sometimes for an hour. While the individual and I rattle on, the stringer records that end of the conversation, without hearing my questions. Meanwhile, back in the Vancouver studio, our technician is recording my questions only, but we can hear both sides of the conversation. At the conclusion of the interview, the stringer runs like hell to a mail box and sends us that end of the chat. We wait at the mail-drop tray for it to arrive, and then the two ends of the conversation are mixed together. *Voilà*—it sounds almost as if we are in the same room. Isn't that clever?

Sometimes the funniest part of a conversation conducted as a double-ender takes place before the tape is rolling, and that is a pity. Even if the preamble is recorded, we rarely use it because it's unfair and cheap, given that the victim has not been told that we are away and rolling. This short excerpt is an example of just how cheap we can really be; I don't think film director Billy Wilder would care.

VG So, are you all ready?

BW Yes I'm all set to go. There is a mike shoved down my throat and there is a tube with blood that I am getting intravenously so that I keep alive, you know, while you are hammering at me.

VG A tube of blood?

BW Yes, you know, a sack of blood.

VG Are you serious?

BW No, No, No.

VG I'm so relieved. You are well I take it?

BW Well is exaggerated. But let me put it this way—I'm not sick, just mildly depressed.

VG You and me both. Look, I will say "good evening" to you because it's a night-time programme and then we'll just have at it, shall we?

BW So, it's going to be a cheat throughout this whole thing?

VG Yes, we are going to cheat.

BW You are going to say good evening to me, this being like 10:30 in the morning.

VG That is right.

BW Well, that is the way the press operates.

VG You cannot tell me that that is not the way you guys operate too, changing night into day and all.

BW Well, we don't pretend that we are giving them the absolute, down-to-the-bone facts. We just say that what you're going to see now is fictional and the names are invented by us and blah, blah, blah. You know.

VG Yes, it is all illusion.

BW All illusion. It's all done with aces up your sleeves.

You might think that conducting an interview without seeing the other party would be a disadvantage, but on occasion it has been a blessing. A good sixty percent of the interviews done between 1982 and today have been done sight unseen. Consider Shelley Berman, for instance. When I was a kid I was obsessed with this comedian. I knew most of his routines, at least the ones he recorded, by heart. "My tongue is asleep and my teeth itch" was one of the lines that captured my attention. I was in a state of excitement at the prospect of interviewing him. He has a notorious reputation and I wasn't at all sure I could control him. I had heard that he had walked out of a r.v. interview in Toronto, where he was appearing. That did not bode well. As I sat in my Vancouver studio—a lovely joint, with plastic flowers in profusion—I awaited his arrival in the Toronto studio with some impatience.

We started off awkwardly, as is often the case, trying to establish a rhythm. When you can't see someone it is difficult to get the metre of his voice and his sentence structure. There is a tendency to interrupt before his thoughts are completed. Generally, after a few minutes that problem is solved and we forget, more or less, that we are separated by 3,000 miles of cable.

After several fairly standard questions from me, Berman barked, "What do you look like, anyway?"

Luckily, the people attending to Berman at the other end had not provided a photo of me, and I was able to state that, to be perfectly honest, I looked almost identical to Marilyn Monroe. From that moment on, Berman behaved not unlike a lamb to the slaughter. I could almost hear his mind working. "What if she does look like M.M.?" He clearly couldn't get the image out of his mind. Lucky for me, because he was a perfect gentleman and made me laugh and laugh.

You can be assured that I have used this tactic on at least a hundred occasions, and it seems to work every time, except when you get the earnest types who don't find the statement amusing at all.

Contrary to popular opinion, most people like to be interviewed. So when people say to me (and I would venture that they say the same to other interviewers), "How did you get that person to be so forthcoming?" the answer is so simple it's frightening. They do it without much prodding. Truly. The trick is to just let them do it. Frankly, authors with a new book are without doubt the easiest. Mind you, if they don't have a recent book they are considerably less interested. But one guy, new book or not, who was as tough as nails was Joseph Heller, the American author. Heller has built a huge following on the basis of a surprisingly small body of work, *Catch-22* being his most famous. At the time of our conversation in December 1984 he had just released his comic diatribe delivered by King David on his death bed, *God Knows*. Although there were a number of things to talk about and he is after all considered a rather dashing figure, I seemed to get myself boxed into a corner at the first bell.

> **VG** You are quite the guy—you sound like Bennett Cerf and look like Paul Newman.
>
> **JH** I don't look like Paul Newman. I look better than Paul Newman. I look younger than Paul Newman and I'm a better actor than Paul Newman. And I am surprised to hear that that is my cadence, but if that is the way I sound, well . . .
>
> **VG** Is this the end of your book tour for *God Knows*?
>
> **JH** This the end of the Toronto interviews but I hope to see a European tour to assist in the publication of this book there. And in between then and now I hope to take it easy and get back to work and listen to my favourite music.
>
> **VG** Which is?
>
> **JH** J.S. Bach, his suites, his "Air on the G String," all the works that are mentioned in *God Knows* as having been composed by David are by Bach. The "Air on the G String," the "Goldberg Variation in B Minor."

At this point the record was played and he in Toronto and I in Vancouver listened to the piece, after which he laughed uproariously.

> **VG** Why are you laughing, Mr Heller?
>
> **JH** Why am I laughing? Because it was *not* Bach's "Air on the G String." That was played on an accordion and not on the violin. And if King David ever wrote anything that sounded as sour as that, I would not have boasted about it in that novel of mine called *God Knows*.
>
> **VG** Joseph, Joseph, Joseph, that was the English Consort and that was a harpsichord, not an accordion.
>
> **JH** It may have been a harpsichord where you are. It sounded like a sour accordion over here, or a defective organ.
>
> **VG** Oh, my God.
>
> **JH** It was not a harpsichord.

VG So, you hated it, right?

JH I'll tell you what to do with the record. That was not Bach's "Air on the G String." It was supposed to be played on a G string accompanied by an orchestra and a suite. And it is not the overture. Well, it may have been an overture that you played and may be the same melodic line as the "Air," but that was not J.S. Bach's "Air on the G String." It might have been William Fitzbach or something but not J.S. Bach.

Just to set the record straight here, I volunteered to send him the disc; he declined my offer.

VG You are argumentative, aren't you?

JH No. I'm the most tractable person in the world and I was feeling fine until I heard that piece of music.

VG Did you ever have occasion to play a musical instrument yourself?

JH No. All I do is listen to music and remember pieces. I remember how they are supposed to sound.

VG Oh, you are cruel.

JH I will defy a response. And have respect for the occasion.

VG Will you tell me something?

JH Tell me how wonderful you are.

VG What do you want to talk about? Surely you are slightly weary of telling the same story?

JH Yes, I am, so ask me some new questions.

VG What are you doing for dinner?

JH It depends how far apart you and I are

VG I don't think we'd get along at all, to tell you the truth.

JH I would like to have dinner with somebody I don't get along with. I'm sick and tired of all the harmony in my life

It is not fair to continue using excerpts from this conversation without pointing out that there were actual moments of straightforward give-and-take—how do you work and that sort of thing—but it is this looney part that I remember with such fondness. I hardly recall the "smart" bits. Thirty minutes later:

VG Well, I'll let you go now.

JH Wait a minute—I'm wide awake now. I want another two minutes to straighten this out. But if you feel we are finished, will you check on that recording and then you will see that I am right?

VG Yes, but you are dead wrong.

JH I'm dead right. Say, would you like to hear me sing the whole of Mahler's "Second Symphony?"

VG I certainly would.

JH Do you have another hour and twenty minutes?

VG Well, I'd go for two minutes of it.

JH No. I can't give you two minutes of it. It takes Mahler two minutes for the first note to go by. How about just the last two movements?

VG For you darling, anything.

JH OK. Put on another tape because I'm going to give you all of Mahler's symphony as conducted by Bruno Walter rather than Leonard Bernstein. Are you ready?

VG Yes.

JH Here we go. [*Huge silence.*]

VG You're not going.

JH Well, Mahler is best in his silences.

VG You've been waiting a long time for that joke, haven't you?

JH Well, I haven't told it before, but I guarantee I'll tell it again.

VG Thank you, Mr Heller.

JH It has been a pleasure. It may not have sounded like it, but I have enjoyed you very much.

It was over and I had been reduced to a pile of rubble. A heller he was.

Studs Terkel, another giant in his field, a man who documented the American working class in his classic book about jobs, *Working*, turned out to be a lead-pipe cinch. His new book at the time of our interview was *The Good War*, a series of reminiscences of the Second World War. There is a reason why he is so expert at oral history—orally he is relentless. Within the body of a fifty-minute interview I asked three questions, and he talked for the remaining forty-eight minutes. He was like an ack-ack gun. I think I could have got away with asking only one question.

Mike Royko, the syndicated columnist from Chicago, was a different story. In our forty-five minute chat I must have asked fifty questions and managed to get a lot of three-word sentences in return. (There is a reason why some people write and don't talk for a living.) To say he was not taken with me is an understatement.

Two thousand interviews later, when people ask me what has been my favourite interview, I still can't come up with an answer. But I can tell you of a humiliating moment that still makes me cringe when I think about it. Gary Heald, one of our Vancouver technicians, and I were in the studio control room listening to some Bob and Ray recordings when the phone rang. It was for me. It was a person-to-person call from Mr James Mason. "Who is James Mason? Not *the* James Mason?" I had not heard that he had been booked for the show. Not that the producers tell me everything that might be coming up, but James Mason—surely I would know. But why was he calling me?

As soon as he said, "Is that you, Mrs Gabereau?" I immediately recognized the voice as that of my friend in Toronto who has been known to give a mean imitation of Mason. I just knew I was being taken.

"Mrs Gabereau, I'm calling to say that our interview date will have to be changed due to some confusion in bookings. Would you mind awfully changing times?"

I was instantly abusive, not wanting to be suckered by my pal, who had been known to make a fool of others by having them gush all over the place, bowing and scraping. I wasn't going to fall for it.

Basically, I was short with the man. He continued on charmingly with his explanation. I asked myself if it really were James Mason, why wouldn't he have had one of his helpers call? Wouldn't you wonder that too? Sure. I allowed as how I wasn't really in a position to change the time of our interview (tongue in cheek), but that I'd have My People call His People, and thanks for calling. "Oh fine," he replied with great dignity. I hung up.

Heald, the tech, wanted to know immediately what that was all about. I told him.

"What if it was *the* James Mason?"

"Couldn't have been," said I. Without taking a breath I leapt from my chair and flew up to the office and asked rather sheepishly if, in fact, James Mason was booked? He wasn't, was he?

You know the answer already. I nearly died.

Susan Englebert, our executive producer and a calm woman, did not think it was the funniest thing she'd ever heard in her life. I begged her to forgive me; she wouldn't. But she did smooth things over and re-scheduled the interview for the following day.

I nervously awaited the start of the interview.

"Hello, Mr Mason, is that really you?"

"Yes, Mrs Gabereau, unlike yesterday."

He took it upon himself to break the ice and the interview went swimmingly. He did, however, want to know who it was in Toronto who could do his voice so well. He was a gracious man.

In 1984 we received in our office a very good book by an American writer, James Haskins. It was a biography of Bricktop. Bricktop was a remarkable soul, an American black woman with red hair and freckles who owned and ran her own night clubs in New York and Paris, Rome and Mexico. She had lived the mad life in Paris in the twenties and thirties and all the fancy people attended her clubs to see the latest dancer or singer. She never allowed any talking during the performances and even if you were of noble birth there was no breach of etiquette allowed, or out you'd go. Champagne was mandatory, single women not admitted. Bricktop left Paris shortly before the Occupation and returned to New York, where she worked her magic once again.

It was decided that the subject of the book was so intriguing that we would try to get her for the interview rather than the author. Unfortunately, Bricktop by this time was terribly ill. She was bed-ridden but miraculously agreed to be interviewed over the phone from New York. We sent a stringer to record her end of the conversation, in the manner I have already described. Here is a bit of our back-and-forth.

> **VG** I'm so happy that you finally got around to telling your story.
>
> **B** Well, that book was turned down many times because I wouldn't write any filth, and I would have died and went to hell before I would have done that. A critic wrote and said he was glad to pick up a book that you

could lay down and a child could pick it up. But I'm not trying to wash myself or anything, because I've slept with every man, woman and—no, not women, I don't like women. Ugh. But I've slept with 9,000 million different men and that's my business. In fact I was trying to count them once and I lost track.

VG Sometimes it's just as well.

B Well, what is the use of remembering all those things. When it's over, it's over. They say there's three things about passion: expectation, the act itself, and then when it's over—was it worth it?

VG I think the first part is often the best, the expectation part.

B Yeah, that's the part that's great. Then when it turns out—

VG Oh, brother.

B Are you Canadian?

VG I am. In Vancouver.

B I lived a couple of years in Vancouver. In fact, one night in this saloon where I was working, those lumberjacks got to fighting. And you know when those lumberjacks get to fighting, everybody gets to fighting in the place. And I kept running in. Me and my drunken self. It was New Year's Eve and I kept running in the middle of the right and they kept pushing me out and pushing me out and next thing I knew I found myself in the hospital with a broken ankle.

VG But when the time came and you had your own night clubs you had very strict rules about behaviour. There weren't too many fights?

B No, there weren't. Practically none because I had a little thing. If people looked as if they were going to start trouble, I'd go and say, "Now you wouldn't do that to me, would you? I'm a little girl and I'm alone by myself." I don't care how bad they were, they'd calm down and stay that way.

VG You are a born diplomat.

B Well, my mother brought us up to think big and you'll do big. That's all I've ever thought in my life.

VG You ran a very tight ship.

B I did. And that is why it always had to be a small place so I could have my eyes over the place all the time. There was never any kinda hustle in my place. One of my biggest rules was when somebody was on the floor singing, then everybody had to be quiet. Truman Capote once said, while some guy was singing about lions, "Heck, I didn't come in here to hear about no lions." And I said, "Well, somebody must have asked him or the singer wouldn't be singing it." "Well," he said, "if you don't stop him, I'm going to walk out." I said, "You wouldn't dare walk out of Bricktop's while somebody is on the floor singing." And of course, two hours later he was still there.

VG Did you really teach the Prince of Wales some fancy dance steps?

B Yes. He was the best dancer of all. He really could dance and was the most polite person I've ever met in my life. To everybody he said, "Could you please," and "Thank you so much." I never saw him insult, but he let you know right away quick that he was who he was.

VG What do you do during the day now?

B Lay in this bed.

VG Are you in bed now?

B Yes, ma'am. And you know, it's like this. When you're sick, you're up today and down today. You can't make plans and if you do you can just hope that everything will turn out all right. But I'll live, and if I don't, I *have*. I've had one of the most beautiful great lives in the world and I'm grateful, and God knows it.

The interview was recorded on a Friday. On the following Tuesday she died, at age 89. We ran the interview that night. I must assume it was her last.

Melvin Belli, the infamous American lawyer, has defended the likes of Jack Ruby, Lenny Bruce, and Mickey Cohen. Even though he is just short of eighty, he continues working, seemingly uninterested in retiring. When I spoke with him in January 1985 he had just bought a 110-foot power yacht.

VG What are you going to do with this boat? Take it from where to where?

MB Well, every time I win a case I'm going to go out and celebrate with some booze, on the boat. Every time I lose a case I'm going to go out and drown my sorrows. So it is going to be a wet boat.

VG How far will it go, this vessel?

MB Ah, hell. This will go around the world. This boat can travel. Some eccentric Scotsman bought it years ago and never got a chance to use it very much. It has been up in Vancouver all of this time in one of your ship-yards.

VG So it has gone from an eccentric Scot to an eccentric American?

MB Thank God you didn't say flamboyant. I'd rather be eccentric.

VG Flamboyant is the word often associated with you.

MB Yeah, every time they see my red lining inside my coat.

VG Well, don't you have anything with blue lining?

MB No, not a thing. My overcoats and even my dinner jackets are red. But I wear cowboy boots through the year. They look great. Cowboy boots, if they are well shined, look great with dinner jackets or even with tails to the opera.

VG Are you on the best-dressed list?

MB Yes. By the way, *Gentleman's Quarterly*, I think, had a story of some MP of yours who wrote to a haberdash-ery that is number one on Savile Row. He said he wanted some clothes just like Belli's. So he got outfitted with everything that I had. They thought that that was peculiar on the part of your MP and peculiar on my part, too. Neither he nor I thought it was peculiar.

VG I wonder if it was Eugene Whelan?

MB I forget the guy's name but I remember when I was talking to him once, I liked him at once.

VG Well, Whelan is a sartorial sight. He's taken to wearing green cowboy hats.

MB Oh, for heaven's sake. No kidding?

Melvin Belli pronounces his name with a long I, but the original pronunciation was as in belly. His grandfather was named Caesar

Belli, as is Melvin's son. This part of the chat came after his musical selection from *Rigoletto*.

VG How is *your* Italian?

MB Awful. I can hardly say anything. I can say *Buon giorno* or *Buona notte* and then they start with a steady stream and I stand there like a dunce.

VG Well, you can say *La Donna e Mobile*. I take it you know what that means?

MB The woman is fickle.

VG Do you find that to be true?

MB No, I think the *homme* is more *mobile*. At least that is what four of my wives would say. You know, I've been cheating on you.

VG How's that?

MB Your friend (our San Francisco stringer, Rose Tobin) who has been recording this and I have been trying a bottle of, let me see, a 1982 Pommard. We have a case and I just wanted to see if it was any good or not. I am having fifty people out to the house tomorrow and I want to see that the wine is good. And besides, it is the only day during the year that my two dogs, the parrot, and the cat join us and they have a little wine, too. My dog is wonderful. He's an Italian greyhound.

VG Oh, they are very nice, but they are nervous.

MB They are not only nervous, but you can't house-train them. His name is Wheldone Rumproast IV. I'm not in the phone book, so if you want to call me when you come down, you look under Wheldone. They call from the university, usually about two or three in the morning, and ask "Is he well done?" Har. Har. So we are going to have to get him out of the phone book if he can't learn to answer the phone himself.

Belli's final musical choice was "The Stars and Stripes Forever."

Red Fisher, fishing ace and proprietor of T.V.'s "Scuttlebutt Lodge", is a guy I really fell for, again without ever meeting him. His weekly fishing show is relaxed, to say the least. It generally follows the same format. Red invites a friend or two over to the mythical lodge, and then they set off fishing (that's the real part). They actually go fishing, and they talk about life and fish.

> **VG** You must have been pretty impressed when you realized that one of the most-requested Thrill-of-a-Lifetime wishes (as in the T.V. show) is a fishing trip with you.
>
> **RF** Yeah, and what they got was herring. I told these guys, "Well now, if we're going to go, let's get up early in the morning or late at night, because up at Lake Nipissing—and I've fished that lake for twenty years—the fish do not forage for food or anything during the daytime. We never caught anything. In fact, we'd go in and play cards and have a few canoopers and then get ready to go out again at 5:30 P.M., but the director had to have his way and so we went out about 11:00 o'clock and the poor guy [the thrillee] and I caught a couple of herring.
>
> **VG** Oh well, it was still a thrill. Say, what is a canooper?
>
> **RF** Well, a lot of people call them cocktails.
>
> **VG** Oh.
>
> **RF** I made that up years ago for a fisherman.

Red Fisher spends a lot of his time at sports shows. One year, in St Louis, Missouri, he somehow managed to purchase a trampoline.

> **VG** Have you given up the trampoline?
>
> **RF** You better believe it. I don't even want to think about it. I damn near got castrated on that damn thing so I'm not going to talk about it.
>
> **VG** Can I tell it?
>
> **RF** Eh?
>
> **VG** Isn't this the story about your going through a wall?
>
> **RF** Oh, that was the second incident. The first one—OK, we were at the St Louis Sports show and I guess we were full of canoopers and I didn't know it but I bought it [the trampoline]. Later on, the sports show came to Akron, where I was living at the time, so I was going to go out and perform for the gals. I'm doing back flips, but I made one tiny mistake and I went through the springs and there I was with the springs acting like an accor-

dion and I couldn't reach bottom. I said, "That's it." The University of Akron got that trampoline in exactly fifteen minutes.

VG Actually, Red, I was thinking about the time you went right through a wall.

RF Oh, yeah. Well, see, the Keel Auditorium, where they held the sports show, was a double hall. We didn't know this. A huge big hall with a tank [for fishing displays] and booths and everything. We thought, well, why not walk around that long tank. We'll cut backstage. Our booth was on the other side of the tank, see. Well, here right in the middle of the stage was a trampoline. It belonged to a guy I knew, one of the acts there. I had a casting act so I said to my buddy, "Hey, putterhead"— he was a golfer—"did you ever work out on one of these things?" He said, "No." I said, "Let's go." You could hear this music, Vicki, it sounded long-haired. You know, this Tchaikovsky's Fifth Symphony or whatever it was. I thought it was being piped backstage. So, I got on and said, "This is fun, I'm going to go up and touch the valance." Well, the valance is about eighteen feet up and goes across the stage. And I'm a porky guy. And I'm jumping and coming down harder and harder. And the last time I came down on the end instead of the centre and there I go for the wall. I didn't know how to stop and I covered up my head 'cause I knew I was going to hit this solid wall, and I did. It gave way and here this old guy is, standing there with a baton up in the air and his eyes looked like a couple of yo-yos on the end of the string. And here are all these people in this little theatre, you know. And it was Sunday morning. It was the St Louis Philharmonic Orchestra and they were all listening to this Tchaikovsky rendition and I come in and hit the kettle drum, roll over into the cellos and knock everything all to hell. And I'm all bloodied up and running back through the hole. I tell you, it was really something. The poor old guy. If he could have died then—

VG Did the people laugh?

RF Oh, God, yes. It was the end of the Tchaikovsky, I tell you. Big write-up in the paper and all that stuff. It was the Celotex divider, see, which divided the big theatre from the little theatre.

VG I guess it didn't do a very good job.

RF Oh, it did, but when I came through the air like a cannon ball, that Celotex ain't gonna hold me.

During the early years of his career William Peter Blatty wrote funny stuff. In 1966 he wrote the screenplay for *A Shot in the Dark* and launched the unforgettable Inspector Clouseau, immortalized by Peter Sellers. In 1971 he wrote the equally unforgettable, but far from funny, novel and screenplay, *The Exorcist*. He was in Los Angeles when I interviewed him about his new novel, *Legion*.

VG I've got a copy of the paperback edition.

WB Isn't it hideous? The ugliest cover I've ever seen.

VG Have you ever? What in heaven's name is it about? It is the worst—the priest with the red eyes.

WB Can you believe it? I was in Washington, D.C., when someone told me that the book was out and I said, "Well, that was nice of my publisher to send me a copy and let me know." So I went out to a bookstore around the corner, and finally my eye caught a stack of these monstrosities. I literally slunk out of the store, lest anyone connect me with it.

At this very moment the phone went dead. We tried to call him back immediately, but all our lines in the studio were dead, too. This situation lasted at least five minutes, until we were able to establish contact again.

VG Shall we carry on? Does this happen to you all the time?

WB Yes, actually rather frequently. There is a story I tell. Few believe it except my close friends. When I was staying at the home of a professor of law who went to school with me in Washington, D.C., a call came. I'll cut this short. Twice in my presence, and that of two or three other people, this particular telephone rang a couple of times and it simply—I can't say it levitated— but it lifted up enough to clear the cradle and fell to the floor. Now, I called the telephone company about this. I called a number of people because my theory was that perhaps the ringing of the phone generated sufficient energy to knock the receiver off. The engineer at the phone company, I remember vividly, said, "NO, our telephones don't fly, Mr Blatty." I did point out that it was a princess phone. Then he hung up on me.

VG Why would you go from writing comedy to this other stuff?

WB A couple of things. One of them was coming back to terror. Terror of the bill collector.

VG But you were a hot shot.

WB Yeah, but they didn't want comedies any more. The only screen writing jobs available seemed to be in the area of serious dramatic work, and I said, "Hey, I can write that." And everybody said, "No, you can't write that. Go back to your room." I had been planning *The Exorcist* since I was an undergraduate at Georgetown, and I was fearful of whether or not I could really accomplish this. God knows, I certainly had the time. My intent was to get a small advance, which I did, a very small one that would tide me over for a while and help me pay the bills, and finally I would complete something that would be decently received and would be a signal to all the producers in town that "Hey, gee whiz, Bill Blatty can write something other than comedy."

VG And my, you did hit with a vengeance, didn't you?

WB My lucky day. However, when it was published, I must tell you that they were returning it by the carload from the book stores all over America.

VG You mean it didn't sell?

WB No. It was selling only in Los Angeles. There it was number one. But I remember arriving in Cleveland to do some talk shows and interviews, and the Harper and Row salesman greeted me at the plane with the words, "Well, a department store has just returned ninety-nine out of a hundred copies they ordered."

VG That must have cheered you?

WB Oh, really. And when I went back to New York, Dick Cavett lost a guest on his show. The evening of the show the producers found me in a restaurant and rushed me in to fill the author spot, usually about five, six, or seven minutes. Fortunately for me, the first guest was very boring and Dick gave him the hook. And with forty-five left to go, there was nobody left but good old Bill. I was happy to talk about the book non-stop.

VG Did you notice in the days following the telecast that the book sales went berserk?

WB I left New York with my tail between my legs. They were, as far as I knew, still returning the book. At the airport, whiling away the time waiting for the plane, I picked up a copy of *Time* magazine. I idly turned to the book section and to the best-seller list, and I was suddenly electrified. I saw *The Exorcist* and my name— number four. And I was so excited I called my publisher. He said, "Oh, that's nice."

I am sure that Mr Blatty's publisher thought then and thinks now that the whole thing is very nice, indeed.

The Toronto T.V. chef and cookbook author Pasquale Carpino made both the Toronto and Vancouver studios shake with laughter. To say that Carpino is an enthusiastic soul is to understate. We hardly ever do cooking items, because cooking stuff on radio is a bit odd. But in Pasquale's case an exception was made and he was asked to prepare a Veal Scaloppine Marsala in the Toronto studio and I would (under his instruction) prepare the same dish in Vancouver. A little chit-chat took place. The regular sort, about his new book and his television show. And finally we got to the ingredients for this dish. In front of me was a table with all manner of kitchen utensils (none of which do I own in real life), a hammer (wooden, to flatten the meat) and an electric frying pan. He told me the sequence of events that were to follow and I prepared to cook it up.

Because I had never seen Signor Carpino's T.V. show, I did not know that in addition to liking opera very much, he liked to sing it—while working. He especially likes to sing opera tunes while hammering veal. The instant the transcontinental pounding began, so did Carpino—loudly—as if to drown out the meat bashing.

The more he sang the louder he hammered.

I fell on the floor. The mental picture of a truck driver, whipping along the Trans-Canada highway and hearing this, made me and the crew hysterical. I would have been in the ditch. The veal turned out beautifully, as the vultures from the studio next door can attest.

The late Don Jamieson, former Liberal cabinet minister from Newfoundland and Canada's High Commissioner to Great Britain, admitted that he darn near drove off the road while listening to my guest, Louis Del Grande, one of the brains behind and the male star of CBC television's "Seeing Things."

There is, by the way, no point in trying to supervise Louis. He cannot be manipulated into participating in what has come to be known as a standard interview. First of all, I don't think the man breathes; he talks at Mach 2. The transcript of this interview is twenty pages long and (trust me when I tell you) I said hardly anything. The thing about these long-distance interviews is that I get the impression that I know these people, so they must know me. When I saw Louis some months after this conversation, I grinned like a fool and he, not knowing who I was, looked somewhat puzzled. This exchange took place in January 1984. You'll be surprised, I'm sure, to note that Louis started by asking me a question.

LD Hello, wait, you promised to tell me what you are wearing. So what? So tell me.

VG Oh, all right. I've got on a grey sweatshirt that says Burns Town, Ontario, on it and I am wearing a pair of attractive grey elephantine pants.

LD I love this.

VG You do? What is it that you are wearing, Louis?

LD An ugly green sweater knitted by my wife, but she has knit some beautiful things.

VG Louis, do you think that "Seeing Things" could be considered a runaway success?

LD I don't know if it ran away. The people who like it, like it emphatically. The most important and exciting aspect of it is anthropological. It is said Canadians don't get excited about anything and people *did* get excited about this. They perhaps are not staying home to watch, but we have some diehard fans. That's lovely. The biggest achievement of my life is that people actually got excited about something I did.

VG Are you in any condition to tell me the story of your life at all?

LD Sure. And I'll be good. I was born in New Jersey.

VG What made you cross the bridge?

LD I wanted to be an actor, a Shakespearian actor. I spent a lot of money studying to get rid of a New York accent and now I get paid for having one. But I don't put it on as much as my brother, who really has it. His name is John Del Grande and he is a very famous maintenance man in New Jersey.

VG Not in the theatre business?

LD He's cleaned a couple of theatres. He's coming here on Friday. I love him, he's one of my closest friends.

VG Did your family approve of your theatrical pursuits?

LD We were poor, but they loaned me money and I quit school when I was sixteen. I had a kind of pretend autonomy. The first show I did—well, I was working in a shoe store and I got this job acting—it was very exciting. Jayne Mansfield's husband hired me. He was the director of this production and I read very well. I was a very nervous youth as you can imagine and I read very well, but I sat down when I read. And the part was enormous. It was *Intimate Relations* by Jean Cocteau and the part, the juvenile lead, was the size of Lear. It was ridiculous. But they thought I was going to be better than the guy who was playing it, because I was a replacement. They didn't see me walk. I couldn't walk and talk at the same time. So what happened—I laugh now, but it was tragic—well, I only got one rehearsal. The woman actor, who had cheek bones into the balcony, was older, a former model I guess. At one point when I was supposed to pick her up but I was shaking too much, she said, "It's all right, you don't have to pick me up, darling." I could tell she was afraid I would drop her or something. My hands were humping. Oh, it was so painful. Anyway, I got fired. But thank God my parents gave me the money to buy a suit.

> **VG** You got better, though, didn't you?
> **LD** You can laugh, you're in Vancouver.

To interview Rich Little is not unlike interviewing a crowd. He slips in and out of character with almost no prodding. He is, to put it mildly, a natural. I never once during our chat got the impression that he resented me asking for examples. Mr Little lives in Los Angeles and this conversation, too, was conducted as a double-ender. I have yet to meet him.

> **VG** What do you know of the history of doing impressions?
> **RL** Matter of fact, I did a routine once on stage just on that subject. Traced time through Adam and Eve to King Arthur's Court, and I had a jester—Don Rickles, impersonating Merlin and Arthur and so forth. It was a comedy routine, but I couldn't help thinking that perhaps there is some truth in it. I would assume that the court jester in King Arthur's time probably did a few impressions, but of course he had to be careful or lose it. It was a bit touchier than it is today.
> **VG** When you were little, did you show a great talent for this? Did you drive your mother mad?
> **RL** I used to always do voices—barnyard animals. And then I just fell into it, I think by watching my teachers. I started imitating them, mostly with expressions at first and walks. I think the voices would come later. And I was a movie fanatic. I had a wild imagination. I would come home and act out the whole movie for my parents. I remember my dad saying, "We don't ever have to go to the movies, 'cause Rich just comes home and acts it all out for us, and sometimes it's better than the picture."
> **VG** Your parents were quite encouraging.
> **RL** Well, they didn't discourage me. I think they thought I was—well, strange may not be the right word. I know my brothers thought I was strange. I would lock myself in the room with my tape recorder and I'd tape everything. You know, "Lux Radio Theatre" and "Suspense." I had quite a file of them. Then I used to imitate them and put my own shows on tape. My brothers

would pass my room with their friends and say, "Oh, that's Rich in there, my sort of strange brother who doesn't know who he is." They all thought one day I would grow up and think of a career. Thank goodness I didn't.

VG Do people bug you for routines, on the street, say?

RL Yes, but I don't mind it. Just when I'm tired or in a hurry and somebody wants me to do Nixon on a corner, it can be a little embarrassing. But I'm like the piano player, wherever you go you're asked to perform. I do keep thinking, "Be tolerant and smile. These are the people who have made you, you know."

VG Is older better? I mean, the more mature someone gets, all the more intriguing their voice must become.

RL Yes, yes. That is why politicians are usually good subjects, because they are older, generally speaking, which means their voices have more character to them. You know a gruffness, more distinct.

VG And catch phrases, too?

RL I have always said that even the person with the blandest voice, if they become president or prime minister, with the pressures they develop things. Or the littlest things they have always tried to cover up, little idiosyncracies that they have forgotten about, will come to the surface. And that is what I look for.

VG Must make 'em nervous, eh? I wonder if they—let's say, Reagan—are aware that you watch like a hawk.

RL I think they are, because when Reagan first came on the scene, everything was "W-E-L-L-L-L, uh," and I drew attention to it and since that time he hardly says *well* at all. So obviously I made him aware of it and he got rid of it. He is kinda hard to do until you realize how visual he is and [as Reagan now]: "It's that, that hesitation, and, um, the humming and hawing, and, um, you know that um, that little smirk, and the head movement, and the tight mouth, and um." He is a good one, all right.

VG One of your great fortés is doing Canadian politicians. But is all that lost on the Las Vegas crowd?

RL Yes, but once in a while in Vegas I'll be in the middle of a routine and I'll hear somebody in the back yell out, "Do Kate Aitkens," or "Do Charlotte Whitton." I know they are out there. But [as Dief now]: "Of course Diefenbaker was the big voice for me in Canada. I did him for years." [Now as Lester Pearson]: "Then of course, there was Lester B. Pearson with that marvellous lisp." And Stanfield too—a lot of great characters. Louis St Laurent was the first political person I ever did. I do remember him at some convention or other when they introduced him. It was the funniest thing because he came out and said—actually did this, I had it on tape, I had everything on tape. They introduced him as the former Prime Minister of Canada and he came out and went "eh an, eh I, eh it, eh and it eh, ah and I uh, say that from the bottom of my heart." He actually said nothing. I have often thought it would be great if Jimmy Stewart had a conversation with ah, Louis St Laurent:

Jimmy: "It, it, it would, it would, uh, well Louis, um I'd uh.

St Laurent: "Eh, an, I, I eh um, well . . ."

Wonderful, eh?

FOUR

Author, Author!

I am crazy about interviewing authors. They spend so much time alone that when they are finally out of their cages and encouraged by their publishers to be charming, most will perform beautifully. One of the reasons why you hear so many authors on the CBC is because they appear for free. Cross-promotion is the banner under which these appearances fly. In fact, Canadian radio hardly ever pays anyone who isn't performing or writing. In England even politicians insist on payment; not in a scrum situation, but for a full-length, in-depth piece, the crossing of the palm is *de rigueur*. Can you imagine the chaos if the practice were adopted by Canadian politicians? Needless to say, the programmes on which I have worked hardly ever included a British politician.

But then there is Jeffrey Archer, who does seem to hit the front pages with some regularity. He is quite a dapper fellow, slight, well dressed, a bit full of himself. He has an on-again, off-again relationship with the British Conservative Party I suppose in that he is not alone. He resigned his seat in the House of Commons in 1975 because of a conflict-of-interest problem; he was also bankrupt. Unfortunately, the quick-witted Archer had been out-witted by a high-flying American con-artist who was for a time the vice-president of the Bank of Boston. Flat broke and facing the prospect of unemployment, Archer conceived the plot for his first novel, *Not a Penny More, Not a Penny Less*, the story of four men of great wealth who were cheated out of their fortune. Their scheme to get back the dough made readers wild, thus making the author a very rich man indeed. His 1979 book *Kane and Abel* was made into a mini-series for television, a fate that will no doubt befall *First Among Equals*, his 1984 blockbuster.

Most recently Archer has been, yet again, forced to resign. This time he has left the post of assistant to the Conservative Party chairman, a job he performed without pay. Jeffrey Archer is some kind of contender, for what I'm not sure. I spoke with him in the fall of 1985.

VG When you came out of the House of Commons and wrote that first book, did you think it would go over as well as it did?

JA Frankly, I thought that if it sold a few thousand copies and then I went out to look for a real job, that it would be wonderful. And it all came as a shock because it was what is called in the trade "a slow burner." It sold a few thousand and we were all happy even to sell a few thousand more and a few thousand more and then more and then it sold over ten million.

VG Did you promote it like a mad fiend?

JA No. They didn't want me to. They thought, "Well, he was a Member of Parliament, he has written one semi-autobiographical or quasi-autobiographical book; why should we back it—we won't get another one." So, ironically, it sold itself. Because no one would spend any money sending me around the country, or certainly they wouldn't have sent me over to you.

VG But you are a born promoter.

JA This is true, but unless you sell the book, you're not able to buy the ticket.

VG And you were financially embarrassed, so to speak.

JA Embarrassed is an understatement. You have under-played it. I left the House of Commons with debts of £427,000. Now, that may be minor where you come from, but where I come from, that is pretty major, especially as my income as a Member of Parliament would have allowed me to take 142 years to pay it off. You know I am an ambitious man, but I couldn't see how I would live to 186. And when you have an overdraft of

£427,000, your cheques have a tendency not to bounce but to sort of run around you.

VG Did you get yourself into that mess overnight, all of a sudden?

JA Uh, yes. It was a piece of extreme stupidity and *naïveté*. I invested in a company called Aquablast, on the advice of the Bank of Boston. The vice-president said that his bank had put in $2 million and I thought, "This is a winner." And indeed they *had* put $2 million in. So I borrowed a quarter of a million and then cashed in everything I was worth, which was another quarter—the whole lot. The shares went from £3.82 on a Monday morning to 17p by Wednesday morning. They disappeared overnight. No one wanted them. It was fraudulent and the vice-president at the bank got on an airplane with about eight million quid and shoved off. And he hasn't been seen since. This was a Canadian company, just for your interest, so you know I love the Canadians. It is going to take them a little while—they gotta buy a lot of books to pay back the money.

VG But you are such a smart cookie, could you not have smelled a rat?

JA I agree I was naïve. I agree that the degree of immaturity was akin to Hannibal crossing the Alps. Nevertheless, where I come from, in Somerset in the west country of England, my dear, you don't expect to find the vice-president of the bank is a crook. In my country this doesn't happen.

VG Well, what exactly did Aquablast do?

JA It cleaned high buildings, those great massive things, but it claimed to have invented something that could be put on the exhaust of the car and cut down the fumes and therefore the shares should have doubled overnight. They had reports from German and American police indicating that it was a wonderful thing and that the Senate were going to demand it on every car. The bank fell for it, and I fell for the bank's reports.

VG Are you still an athletic whiz?

JA I play squash four times a week, badly, and I referee cricket matches on weekends. I still have ambition to

> captain an England cricket team, but the selectors seem to have missed me completely.
>
> **VG** But you were such a good runner you would have made the Olympic team in Tokyo in 1964.
>
> **JA** I was lucky enough to run for Britain but frankly, I wasn't good enough. I shared rooms with Adrian Metcalfe, who at the time was an Olympic silver medallist, and I sort of lived on his coat-tails because I was on the same team he was on. So that was a bit of luck, but if I had shared rooms with you, let's say, I don't think I'd have made it.
>
> **VG** If you'd shared rooms with me you'd have been doing the laundry. How fast did you go in the hundred yards?
>
> **JA** I did 9.6 for the hundred. I remember running in Canada; in fact the best time I ever did was against a man called Harry Jerome. He is, tragically, dead now, isn't he? But Harry Jerome, God bless him, showed me his heels. I never actually saw his front, only his back. He was fast, that one. It was a terrible business, his dying. He was a great great runner.

Just for your information, to run one hundred yards in 9.6 seconds is not all that slow, but it ain't all that fast. All things being equal, and they're not, that would be a pace of about 10.7 if he ran the hundred metres instead of the hundred yards. Not fast enough, given that the world record for the hundred metres as of January 1987 is held by Canada's Ben Johnson at 9.6 seconds. Harry Jerome ran the hundred yards in 9.1 seconds.

Somehow the next four men, all writers, stick together in my mind. They were all taped within days of each other and in the same locale, the London studio, where I was temporarily stationed. But I think it was the fact that for a substantial length of time and in reasonably intimate surroundings, I was exposed to many first-rate writers: 1986 Booker Prize winner Kingsley Amis, the sardonic and argumentative Clement Freud, the American (living in London) novelist and travel writer Paul Theroux, and the only one with whom I have had lunch, John Mortimer.

Mortimer is quite a big guy. He is tall and robust but he is hardly tiger-taut or lion-fit, as CBC's own darling Clyde Gilmour would say. Mortimer's glasses slide down on his nose, and I must say I like that in a man. He is genuinely witty, with punch lines delivered so gently, with so little change in register, that it is possible to miss them completely. And that's a loss. In addition to being a practising lawyer (at least at the time of this interview in 1984), he is the author of the T.V. series, "Rumpole of the Bailey." His book *Clinging to the Wreckage* documents his extremely unorthodox childhood as the only child of parents who gave new meaning to the word "eccentric." His play *Voyage Round My Father* singles out old dad as a protagonist. His book *In Character* is a collection of interviews he has conducted for *The Sunday Times*. So, Mr Mortimer is hotter than a bandit's pistol.

On the law:

    VG What is your success ratio?

    JM I think that most cases win or lose themselves really and you can have a run of cases which are possible to win and a run of cases which have to be lost. I think you can *lose* cases but I'm not sure whether great advocates win cases that can't be won.

    VG Can you tell if you are going to win it or lose it from the first encounter with the charged one?

    JM Well, not from the charged one but as soon as you open the papers, it's like opening your hand at bridge; you take a first look at the cards and you say you're either going to win it or lose it. Then as you begin to work on it, you think you've got an answer to all the problems. By the time you get into court, you've persuaded yourself that you could win. And the result is almost invariably what you thought it would be when you first opened the hand.

    VG You seem awfully partial to obscenity and murder cases.

    JM I've given up obscenity cases. I don't like them any more. The bottom's gone out of the pornography market, as far as I am concerned.

    VG Har har.

    JM So, I don't do them any more. I like murder cases because I find murderers probably the nicest clients. Compared to people in divorce cases, they usually behave rather well, and they are no trouble. They are usually under lock and key. And they can't ring you up at night. And they are very grateful for what you can do for them and they've also probably killed the one person in the world they wanted to kill and they're in a rather peaceful frame of mind. I like murder trials. They are rather short.

VG Yes, but what if they are innocent?

JM That is all very worrying when people are innocent.

VG Don't you have to assume they are?

JM I don't make any assumption. I mean it *is* very difficult to explain this to people.

VG Try me.

JM Everybody thinks immediately that lawyers are terribly dishonest because they are always defending people they know are guilty. It becomes perfectly easy to do what we have to do, which is not make an assumption about whether they are guilty or not. It is for other people to decide—the jury, the judge.

VG Your legal life was almost preordained. Was there any question that you would be a lawyer?

JM No. My father decided that I should be a lawyer and I decided that I would be a writer, in the way that girls who want to go on the stage are offered typing courses so that they might have something to fall back on. He just said, "Learn a little bit of law and you'll have that to fall back on." As he said, writers' wives have terrible lives because writers are always hanging about the house making cups of tea and stumped for words. Your wife would be much happier if you'd get on the Underground and be off to the law courts. And he said, "You don't need anything for the law except a certain degree of common sense and relatively clean fingernails." And courage. I mean, you've got to keep on saying something when everybody's telling you to shut up.

VG Do you still have *Private Eye* as a client?

JM Well, I suppose I've given them up now. They are quite good at managing their defamation cases and they manage to settle most of them.

VG Practice, I guess.

JM Yes, Of course, the trouble with *Private Eye* now is that it's got very successful and it makes a lot of money. In the past, people never bothered to sue *Private Eye* because they thought there was no money to be got out of it. And now there *is* and they're in a lot more trouble. But I really think *Private Eye* keeps England sane. I couldn't think of England without it.

On Rumpole, the eccentric and mildly dotty QC, played by Leo McKern in the British television series. North American audiences were so taken with Rumpole and his dictatorial wife that the expression "she who must be obeyed," as applied to Mrs Rumpole, became a catch phrase.

VG Who coined the phrase, "She who must be obeyed"?

JM I got it from a book—African adventure stories from the beginning of the century. One story involved the search for SHE who must be obeyed. She was about a thousand years old and lived in a cave somewhere in Africa. When she was discovered she crumbled into dust, because the light got on her. I think that is where I got it. It's a very strange thing—she's become a very popular figure. Rumpole won't let anybody else say it. But in the latest series of plays and in the latest book they've become really much more dependent on each other and she's got bigger parts, which makes her even more intolerable.

VG Do you make Rumpole do what you would never do?

JM Well, Rumpole is a more brave barrister than I am. His life is all about being a barrister. I think he lives a more stoical, brave, and courageous life than I could put up with. So perhaps in that way I rather like a more comfortable existence.

VG It appears you don't care much for sporting activities of any kind.

JM Hate it. I don't even like playing Snap. I don't wish to compete in any form. Actually, I don't mind going to the horse races but I hate anything to do with people wearing gym shoes, sweating. I live in constant fearful memory of the smell of gym shoes.

VG Don't earnest types say, "Come on, old chap, you really ought to do something?"

JM They gave up that very early. At school I was expected to go outside and play with a football, and I made it quite clear that I had no intention of doing anything like that. So they used to give me a bar of chocolate and send me to the theatre.

VG Are you an only child?

JM Yes, I am.

VG Were you lonely?

JM Very lonely. But it's a marvellous opportunity for a writer. Added to my loneliness was the fact that my father was blind, so he didn't want to have people to the house in case they should feel sorry for him. So we didn't see many people when we lived in the country. I used to act all these plays. I did *Hamlet* and *Macbeth* and *King Lear* and I had to play all the parts. I had to duel with myself and drink my own poisoned chalice, and make love to myself as my own mother, and all that.

VG It is a wonder you're not more odd.

JM Well, I am strange—quite odd.

Two years later Mr Mortimer had occasion to visit Vancouver as part of his book tour for *Paradise Postponed*. His accompanying publicist called and invited me and Tom Rowe (with whom I live) to have brunch at a snappy hotel downtown. After we ate more than was necessary, it was decided that we would motor up the highway towards Whistler.

Mortimer never stopped telling unrepeatable funny stories. We were all in convulsions. Hardly able to move from the huge lunch, we stopped for a beer in the once-booming mining town of Britannia Beach. The law has changed now, but then a person could not have a beer on a Sunday without eating something. This particular restaurant served standard Canadian fare, and in addition, pyrogies. John Mortimer had never seen a pyrogy so two orders were placed. That meant that two people could have beer. The publicist and I drank coffee. Tom and Mortimer were delivered two of the biggest plates of pyrogies you have ever seen, laden with sausages and cabbage, swimming in butter and covered with sour cream. The pyrogies were judged to be fine, but none of us was able to eat more than one bite, so they were left to solidify in the butter.

Directly across from the CBC studios in London, England is an essential shop. It is an off-licence establishment called Frumkin's. It sells alcohol, and remains open even during the hours in which the pubs are closed in the afternoon. In the home studio, guests are rarely offered alcohol, but I guess it is the festive nature of being away that causes us to alter our normal offering of cafeteria coffee. To tell you the truth, I think the practice began with Kingsley Amis, a fellow who loves his single malt. Kingsley Amis was one of the original "angry young men," and when his novel *Lucky Jim* hit the book stores in 1954, he became a substantially better known and better-off angry young man. In 1963 he published *One Fat Englishman*, a satirical novel set in America. He is nothing if not versatile, and he has written a thriller, *The Anti-Death League*, and at least one detective story, *The Riverside Villas Murder*. For some years Kingsley Amis wrote a popular alcohol column for *Playboy* magazine.

VG Tell me what is swank to drink now? May I hope that the days of Campari and soda are over? It's a drink for those who like medicine.

KA Well, you may say that. But always take it with a slice of orange—not lemon—orange. Look, I said more or less what you said about Campari and soda to one of our best drinks writers and she said, "Well, everything you say may be true, but I don't think you could have tried it after coming in from a couple of hours of shopping on a hot and crowded morning. Then it really restores you."

VG Are you a purist? Do you like things neat?

KA Scotch malt whisky, with a little water and no ice. In fact, signs of my old fogey-ness came up about that the other day. You can ice the common or garden blend. My son Martin brought this young lady along and I said, "Well, there is the malt whisky." And she said, "Oh, could I have some of that?" I said, "Yes," She said, "Ice." And I said, "You are not having ice in your malt whisky."

VG Oh, she must have thought you a corker.

KA Well, before I knew it, it had slipped out. "Don't you say," she said rather cunningly, "that people should have what they like?" So I said, "Well, it doesn't apply in this case." But she was right, people should please themselves.

VG What has really gone down the tubes are the mixed fancy-lady drinks. We don't go in for them any more. A Pink Lady, for example.

KA There are some pretty ropy things out there. In the last four or five years the cocktail has bloomed all over the place in London in the most amazing way. I mean, a friend of mine about my own age said to me rather worriedly that his son had asked if he had a cocktail shaker. The chap of course had not seen or used his cocktail shaker in twenty years. You see, you go into the pubs and it says, "Whisky Sour, Piña Colada, Harvey Wallbanger," these names—nasty drinks, I think. They like going to the pub; they like playing the fruit machines. They come in straight off the bike—the motorbike, that is—and the girls have awful concoctions of coconut cream with rum and grapefruit juice.

VG You are not too partial to the slot machines in the pubs?

KA No, I am not.

VG What do you do for amusement then? Go to the races?

KA I hate all that. It is a tribute to Dick Francis's power that I love his books and hate horses and detest race meetings. I do go to my club, the Garrick. It is noteworthy and wonderful. Occasionally I go to the cinema. But I don't really go anywhere to amuse myself.

VG You and your son Martin have something in common other than blood. Both you and he have received the Somerset Maugham Award. Now, that has to be a rarity—both father and son?

KA I suppose so, yes. He is a very different writer from me. He is a very clever lad. But the funny thing is that it shows you how, I would say, we write very different sorts of books. My style is comparatively straightforward; his is comparatively devious, as it were. Indirect.

VG You mean to tell me he didn't get it all from you? You didn't teach him everything he knows?

KA No. He shut himself away, religiously almost. I knew he was writing a novel. He let us know that much. I went into his room to say—and I knew he was writing it, I could hear the typewriter going—"Come on, time for the pub." And as I looked in the door he put his hand on the typewriter, so that I could not see a word that was there.

VG Do you blame him?

KA No, I don't. It is odd and it shows you how little perhaps literary or critical talk matters. He and I agree completely on all his problems, what a novelist is trying to do, where he gets his characters from, all that kind of thing. There was one time when we were interviewed together and every time he answered a question, I was asked my opinion. I said I have nothing to add to that. The interviewer thought we had a conspiracy. I said we've never discussed it before. So I often wonder if there is any sense to criticism at all. You see, learning about literature at school or university, I think, produces good readers, or can do if it is at all intelligently done. A good teacher can help you see things that you didn't know were there, or point out to you things you have only half seen. But I think it makes bad writers.

VG To be taught you mean?

KA To learn literature. Philip Larkin simply said, "Studying literature teaches you to think you know what good poetry is; then it is your duty to produce some, isn't it?" I'm not saying that writers ought not to read. In a way, the more they read, the better. But I think haphazardly. They should not read anything because they ought to, because they've got to. And they shouldn't study it. The only thing that matters is enjoyment. Larkin again, interviewed by an American, when asked what he had gained from his study of the poetry of Hardy, said, "For Christ's sake, you don't *study* poets, you read them. That is what they are there for." And I think when you read what you like, you find out a lot about what you can do. You see how people do things. Seeing how Dick Francis, for example, a wonderful writer, works, you say, "Look, how has he done that?" The man has got out of his car, gone into his house and met this chap who is a stranger to him. It has taken only eight lines and he has told me what the house is like, what the room is like. *Those* are lessons that are worth learning.

VG Do you ever read jealously? Do you think to yourself, "Oh, I wish I'd written that?"

> **KA** Yes. I think, "I'll never be able to do that." I think that with Francis. The only consolation is that perhaps there are some things I can do that he can't do or can't be bothered to do.

Kingsley Amis is a great guy, and I surely did get a kick out of seeing the expression on his face when, after being on the short list for the Booker Prize several times, he finally got it. He looked genuinely surprised.

I suppose you think that I just love everybody and this entire tome is going to be full of accolades for all. Well, it stops here. I am not alone in saying that Clement Freud is not a piece of cake to interview. He is caustic and occasionally rude. Not being a journalist in the true sense, I am rather unused to being pushed around too much or having my questions evaded. Mr Freud gave me a bit of a runaround. He is, of course, something of a legend in his native England. In addition to being the grandson of Sigmund, he has been a restaurateur, a university rector, writer, horse owner, after-dinner speaker and general bon vivant. He used to do dog-food commercials with Henry, a bassett hound. They were almost indistinguishable from one another.

The Kingsley Amis interview took place immediately before the one with Clement Freud, and when Mr Amis learned who would be next, he said, "I see. Well, he won't like you or this studio much. He loathes cigarette smoke." As Mr Amis and I had puffed up a storm and the studio was clouded, he suggested we air it out, or Freud wouldn't come in. He then mischievously suggested that perhaps we ought to smoke even more, to truly infuriate the man. The prospect of seeing Clement Freud in a rage seemed to provide a certain joy for Mr Amis. He departed howling with laughter.

I was now in a state. I opened all the doors to the studio and fanned like mad. I do respect a person's dislike of smoke and I didn't care to start off on the wrong foot. One hour later the punctual Mr Freud arrived, and within seconds I had riled him. He questioned me about why I was in London and whether I had come unaccompanied (not a come-on). I replied that I had come with my mother, because she had never been to England before and because she was recently widowed and I had not wanted her to stay alone in Canada. He was stunned by my reply.

"It was her second husband, then, and not your father?"

"No," I said, "he was my father."

He thought it curious in the extreme that I had referred to my mother as being recently widowed, and I got the impression that he thought I should go for immediate psychoanalysis. I thought I was being polite, if not formal, not wanting to elicit sympathy about my father's death from a complete stranger. Anyway, he thought I was an odd duck and it got worse from there.

VG Are you a bit of an institution? It seems everybody has an opinion of you.

CF Yes. A child said to me the other day, "When you die, who is going to be Clement Freud?" I thought he was awfully nice.

VG Your hangover cure book is out in paperback now. Would you say that Angostura Bitters is a cure?

CF I wouldn't have thought so, no. I think drunkenness is very overrated. I've always felt that if you can lie on the floor and not hold on to anything, you are not drunk.

VG What, then, provoked you to write a hangover cure book?

CF I started my working life in France with a limited knowledge of French and mistook the words of a managing director who said, to encourage me to pursue the French way of life, that they would let me have a litre of wine with every meal. But he actually said "every week." So for the first three weeks, before I got my first monthly pay cheque, I thought I would do the right thing by him and I drank a litre of wine with every meal. Even on my day off I would come in and drink a litre of wine. A litre of wine is a lot of wine. I lived in a sort of oyster light of a drunken glow, giving the wrong people the wrong keys and calling gentlemen "madam."

VG Was this Paris?

CF No, Cannes.

VG Scenic?

CF Warmer. I didn't see much of the view.

VG Blurred at all times?

CF Well, drunk.

VG Are you more cautious now? You don't slug back a litre of wine at the drop of a hat?

CF No, no. I very seldom drink a litre of wine at the drop of a hat. I don't wear a hat.

VG Never?

CF Nor a coat.

VG Well, how do you manage? It's quite pleasant today but—

CF You know, I keep meeting people who complain about how cold they are and they have coats. I'm cold and I don't have a coat.

VG And no hat. But that's where all the heat escapes, from the top of your head.

CF But it does mean that I am considerably richer than people who keep buying coats and hats, and I'm no more or less warm.

VG Will you choose some music?

CF I'm not big on music.

VG I know. When you told me your musical choices, I hardly knew what to say.

CF Well, they are things that come most quickly to mind, music that I hear most often. I hear "God Save the Queen" every Christmas Day and at the end of television programmes. I don't want to hear it again.

VG Well, we will play it in your absence.

CF That is very good of you.

VG Perhaps we should play "Land of Hope and Glory," another stirrer?

CF I get those two mixed up quite a lot.

This *thing* went on and got nowhere and I was disappointed and a trifle embarrassed. So shall we forget the whole thing right now and get on to the next guy, who was swell?

I think that Paul Theroux is this decade's literary darling. That is not to say that he would like or even covet such a handle. Responsible most notably for *The Mosquito Coast,* a novel and now a movie, *The Great Railway Bazaar, The Old Patagonian Express, The Kingdom by the Sea,* and a whole lot more, he is quite a steamy guy, lean and intellectual, charming and distant, not goofy. I was impressed by his manner. We drank tea.

VG Did you write *The Kingdom by the Sea* for the British to read about themselves, or did you write it for North Americans?

PT Well, I think I wrote it for myself, the way I would write any book, to amuse myself for a year, to pay for the children's school fees and also, I think, to give myself the satisfaction of nailing the place down, of giving it some order. That's why any writer should write. It is a very good reason. But I wasn't writing it for the market, no. If one wanted to write for the market you would write about cannibalism or incest or something like that—get a really good topic. You certainly wouldn't write about English seaside resorts. But *The Kingdom by the Sea* was a book I'd always wanted to write. There were places I'd always wanted to go—Northern Ireland, Wales, the North of Scotland, Aberdeen.

VG In Aberdeen this past summer [1983], you were a hot topic.

PT I doubt if I could get a T.V. dinner in Aberdeen, but that's how it goes. Actually, you don't win many friends writing.

VG Do you always travel alone?

PT Yes, nearly always. If I'm writing, always and without exception.

VG You go away for great spans of time, months sometimes. Do you phone, do you keep in contact, write letters?

PT Yes, I'm a great letter writer. It is not unusual that I should be away. People listening to this would say, "What a twinkie, he's only away a month or two. I work on an oil pipeline. I'm on a fishing boat. I'm in the army." Somebody else, let's say a fur trapper in Yellow-knife, thinks, "What is so great about this guy? He just goes and stays in a bed-and-breakfast place in Aberdeen or he goes to Patagonia."

VG It's not so rough.

PT It's not so rough.

VG You don't isolate yourself when you are away? You don't pretend that the rest of your life doesn't exist?

PT   Yes, I do. I pretend the rest of my life doesn't exist. I think that in order to travel well you have to throw yourself more or less completely into the other culture. You need a sense of detachment, but you can't make too many plans ahead and you can't be compelled to keep in close touch with people. But I think also if you are alone you have a greater opportunity to write about it. Your time is your own and so you can work late at night and you can do all the antisocial things that writers do, or have to do.

VG   In *The Kingdom by the Sea* you talk about running into punk kids—

PT   Yes, little gangs of boys with very spiky hair.

VG   Did they make you nervous?

PT   Occasionally they made me nervous. But actually, being English punks, they are pretty harmless, soft-spoken, and polite little people. One of their favourite groups was the Stranglers. I thought, I'm game for anything. You have to be, in my line of work. So I thought I would play them. You can't be too contemptuous and I discovered that I actually liked one of the songs on the album *Raven*. It's called "Shah-Shah A Go-Go" and is about the fall of the Shah and the rise of the Ayatollah. The words are—the Ayatollah promising peace and prosperity—"We shall see, we shall see." It's actually much better than I thought it would be and it is a catchy song.

VG   Why do you appear on the book jacket wearing sunglasses? Is it so people won't point at you and grab you?

PT   It is not the reason, but it is fatal for a writer to be a conspicuous kind of celebrity. This is one of the appeals of radio, I think. People aren't looking at my necktie and saying, "He seems a nice chap, where do you suppose he bought that tie?"

VG   And they don't see how badly the suit fits.

PT   If they knew I was sitting here stark naked.

VG   They would be as thrilled as I am.

It is hard to imagine anyone not having seen or at least heard reports of the remarkable creature that is Barbara Cartland. We should all be so lucky to possess the vigour she has for life. And what a life it has been. Now well into her eighties, Cartland has never let her style erode. She dresses with great flair and indeed continues to wear seamed stockings that are always in perfect alignment. While most women have given up on three- and four-inch sling-back pumps, she still manoeuvres up and down stairs in them with great facility. Mind you, she is well attended. She is driven to interviews in an expensive white auto and accompanied by a driver who is ever on the alert. There is a metal strip on the side of her car that allows for a coloured piece of plastic to be inserted. The day she and I met, the coloured strip was turquoise to match, exactly, her outfit. She is as glamorous as anyone I have ever encountered. The fact is that even if she were not responsible for over four hundred romance novels and other works, she would be a force to be reckoned with. This woman churns it out. Although she is formidable and allows few liberties, she is affectionate and charming and I loved her immediately.

As the appointed hour of her appearance at the London studio neared, the staff there began to lurk around the entrance. Everyone in the place wanted to get a look at this woman who, in addition to everything else, is the mother of Lady Spencer, the second wife to Lord Spencer, father of the Princess of Wales. Barbara Cartland came bearing gifts (her books), carried in a modest shopping bag. One for each of us. *Us* being the producer, the researcher, and me. The presents were all wrapped beautifully and autographed accordingly, all names spelled correctly. Now, that is training.

You don't so much interview Cartland; you sit and listen. Her age, position, and series of accomplishments dictate a certain demeanor and I behaved.

> **VG** You must have been interviewed more than any other human being.
>
> **BC** I should think so by now. They come every day. I have press practically every day, at four o'clock. By then I have written all my chapters for the day, and then I give them tea. I can't give them lunch because I'm working. And they all come, you see, and ask the same questions. So do ask some new ones.
>
> **VG** I'm going to try. That is the thing—you must be awfully weary of it.

BC Well, I am sick of virgins.

VG You seem to have a huge capacity for work.

BC I like working. What else would I do at my age? I am eighty-four and I should find it frightfully boring if I just sat about waiting to go to a party somebody hasn't asked me to. I couldn't bear it. I love doing my books. And when I get letters like I got this morning, saying how much my books had helped somebody and what a difference they made in her life, it is all worthwhile. Well, I'll tell you. You know who I mean by Mrs Billy Graham?

VG I do.

BC The evangelist's wife. Well, she was ill in Los Angeles and a great friend of mine took her twelve Barbara Cartlands. She said it was the only thing that stopped her from feeling pain. She loved them. Now Billy's reading them. I can't do better, can I?

VG I guess not. You are assuring your fate, anyway. You say "She was taken twelve Barbara Cartlands" as if a Cartland is something else, apart from you. "Barbara Cartland" is something bigger than just you, isn't it?

BC It has become a sort of adjective, almost, in America. As you know, I get about a hundred press cuttings every day, and they say, "Oh, *it* is like a Barbara Cartland," or *"She* is like Barbara Cartland." A sort of adjective. I think it is because I'm so old, quite frankly.

VG You have the most extraordinary wardrobe.

BC You are kind. Well, you see what people expect from me is for me to be glittering in diamonds all over. It was very funny when I went to France the other day and I hadn't appeared there for some time. I sell enormously in France, more than anywhere in the world now. And my son, who is very keen on France and has spent a lot of time there learning French, said to me, "Now Mum, the French don't like people to be over the top. You must go chic and quiet and subdued." So I rang up one of my publishers, who happens, actually, to be a Russian prince, and I said, "Do you want me pseudo-French or the *Folies Bergères*?" He said, "The *Folies Bergères*." So I went *Folies*, covered in diamonds from head to foot, and was a huge success.

VG Their mouths must have been agape.

BC They were very sweet and they said it was all very funny. And I do understand, more or less, the French humour.

VG Well, perhaps you could explain it to me.

BC The French think only two things are funny—love and food. You can take your choice. I was interviewed once and, of course, it all had to be translated, so I said to the interviewer, "Ask me why I like France so much." Then I replied, "Well, France is a country where you can make love after luncheon, and people don't hammer on the door and ask you if you're ill." The French thought that was very funny. Very likely the Canadians won't, and the Americans wouldn't, but the French—that is just their sense of humour.

Miss Cartland had recently recorded an album of songs she loves, with the Royal Philharmonic, no less. She admits she sort of "whispered' the lyrics, something like Whispering Jack Smith did in the twenties.

VG Were you happy with the sound of the record when you heard it all back?

BC Well, I rather like it now. I said to them, "The only thing I want, and there is only one thing I insist on, is that I can be heard in the car." The only person I can hear when I am motoring is Frank Sinatra or Perry Como, who I wish to sing at my funeral, and myself.

VG You've booked Perry Como?

BC Well, I want him to sing "I Believe," which always makes me cry. I think he is absolutely marvellous.

VG I can't believe you would be planning such a thing. Did you say that in jest?

BC No, no, no, no. My children keep saying to me, "You're not going to plan your funeral like Mountbatten did." Lord Mountbatten used to come out to lunch with me and say, "I've just been choosing the hymns for my funeral." And I'd say, "Oh, don't go on, don't talk about it." But he liked doing it, so in the end I shall plan mine. He planned his so beautifully. The man who really does all the royal funerals said he had nothing to do.

VG You must miss Mountbatten.

BC He had this terrific charm, everybody says so. You couldn't get away from it, you see. He always got his own way in everything, because he did it so charmingly. It was so different from other people, who gave orders.

I remember going to the Kerrisdale theatre to see *Love Is a Many Splendoured Thing,* the story of a romance between an American journalist and a Eurasian doctor. They were in love with a kind of desperation that wartime causes. He was not free to marry and she was endlessly patient. The male lead was William Holden, and when he died I wept, as did the whole Saturday afternoon movie-going crowd. But we all knew that the woman, Han Suyin, played by non-Eurasian Jennifer Jones, would carry the memory of this great love forever, and I suppose she has.

The real Han Suyin, daughter of Chinese father and Belgian mother, has had an amazing and varied career: doctor, diplomat, television personality, lecturer, and writer. It was in her capacity as writer that I interviewed her in Vancouver, a city in which she has a considerable number of friends.

HS I have been to Vancouver many times to visit my friends in the Chinese community and I have many Canadian friends. My friends in Victoria I shall always remember, because of the time in 1950 when I was in Hong Kong with my daughter, all alone, with no place to go, because there was accommodation for single doctors but not for those with children at the hospital where I worked. My friends from Victoria took us in. I recall the horror among this woman's friends. "What? You are taking in a Eurasian? Don't you know the danger?" Well, my friend said, "I like her and enjoy her conversation." And I thought that was terrific. At that time there were still so many, many prejudices against Eurasians.

VG What was the danger to her?

HS Her husband. They all thought that I would make a pass at her husband.

VG Oh, no.

HS   Oh yes! Eurasians were thought to be born prostitutes,
and that is what was insinuated to her. I have another
friend on Vancouver Island. I met her in London during
the bombings, and we used to comfort each other. At
first we refused to go downstairs to the cellar. We just
sat together drinking tea quietly while the bombs fell.
She was a very courageous woman.

VG   I have seen a number photographs of you over the years
and in none of them are you ever static. Your hands are
always on your head or somewhere. You move all the
time.

HS   Yes. That is why I don't need to do any physical
exercise. When I read about these people who go in for
the body beautiful and all that and then they say to me,
"My, you are keeping your figure," I say that is because
I am moving all the time. It is a way of saving time. You
have to move from a kind of focal point in you, and the
focal centre as all the Chinese know is in the belly.

VG   Not the heart?

HS   It is the belly. When we have a pain, we don't say, "My
heart is broken"; we say, "My bowels are twisted."

VG   Well, I've always thought it was lower down.

HS   Well, you are right. That is, of course, where you feel the
pain, isn't it?

VG   That gives a whole different meaning to the way we
look at romance.

HS   You bet.

VG   You work like a Trojan.

HS   I am a striver and a workaholic. I tell people it's because
I have the Chinese striving, and I think the Chinese
revel in work. In fact, I don't really know what a holiday
is. This book tour for *The Enchantress* is my holiday.

VG   No days off to sit around and knit?

HS   Knit? My husband would kill me if I knitted. In fact that
is why I like him so much. Because the first thing he
said to me was, "You don't knit, do you?" I said, "No."

VG   With what frequency do you go to China?

HS   I go about twice a year. I try to do four or five months a
year. I have to or I can't keep up with the changes. I
started to go back in 1956 and have been ever since,
except for two years during the Cultural Revolution

when I was labelled an agent of the CIA and therefore not allowed to go back.

VG You were not, I take it, an agent of the CIA?

HS Well, what do you think? I was also at the time blacklisted in America. The whole thing was very funny. I think that perhaps because I just laughed, the barriers seemed to melt away. Bamboo curtains, iron curtains dropped and so I just went through. It was a worry, though. I think that is why for ten years I couldn't write a novel because I was so worried inside. And I couldn't go out and say too much publicly because it would have got too many people into a jam in China, even some very high-ups. I'll write it all one day but I'm not quite ready. I'm still recuperating. One day I'll write about the younger generation and how they look at these past thirty or so years. They don't know what the old China was like. When people tell them, they don't believe. But they believe Han Suyin and that is why my books are being translated into Chinese. My biography, for instance, which is the real biography of my family.

For many years my father was the Publicity Director at Exhibition Park racetrack in Vancouver, and I loved to accompany him on his early-morning treks around the backstretch. He liked nothing better than to stand at the rail and watch the morning workouts. There are very few books that capture the sensation of life at the racetrack before and after a day's meet, but Peter Gzowski's book *An Unbroken Line* is an example of how well it can be done. The fact is that the greatest critics are the racetrackers themselves. They are very touchy about their sport and how their way of life is represented. In other words, racetrack books are very rarely big sellers.

The giant exception is the work of Dick Francis. There is no doubt that his background as a jockey has provided him with insight and a firm grasp of the facts. One of the harsh realities in the life of a jockey is weight. It is a constant battle, fought especially hard by North American riders, and until vitamins came into popular use it was not an uncommon sight to see toothless jockeys practically suffering from malnutrition just to keep getting mounts.

Most jockeys, however small, spend an unbelievable number of hours in the sweat box. Not unlike other businesses that depend on the big payoff (theatre, publishing, and movies), the racetrack world is full of gossip and intrigue, grist for the mill of a guy like Dick Francis. He and his wife, Mary, were in Vancouver in 1985 to promote his most recent book, *Proof*.

VG You're awfully big to be a jockey.

DF Well, I was what they call a steeplechase jockey, of which there are very few in North America—a few in Pennsylvania and Maryland. When I was riding I was about 140 pounds, which is really the minimum weight steeplechasers carry. It can go up to 167 pounds, so being 140 was ideal, and I never had to do any fasting or go into sweat boxes or anything. And since I have given up, my diet has remained the same and I have only gained about 20 pounds.

VG Do you miss all the action?

DF Not so much now, but I missed it for years after. Immediately after I gave up race riding I wrote for the Sunday paper *Express*. I went to a lot of meetings every week and I felt very jealous of those jockeys who were going out to ride in the big races that I used to go out in, especially those jockeys who were going out to ride horses that I had initially brought to the course. You know, they were green horses, but by the time I came back and was writing they were old experienced horses. I was so jealous of them all then.

Mary Francis was asked to join in on the interview, because they don't do much separately.

VG Mary, did you notice a change in his disposition when he stopped racing?

MF No. He is always very easygoing and good tempered. I mean, it is a terrible thing to have wanted to do something all your life, to have done it, to have been at the top of it and then have to stop because, like all athletes, age stops you and you can't go beyond a certain point.

VG Were you relieved in a way?

MF In a way. I was relieved not because he was not going to get any more damaged—broken bones and so on—but because of that old phrase about it being tough at the top. It is quite true. A jockey has to prove every single race that he's still the top jockey. That is the strain, and in a way I found that the removal of that strain was more of a relief than the removal of the threat of injury.

VG Well, you've replaced that kind of strain with yet another. Now the entire world judges your work.

DF Yes. Being a jockey you win and everyone pats you on the back. Your acclaim is immediate and it is lovely. When you write a book the acclaim is much more long lasting but longer in coming. One hands in one's manuscript like I do every year about May and then the book isn't out until October. And then you wonder, "How will it be received?" And you don't really appreciate it until the book has been out a month and people say they loved it.

VG Have you never had one book that people yawned at? Not ever, since you started writing?

MF He is always afraid that he's actually writing *that* book.

VG You wrote the autobiography first. Were you nervous about doing it?

DF I was nervous and I didn't really think it would go, but you see I had had a wonderful life and I did have two ambitions. One was to be a champion jockey, which I achieved. And the other was to win the Grand National. And that was snatched from me in the 1956 Grand National when the Queen Mother's Horse Devon Loch collapsed with me thirty yards from the winning post. The Grand National is two circuits—you jump the water-fence to the winning post on the second circuit. We were winning easily. I was about ten lengths in front and going away from the opposition with every stride. Just as we got to the jump, Devon Loch caught the jump in the corner of his eye: "Ah, I was here last time round." He pricked up his ears and as he did it—I've looked at the newsreel so often—his hind quarters refused to act, as if to say, "God, what was that?" It was a momentary shock, I think, and down he went on his belly. You can imagine the noise of all the people screaming and cheering. Ah—it was horrible, horrible.

He went down on his belly and slid along the ground, and funnily enough I didn't fall off him. He got to his feet again. If I could have got him going again, he was still far enough ahead—but he had pulled all his muscles in his hind quarters and he just couldn't move. I had to get off him and walk away in disgust. But if I had won that race, would I have been asked to write my autobiography then? Who knows.

Robertson Davies first came into prominence in Ontario as the editor of the *Peterborough Examiner* when he wrote a column under the guise of one Samuel Marchbanks, a gentleman of most unpredictable opinions. National recognition came with his Salterton Trilogy—*Tempest-Tost, Leaven of Malice,* and *A Mixture of Frailties,* three novels about life in the arts in a small conservative Ontario college town. The rest of the world took note with the Deptford Trilogy—*Fifth Business, The Manticore,* and *World of Wonders.* A man of many parts, Robertson Davies has also made a name as a critic and playwright. He spent nearly twenty years as master of Massey College at the University of Toronto where he created an eminently civilized atmosphere for the exchange of ideas. At the time of this interview he had just finished his latest novel, *What's Bred in the Bone,* the story of a Canadian who becomes an international art critic with an international secret.

You have no doubt seen Robertson Davies on television, but that is not preparation enough. He is formidable, much larger than I had imagined, and much less stern.

> **VG** I have a feeling that it really doesn't matter what I ask you because you have pretty catholic tastes and everything interests you.
>
> **RD** Everything. Absolutely everything.
>
> **VG** Does that mean that you will read anything? Scientific journals let's say?
>
> **RD** I'll read scientific journals if they're about something that interests me. I read an awful lot about gastroenterology because I'm interested in digestion. It's fascinating.
>
> **VG** It is? Have you had problems with digestion that would make you fascinated?

RD Oh indigestion runs in my family. But also a great friend of mine is one of the world's foremost experts in gastroenterology and he keeps me posted on all the news that's not fit to print on the subject. In March-banks I quote him as saying it doesn't matter whether you chew your food or not. Whether you gulp it down in hunks, it's still digested and does the same amount of good. It may give you indigestion but it will do exactly the same sort of things inside you.

VG Might you have chosen a medical career?

RD No. I would have been an impossible doctor because I couldn't have played fair with boring patients with boring diseases. There are only twenty diseases that a doctor sees in the course of a week and he's delighted when somebody comes in with something really extra-ordinary to catch his attention.

VG I take it that students never bored you?

RD Well, no. Students are perpetually interesting. I was extremely lucky with my students and I had some very good ones, and very few were just dull.

VG You have even said that you got a lot of new ideas from them.

RD That is true. And if you bring enthusiasm to them, they will bring it back to you. And that is interesting.

VG You and your wife had a great deal of entertaining to do when you were master at Massey College—students and faculty. Were these evenings pretty high-falutin' affairs?

RD It was not high-falutin'. It was a very good occasion because what we did was to invite a number of guests to come and have dinner with ourselves, that is the seniors of the college. We chose a group of young people from the body generally, and everybody got asked at least once a year. But we didn't ask crowds because you can't get good communication with crowds of people. But what we tried to do and what we said to the young people is "We're asking you to come and meet some people in whose shoes you may expect to stand in another twenty years and you'll want to see what they're like and you'll find them interesting." And they did find them interesting. We had all kinds of

people, and I remember one of the most successful
dinners of that kind we ever had, our two chief guests
were the Chief of Police of Metropolitan Toronto and
Veronica Tennant, the ballerina. They were both runaway successes. The students loved them and they
were wonderful talkers, delightful people. That was the
kind of party we gave and we didn't have fancy
nonsense. That was just something said by people who
were wanting to say something disagreeable or were
jealous or something of the sort.

VG I wonder if jealous is the key.

RD Well, jealous was some of it. But you know there's silly
talk of us taking snuff and rubbish of that sort. We had a
snuff horn because somebody gave us one and we used
to put it on the table. But nobody was forced to take
any snuff if they didn't want it. It was just, you know,
what the Masseys said to me was "We want this place
to be a centre of hospitality." So we made it a centre of
hospitality and I think hospitality is part of the very life
blood of a university. If students don't get a chance to
meet the faculty and older people on pleasant terms,
the university hasn't done part of its job. If they only
meet in the classroom, that's not good enough.

VG Well, would things ever get out of hand? Would you be
faced with a rowdy crew once in a while?

RD Oh we had crews but they never got very rowdy. We
used to have entertainers sometimes. I remember Don
Harron and his wife Catherine McKinnon came one
time and they sang for us. And that was great and we
loved it. But it just happened spontaneously. We didn't
say "And now will you oblige us with a number?" They
were talking about their work and they started to sing
something and it was absolutely splendid. There were
two rules that were applicable to those high-table evenings. No guest was ever to be asked for a favour and no
guest was ever to be quoted in print. And in those
circumstances people could have a really good time.

VG Say, do you suppose this would be too indiscreet ... but
when you and I were coming down to the studio in the
elevator, you made the remark, "Do you think or do you
not think that the woman at the door is wearing a wig?"

Is this a game you play?

RD Well, there is nothing wrong with wigs. I rather admire wigs. If you have a poor head of hair, it's sensible to wear a wig but I like to detect them. I have a mental game where I add up how many wigs I see.

VG How many have you seen this week?

RD Oh, I think I've been very poor on wigs this week. I think I've seen only about two or three.

VG No wig needed for you—you have hair aplenty and all white it is too. Look a bit like Santa actually.

RD No, I don't. Not a bit. Not really. Not if you look closely. I had a high old time in Calgary last time I was west because I was sitting in a restaurant having an innocent cup of coffee and the waitress, who thought she was very funny, approached me and said, "Say, are you Santa Claus"? And I said, "No, I am his brother Sharp Claws and I am going to bring you a dead rat for Christmas." And she went, "Ha ha ha, he he hee." Fool—she shouldn't have been so impertinent.

VG Oh, dear. It's not worth it to try and win with you is it?

RD Well, I didn't want to make a scene. I just gave her a snappy reply.

VG Scenes are not your thing; after all you did grow up in a quiet, rural Ontario town. But you were sent away to boarding school at age fourteen. Did you find that wrenching?

RD I found it a very, very extraordinary change. It was very interesting and good in some ways. Rather desolating in others. But I think it was probably a very good experience because you see an awful lot of life in the raw in boarding school. I always say if you can go through a boarding school and come out with your sanity, very little else in life is going to shake you.

VG But how did you like your time or pass your time when you were in a small country school? Did you think of it one way or the other? You seem to consider it a valuable experience.

RD It was a valuable experience because it taught me an awful lot about people and an awful lot about life. It made me somewhat . . . I would not say cynical but rather . . . disillusioned about the romantic notion that

humble and simple people are wonderful and have
noble instincts and are really very great souls who are
being repressed by economics. I beg leave to doubt that.
I've been at school with them, and, as I say in that novel,
don't talk to me about the common man. I've known the
common child and that's really where it all begins.

VG They grow up to be common . . . ?

RD Monsters.

VG When you go to private school rather than a public
school, you come out of that system a different person.

RD Yes you do. Because you have grown up in a much more
contained society where, for one thing, they drive you
very hard to work and for another thing where they
lecture you on your duty, which is a thing you dare not
do in provincial or state schools. Now I remember that
at my boarding school, not less than once a week we
had a sharp lecture at prayers from the headmaster who
spoke briefly, perhaps for four minutes or something
like that, that much had been given to us and much
was expected of us and we must buckle down and
deliver the goods. And I think that that is good for boys,
but you can't do it in a state school or you'll have people
down on you because it's against the Bill of Rights or
something.

VG How long do you think private school will last in this
country?

RD Forever. Because they deliver the goods. They give a
very good education and they do it very professionally.
They're not paid to be social workers on the side. But
you don't have to go. If you don't like it, you can get out.
You don't have to pay the fees. If you don't like the
discipline go someplace else.

VG What about the question of keeping, maintaining a
class system

RD You'll never get rid of a class system because the class
system is always rooted in something or another. In
Canada it tends to be rooted in talent and ability, and
there is always going to be an unfair or unequal division
of that and you can't get rid of it. People are going to
come to the top because they've got the stuff, or they're
going to sink because they haven't got it. When you live

as long as I have, you've seen families where grand-father made money, the next generation managed the money, and the third generation have blown it because they thought money was forever. It isn't.

VG But I would think that *you* haven't got a spendthrift bone in your body.

RD Not one.

VG Are you a man of ritual?

RD Oh very much so, yes.

VG I've got a friend who is of the same sort, and she jogs every morning. She used to see you when you were Master at Massey, every morning at precisely the same time, walking in precisely the same spot. She could check her clock by you.

RD That's right. I took my exercise before I began my work of the day.

VG You don't like spontaneity in things?

RD Oh, I like spontaneity where I think it belongs. But I don't think it belongs in exercise. I hate exercise and take it because I should. I don't want to improvise; I just do it.

VG If you get up in the morning at 7:45 precisely and you never leave anything to chance . . . I mean, one day you might get up at 9:00 . . .

RD Everything is left to chance. Everything important is left to chance. It's just the details of life—the getting up, the time for meals, when you put your clothes on and take them off—that are a routine. The rest of the time is all adventure.

VG Is it a comfort to you then to have these spots of the day that you know certain things are going to occur.

RD Yes, That is why I find a book tour like this rather disconcerting because it's outside my routine.

VG Have you been like this since childhood?

RD Pretty much, yes. I was brought up that way because both my parents used to say that unless you had order in your life you never got anything done. And believe me there's a lot of truth in that. I meet people who rely on spontaneity and they are going to do things when the spirit moves them and they never do anything.

They never get anything finished. Waiting for God to touch them with his finger and God laughs his head off and passes them by.

VG Do you spend most of your days writing now, with a little dawdling around your property?

RD Yes. I write every morning from nine-thirty till twelve-thirty and then a little in the afternoon from about five till quarter to six and the rest of the time I dawdle. What kind of a word is that? I work like a slave. I help my wife in the garden, and she is the brains and I am the cheap labour. You know, that kind of thing.

VG Dig here, Robertson!

RD Dig here! Bring a load of manure! Move that stone!

VG You take orders well, do you?

RD Of course I do.

VG I don't believe it for a minute.

RD If I hadn't taken orders from my wife, I would have been in the grave forty years ago.

VG Before I let you go, there is one thing that I would like to know. Why, in the 1920s when a great number of writers rushed off to Paris, didn't you? Did it not appeal to you?

RD No. What would I want to go to Paris for? Anything I can do, I can do right here. They just went to Paris because they thought it was romantic and that's stupid. Paris is about as romantic as Paris, Ontario.

VG You certainly are a realist, aren't you?

RD I am.

VG You never had a longing to live the exotic life—drunk all night, mad conversations over too many cups of coffee.

RD Hate the exotic life.

VG Oh.

RD Hate being drunk all night. Hate too many cups of coffee. Loathe fascinating women who make goo-goo eyes. All of that I detest. I regard it as corny and very bad for one's work. You see I am now talking like a moralist and that is what I am.

When I met novelist and poet Elizabeth Smart in January of 1983, she had just recently returned to Canada from Suffolk, England, where she had been living for years. That past fall she had accepted the position of writer-in-residence at the University of Alberta. In 1945 her book *By Grand Central Station I Sat Down and Wept* brought her instant notoriety, when her socialite mother had the book banned from Canada. Elizabeth Smart's nineteen-year affair with the English poet George Barker produced four illegitimate children. Later, after the tragic death of her daughter, she raised her two grandchildren. Life was not a cinch for Elizabeth Smart, but it was interesting.

VG In the past you have been candid in your interviews. The story of your life is so public, I have to wonder if you sometimes wished it would be otherwise?

ES Yes, in fact, I did. I kept very anonymous for a long time. And then this American publisher I had in London sort of released all these stories unbeknownst to me. And, of course, they were slightly inaccurate as always. So it seemed to me that there was nothing to do except put the record straight whenever I was asked anything.

VG Do you know why your mother burned copies of your book? Was it because she was so horrified?

ES She wasn't horrified with the story of the book. She was horrified that she was cast in what she thought was an unfavourable light.

VG She thought it too autobiographical?

ES Well, I did make some of it up, but you have to when you are talking about such a subject. You mention the relationship with the parents, because I think it always comes in when you have your first love affair, doesn't it? And of course, I used a few details which made it look as if it were she herself who was the model for the mother and did *all* of those things.

VG And that did not make her happy?

ES No-o-o.

VG Upon your return to Canada, did you expect to be met and feted as a conquering hero?

ES No to both questions. I've been absolutely delighted and amazed every time I meet writers and they say nice things to me. It *is* a surprise to me, a wonderful surprise.

VG Well, your work, especially *By Grand Central Station*, seems to keep rising, and then settling, and then rising again.

ES It is peculiar the way it bobs up and down.

VG It is very short.

ES They used to say that—how short. But now they don't seem to mention that any more. Other people are writing shorter books and oh, did they used to complain. I mean an American publisher was interested years ago, but would I please write two others because nobody would buy such a short book. They wouldn't be getting their money's worth. Well, you know Samuel Beckett, who is a hero of mine, wrote a novel in eight hundred words.

VG You wrote for the magazine *Queen* for many years, about sweaters and things?

ES I had fourteen pages of fashion.

VG Were you ever taken in by the fashion world?

ES Oh no! I mean I adored them and I admired them so much. They were wonderful girls and brilliant. I think fashion is an art form, rather touchingly ephemeral, perhaps, but I adored them. They were totally inarticulate, though, and also they could hardly write. But they had this brilliant feeling for what was coming next. I loved them and I still go in and see them. Quite a few old colleagues are still there. Now it is called *Harper's Queen*.

VG So this work helped you support your family. You gave birth to four children out of wedlock. There weren't too many women in that situation.

ES No, but I found it necessary to have these children. For the first one I went far away from my parents, because I didn't want to embarrass them. And then, well, I just felt I had to have some more, so I went on having them as quietly and inconspicuously as possible.

VG Did they eventually find out?

ES Eventually they knew, but I didn't tell them to begin with. However, I found it very, very hard to keep this to myself; the hardest thing is to keep a secret.

VG Especially when you're sticking out in front.

ES Well, I had the first baby while I was in Washington, and

I used to go into baby shops and talk to the people who sold baby clothes because I wanted so much to talk about this child, you see.

VG Did you ever consider sporting a wedding ring to avoid hassle?

ES No, but when I was in England it was rationing and identity cards, and I used to get little snide looks and remarks from the greengrocers and people like that. So I did have my card changed to another name.

VG Why did you feel this necessity to have children?

ES I think it's part of this type of love. It's just a continuation of the "act,"you might say.

VG Would you call it unrequited love?

ES Oh, no! Totally requited. I wasn't deserted either. I just found the situation untenable. The man was marvellous but not somebody I could live with.

VG Do you keep in touch to this day?

ES Oh, yes! We're very great friends.

VG Are you writing again?

ES Well, I think I have started to write. I don't like to mention it because I'm not sure if what I've written is rubbish or not till I have another look.

VG When this year is up at the university, what will you do?

ES I am hoping to stick around in Canada for another year at least, perhaps forever.

The fact is that Elizabeth Smart did not stick around in Canada. She returned to England and died there in 1986.

FIVE

Let's Do Lunch

Early in 1984 Alan Clark, head of CBC Radio Sports, asked me if I would care to be involved in the Los Angeles Olympic coverage. A team of sporting specialists was being assembled, and because the Olympics were taking place in Los Angeles, it was natural to want to include some of the atmosphere of the place. CBC was preparing to broadcast live to Canada for four hours solid each day, for fifteen consecutive days. My job, which I chose to accept instantly and would have even with every limb broken, was to interview local celebrities, especially those who might have had some former sporting involvement.

Most of the interviews done for the regular show, *Variety To-night* and its successors, have followed a one-hour format, but for the Olympic package six minutes was the limit. So after all the years of trying to get longer interviews, I was faced with having to shut up sooner. It wasn't an easy task, but five were especially memorable, and five more were arranged for later visits.

One of the first interviews was with Robert Stack of "Untouch-ables" fame. He lives in a grand house in Bel Air, which is far fancier than Beverly Hills. A high fence and iron gates keep this house safe from unwanted intruders, and visitors must ring the bell to gain admittance. We had a bit of trouble finding the front entrance and after a lot of wandering around the property with an eye out for giant dogs, we finally found the back door. Mr Stack was horrified and apologized for dragging us through the kitchen. It was a matter of supreme indifference to me because the kitchen, tame no doubt by Hollywood standards, was splendid. It was rather old-fashioned and pristine. The refrigerator looked as if it had been bought in 1960, and the decor looked as if it had remained unchanged for many years. No slaves to fashion, these people. I was struck by Stack's seemingly un-aged face and was unable, peer as I might, to discover any telltale surgery scars. A former roommate and pal of John F. Kennedy, Stack had been a keen athlete in his youth. In fact, he had been a world champion skeet shooter and he was looking forward to attending all the shooting events.

I certainly did feel frustrated with the short-order format when we went to interview Jackie Collins. I would really have loved to do a proper piece with her. Although she is not a former sporting figure, she does deal with a certain kind of athletics. She is much taller than I expected her to be and she must tower over her sister Joan of "Dynasty" fame. Jackie was wearing leopard-patterned skin-tight pants and sported three- or four-inch-high heels. She looked pretty darn glamorous, but I got the impression that this was common attire. The atmosphere of the house was casual—no iron fences around her house. Few pretensions. The living room in which we sat was gigantic and almost everything was white—carpeting and furnishings. Her husband was around the corner in the den watching T.V. and her two kids bopped in and out, begging for car keys or looking for a lost shoe. Pretty standard stuff. But the fact is that Jackie Collins is rather more than standard. Even covered in great chunks of jewellery and looking exotic, one cannot take away the fact that she is a relentless worker and churns out large books that bring her even larger profits.

I was not looking forward to interviewing Michael Landon, big-star movie actor. I was sure he'd be a jerk and the staff around him would be aloof and not particularly interested in us. Wrong-o. The staff in his outer office treated us as if we were from the UN. "Coffee? Tea? A drink? How about a cigar?" They weren't a bunch of glamour queens either. The woman who appeared to run the place was at least sixty, and she was clearly in charge of the office and Landon. His own office was a complete shambles— junk stacked everywhere, piles of scripts and magazines, pictures hanging at a tilt, the desk littered. He, however, seemed to know where everything was. I liked him immediately. He doesn't appear to know how good-looking he is and that threw me. The man is in good shape. In the early sixties he was a first-rate javelin thrower, good enough to be considered for the U.S. Olympic team, but he abandoned that pursuit because he got a job on "Bonanza." *I Was a Teenage Werewolf*, in which he starred, is his favourite movie; I'm not entirely sure he agreed when I suggested it was schlock heaven.

One of the grim realities of working in Los Angeles is that you really never know till the last minute whether you've got anybody booked for sure. Everything changes—deals come up, or the shoot took longer than expected. You get used to hearing excuses, and by now I have heard them all. But sometimes things work out perfectly, as was the case with Bob Hope. When that guy says you can have an interview, you get. And on time. Mind you, we had to drive practically to San Diego to get to him. He was performing on *The Love Boat* and had thought it would not be too inconvenient for us to see him in his dressing room between acts. I had interviewed him once before, but that chat was over in three minutes flat because I was scared to death and couldn't think of enough questions.

This time the conversation lasted slightly longer (about twenty minutes—he talks fast). At about ten minutes in, a rather official-looking man waltzed into the suite; "official" in that he might have been the captain, but I was not sure. He seemed to want to hang around and listen, and he pulled up a chair almost next to us. I didn't mind particularly, because Hollywood types are often surrounded by people and intimate conversations are not the rule. But Mr Hope did not like it much at all. He was happy to receive us (our technician and me) and his manager was there too, but this interloper was too much. Hope excused himself to me and said to him, "I'm sorry, but this woman has come from Canada, from the CBC, to interview me and she requires my undivided attention, so if you will please excuse us." You could have knocked me over. The man left, somewhat embarrassed, but not devastated.

Some years ago, the movie actress Terry Moore wrote a book about her marriage to Howard Hughes. It caused quite a stir and put her back in the limelight, so we drove out to Santa Monica to talk to her. If it is assumed that as the widow of Howard Hughes she was the recipient of big lumps of money, that was not evident in her living quarters. That is not to say that she was living in poverty, but her digs were, although pleasant, hardly extravagant in any way. She lived in a small ground-floor apartment, with her ancient incontinent dog. Terry Moore seemed a sweet woman, not in the least calculating. She was eager to talk about Hughes and spoke of him fondly. Obviously, the world saw him in another way.

Actor Glenn Ford was one of the Hollywood interviews taped for future use. If you manage to get to Hollywood, you might as well make the best of it and not come back empty handed. I was surprised to discover upon arrival at Ford's house that in a matter of hours he and his wife were expecting a huge mob for dinner. There he sat talking to me, not in the least preoccupied with the impending horde. Help helps. His house, what I saw of it, appeared to be built in the round, with an open courtyard extending three floors. There was an elaborate wrought-iron railing circling the main floor. The hallway was completely covered with 8x10 glossies of everybody, all signed and dated, even George Bernard Shaw. My favourite household fixture was a superb long-haired dachshund named Bismark, a present from the actress Maria Schell. The dog loved me and I was so grateful. Bismark never left me alone for one minute. The technical set-up allowed Mr Ford and me to hold our own microphones, so he had one hand free to wave about, but I had to use mine to scratch the dog endlessly. The minute I would get lost in the conversation and stop the scratching, the dog would go mad and jump on my face. Mr Ford tried to take the dog away; I wouldn't have it. I quite liked Glenn Ford, but he did have the air of a man who had been interviewed too many times.

> **VG** Who awarded you the "Best Horseman in Motion Pictures" belt buckle?
>
> **GF** The Rodeo Cowboys Association. And I still have it. I gave it to my wife.
>
> **VG** Are you a pretty good equestrian then?
>
> **GF** I don't know how good I am. Let somebody else say how good or bad I am.
>
> **VG** You have horses.
>
> **GF** Seventeen.
>
> **VG** What kind?

GF Quarter horses and cutting horses.

VG No thor . . .

GF No thoroughbreds you mean? No, no. You mean the kind you bet on?

VG Yeah, that's what I mean.

GF No, I bet on rodeo cowboys, how long they'll stay on. No jockeys on the track.

VG You still like to go to the rodeo?

GF Oh, yes. I still do. In fact, before I got in pictures, I made most of my spending money by competing.

VG Have you broken every bone in your body?

GF Pretty near. Well, let's say my back three times, all the ribs on the left side, about three on the right side, the collar-bone, my arms. After a while you get sort of numb.

VG It doesn't seem to have affected you in any way. You were out there gardening like a fiend when we arrived.

GF Well, I think anybody who doesn't raise their own vegetables is a . . . my goodness why buy tomatoes and onions and potatoes when you can grow them so easily. And I have about two and a half acres here. But you know, I hate talking about the kind of earthy things I do. It's like I'm trying to prove something. I'm a normal person, you know, live a normal life. See, I'm very Canadian. You can tell? When I say "out" and "about."

VG It has never gone away?

GF No, never. In fact, when I have had to do any dubbing or looping, you know what that is, when they [producers] hear me, I have to do the recording over again. I still can't get "house" right either.

VG You played Superman/Clark Kent's earth father in the movie.

GF Yeah, and the reason I wanted to do that was that I wanted to go to Calgary where it was shot. I couldn't go to the Stampede because it was the wrong time of the year, but it was marvellous because my scenes were in a wheatfield. You know, it was supposed to be in the Middle West or somewhere in America, right? But the wheat hadn't grown high enough, so we all had to wait around Calgary for the wheat to grow . . . the whole company . . . an enormous cost. My wife and I took side trips while waiting, and I was hoping it would grow very slowly.

VG I know you don't like talk about earthy stuff, but it's about your house. Did you design it yourself?

GF Oh, yeah. I designed it. It took me a year to design it and build. And I collected a lot of stuff when I travelled around; the glass, the stained-glass windows, and the bevelled things are all from Europe. That chandelier over there is from Czechoslovakia.

VG You have a good eye. Do you paint at all?

GF Yes, it's an exercise in relaxation. I like to do it to relax. It's fun and I give the paintings to friends.

VG You and Winston Churchill.

GF I'm hardly in his class, but he did teach me how to smoke a cigar.

VG He truly did?

GF Mr Churchill, yeah. Just after the war, as a matter of fact. I was eating at the Albany Club in London, and he was there at the same time, and I asked Bill Little, the owner of the club, what kind of cigars Mr Churchill smoked. Then one night, when there were only two of us in the room, Mr Churchill summoned me to his table and said, "You asked what kind of cigars I smoked, boy?" He thought Bill Little said I was a horse owner. If he'd told him that I was an actor, I wouldn't have gotten within fifty feet of him. But we talked about horses. I knew Lester Piggott, the jockey, one of the great ones, so we talked about Piggott. Then he gave me a cigar. When I lit it, he grabbed my hand and I thought he was gonna hit me. He said, "No, boy, no!" And I said, "Sir? . . . What, what?" He took the cigar from me, and he took the match and waved it in front of the end you light, and then he puffed on it and it lit right away, of course. I always remember him saying to me, looking me right in the eye, "Remember, boy, a cigar is like a woman. Warm her before you assault her."

VG Churchill really called you "boy," huh?

GF Oh, yeah, that was very flattering wasn't it? It was marvellous because he took me back to the Savoy where I was staying. I rode with him, and he went to sleep on my shoulder. I was wearing a brand new

Burberry overcoat and he rather . . . he dropped a little bit of . . . well . . . he blessed my coat.

VG Did you keep it forever and all time?

GF Oh, I still have it. I think the nice thing about the business I'm in is that you get the opportunity to meet so many marvellous people. I met Lord Mountbatten, one of my biggest heroes. I served under him in Burma during the war when I was in the Marine Corps. I was in London at an opening of something at the Savoy, and I was standing in the receiving line with Joan Crawford (I escorted her that evening) and I heard him [Mountbatten] say, "Oh hey, Shipman, Shipman!" Well, Joan said, "It's Mountbatten, you've got to acknowledge him." He then stepped out of the line, came down to where I was standing and grabbed me, and left Joan Crawford standing there. She didn't speak to me again. Anyway, he took me in the side room and I spent the rest of the evening teaching him how to do the trick where you flick the poker chip up and do a fast draw and hit the poker chip in the wine glass, like in the picture "The Sheep Man." It's an easy trick, you know. You just fill the shell with a BB shot instead of one bullet, so you've got a pattern there of about a six-foot spread. Can't miss.

VG You left Joan Crawford standing there by herself?

GF Well, what was I to do. There was Mountbatten. I mean, he outranked me after all. And I think I did the right thing as it turned out.

Tom Poston could have been a scientist. I'm awfully glad he pursued his other calling, that of a comic. It seems to have paid off, too, because he is consistently employed. Appearances on the Steve Allen Show in the fifties gave him a huge boost and for years he was a panellist on the quiz show "To Tell The Truth." He was hysterical in the Mork and Mindy series and he continues to get laughs with his character on the new "Bob Newhart Show."

VG Is it true you were nearly a chemist?

TP I actually was a chemist. My dad was a chemist; he owned National Dairy Industries Research Laboratories. I worked there as a chemist, but I didn't know anything. I always had to run and ask him, "Is this right. Is this right?" And I was doing the most simple of things.

VG Was he quick to suggest that you go on the stage?

TP No, because my brother was on the stage at that time and my father didn't like it. He wanted my brother to be in the business with him. What a laugh. My brother certainly wasn't about to be in the business and neither was I, so eventually I went into the theatre with my older brother.

VG Where is your older brother now?

TP He is in California and he goes to the races every day.

VG Bless his heart.

TP He writes books about betting and so forth. But he is still in the business and he performs too—what you might call a one-man transliteration of *Catch 22*. And he does all the parts. Joseph Heller has never written anything else quite as compelling to me, but he writes beautifully still.

VG Your brother and you use the same last name?

TP Yes. He says that at a time when I was starting to become known, I once asked him if he would mind changing his name.

VG He didn't think you were kidding?

TP No, he thought I meant it.

VG I take it there is no animosity between you guys and that you adore each other.

TP Well, we do. But there's a kind of a haunted look in his eyes about how come success and fame didn't happen to him to the same degree that it did to me. But I had other avenues. I did nightclubs and stand-up and different things like that, and that led to all of the other things. Although he has done some of that, he did it in a formal kind of way as a straight man for a burlesque comic, which is not exactly the same route.

VG Well, did you feel an obligation to help him at a stage, or wasn't that a problem ever?

TP He's extremely independent. He would like me to help him in certain ways, for instance, encouraging my agent to submit him for various jobs. My agent won't submit *me* for jobs! I swear! I have to get all my own jobs. But I'll tell you what he wants me to do is perform his plays. And I haven't been able to do it so far. When he writes a play that I think I would like to do, I want to put it in the hands of a director who will mould it into a play, but he objects so strongly to any changes that we just declare a cease-fire and say, "Okay, we'll let this one go."

VG You say your agent doesn't submit you for jobs. What do these people do anyway? They sure are the brunt of jokes.

TP Well, they take a bum rap all right. There's a terrible Hollywood joke: What's the difference between a dead dog and a dead agent lying in the road in Beverly Hills? The answer is: There are skid marks by the dog. So they get a rough go. Some of my best friends in this entire world are my managers, and I've been with the same firm for decades. I wouldn't think of going anywhere else, 'cause they're close personal friends.

VG Well, agent or no agent, you are working now and it looks to me you are working with a great guy and a great mob.

TP Really the best. It's the best working conditions of any-body in any studio in California. That is my experience, anyway. I am Bob Newhart's great admirer. I think he is magic on television. And, you know, he has never been up for an Emmy Award. If you think that's strange, think of this: *I* was up for an Emmy.

VG Didn't you win once?

TP Yeah. That was with Steve Allen. But I was up for an Emmy last year and the guy who won it is an old Steve Allen cohort.

VG Who's that?

TP Pat Harrington, Jr.

VG You know, it's funny that you've played so many be-fuddled characters.

TP Yes, it's true. It may be something that I resort to when I'm asked to be funny in an instant. It may be tremen-dous love and affection for Stan Laurel, and an apprecia-tion for his art. Just helplessly laughing. I couldn't stop laughing at him. So it may be like a shadow of that.

VG You're so straight-faced.

TP Well, that's a practised thing, too, you know. Bob New-hart doesn't laugh on his show, and Bob is probably one of the world's great gigglers. When he first got into the business, he did plays and just giggled his way through the whole play, just helplessly giggling, snorting and cackling. But he doesn't do it anymore 'cause you can't, you know. You just can't do it. But I laughed so hard on a Newhart show one time that tears came down my cheeks. Bob and I were sitting across the table from each other, and the exchange was over whether or not I had known the pig that the pork chops that were being served were cut from. And, as we sat there, eye to eye across the table, Bob had just finished telling me a story about Charlie Weaver . . . remember?

VG Yes, I remember him. But what story?

TP He was doing his own show, live, and was doing a scene where he was playing cards with a chimpanzee across the table. When the curtains parted, the chimpanzee was nervous because the audience broke into a big laugh when they saw the chimp playing cards with Charlie Weaver. Underneath the table, the chimpanzee's little feet, which are like hands of course, reached Charlie's number one zone and put on the squeeze, just a little gentle squeeze out of nervousness. And it's all live. So Charlie continues with the scene, and every time there's a laugh from the audience, the squeeze gets just a little bit firmer. By the time the scene is over, poor Charlie has tears rolling down his cheeks trying not to scream, carrying on with the scene and waiting until the curtains closed again so he could extricate himself from this over-friendly chimp. Bob's just finished telling me that very funny story, and I'm sitting there across the table from him trying to do comedy lines with him. He's looking me right in the eye, and I know what he's thinking. So I just laughed, helplessly. I just laughed and laughed until the tears rolled down my cheeks. That's all in front of an audience you know, so . . .

VG They must have been out of their minds.

TP If I'd had any brains, I would have stopped everything, gotten up, told the audience the story and what Bob had just done to me, and then made him bear the brunt of all of my laughter. But as it was, I just kept quiet and they thought "Hmmm, not very professional."

VG Not like Charlie Weaver.

TP And look it, Bob isn't laughing at all. Wasn't he the rascal. I find him irresistible. I'm surprised that Bob's genius hasn't been properly recognized—I mean people make a big fuss about Bill Cosby. God bless him, he's got a big hit show, and it's the talk of the industry. Bob's show is just as successful, it's just as counted on by a network as Cosby's, but people just take it completely for granted.

VG Yes, but you know, I bet that it's a lot less pressure on Newhart's life, being, as you say, a bit underestimated or not recognized as he might be. But maybe the rewards are that he doesn't have that kind of pressure.

TP It is true that Bob is a private person and he jealously guards his privacy and his quiet time. He's very, very careful about the quiet time. He does the minimum of publicity and promotion.

VG You're tellin' me! We've been trying to get him for three years.

TP Really?

VG Yup.

TP Even by phone?

VG Well, it doesn't seem to be working.

TP Well, tell him I said to do it. But I'll bet you he'll do it. I'll ask him to do it. And you'll love it. And the people . . . your friends that are listening to this show, they'll adore it. He's wonderful.

True to his word, Tom Poston set up the interview with his friend and colleague.

Bob Newhart hit the North American audience with a bang in 1960. His comedy album "The Button-Down Mind of Bob Newhart" set sales records everywhere. Although his first television show in 1961–62 was a hit with the critics, the ratings were only fair. He waited ten years before trying it again, and this time it worked. He amassed a fanatic following and audiences adored his portrayal of a slightly screwy Chicago psychiatrist. This show folded its tent in 1978, and was followed in the early eighties by a new "Bob Newhart Show," in which Bob plays a slightly screwy hotel owner in Vermont.

VG I'm awfully delighted you've succumbed to our incessant nagging to be on this programme. You don't do too many interviews.

BN Well, you wind up saying the same dumb things. You know, I'd like to go back and relive my life and make it more interesting. I would have loved to have been a fighter pilot in World War II, behind enemy lines and to have fought my way out, but it just didn't work out that way.

VG Mercifully you were spared.

BN Mercifully they stopped them in South Korea.

VG I'm talking to you now in your dressing room.

BN Yes, that's right. Today's blocking day. We go in and block and set the cameras and then tomorrow we actually go in and shoot it.

VG How many days do you take to do the half-hour?

BN Well, you know, that's like the question people ask, "What do you do during the day?" I mean, they know you do a television show at night, but what do you do during the day? Do you have another job? We come in on Monday and read the script and sit around and discuss it, and then the remaining four days are spent blocking it and shooting it in front of an audience.

VG So, five days?

BN Five days, really, yeah.

VG You did the first show for six years. Could this go as long?

BN Well, when I came back, people said, "I thought you said you would never do television again?" I don't recall ever saying that, because I wouldn't say something like that. I was sure I'd be back on television in something, because it's my medium. That's where I'm most comfortable and what I enjoy doing. My reason for leaving the old show was I was concerned about the quality of it. We had done six years and I was very proud of it, and didn't want it to suffer and trail off. I'm enjoying this show very much. We're going into our fourth year and it seems like our second, and the writing staff is marvellous. This is our fourth show this year that we're taping, and they've given us great scripts and the cast is wonderful to work with. And as long as we can maintain the quality, I'll ride this one till it drops, you know.

VG You may or may not know this, but a while ago I talked to one of your co-stars, Tom Poston. His name on your show is very funny. I mean, I don't know why the name "George Utley" is funny, but it's a funny name.

BN You're right, you're right. And Tom is a George. It fits him.

VG Well, that must be great fun . . . naming characters.

BN It is. When we started doing this show, we tried to get as far away from the old show as possible, because we knew there were going to be inevitable comparisons. And the old show was a hard act to follow. It had good writing and a marvellous cast. I would say the first two years of the new show was an uphill battle, but now I think people accept it for what it is and enjoy or don't enjoy it, rather than comparing it with the old show.

VG Well, when you did the old show, were psychiatrists' conventions asking you to come and speak a lot?

BN A lot. I still get calls from psychiatrists.

VG Have you ever been to a psychiatrist?

BN I went to a psychiatrist, a therapist/psychologist or whatever term you want to use. I had a fear of flying, which I still kind of have, and I thought that might help. When we finished the first session, I said to him, "Do you validate?" You know, 'cause he had this big building, and the parking was downstairs. And he said, "Well, what do you mean, do I validate?" And I said "My car's downstairs. I wonder if you validate?" And he said, "No, I don't validate. Do you think I should?" And I said, "Well, whether I think you should or not has nothing to do with it. I just wondered if you validated." And he took it very personally. And so I counselled him for a while about not feeling too bad about it. It wasn't rejection on my part, I was merely trying to find out whether he validated or I had to pay. And that was about the extent of my therapy.

VG Well, it sounds fascinating. Maybe he thought you were trying to see if he would validate your existence. All right, do you want to play a piece of music here? The first on your list is "April in Paris" by the Count Basie Orchestra.

BN There's a reason for picking that. Most of those are jazz tunes, and the Basie Orchestra is, I think, one of the funniest orchestras that have ever played. They lead you down this garden path, and you think they're going somewhere, and all of a sudden they do a 180-degree turn, and it's kind of illustrated in "April in Paris." You think the song is over, and then all of a sudden this tremendous band comes back in. They just constantly surprise you.

VG Have you ever been to Paris in April?

BN I went this last May to Paris with Barbara and Don Rickles, and my wife. The three of them seemed to have a good time.

VG What? Did you follow around like a dog?

BN No, I'm always in charge of the camera. I'm the one who's never in the picture. We had a wonderful time. Don is not too well known over there.

VG That must be a relief.

BN Uh, yeah. He's just a very loud American to most of 'em, you know. They don't realize he makes his money doing that.

VG Does he wear plaid shorts, with a camera round his neck?

BN No, not that bad, no.

VG What is he like? What are the two of you like? Because you're a kind of cool guy, does he calm down when the two of you are playing golf, or on a vacation?

BN Well, oddly enough we try not to examine the chemistry; it just works. We get together and have a million laughs. We enjoy each other, and somehow we complement each other, and our wives get along marvellously. You know, everybody has a very close friend that they love to travel with and Don happens to be mine, even though we're exact opposites.

VG He has shorter hair.

BN And less.

VG Are you still making records?

BN Ah, no, I'm not, Vicki. I haven't for the better part of seventeen, eighteen years, I guess. There was a time and a place for that, and I'm not sure it exists out there any more.

VG It really made you, though, didn't it?

BN Oh, yeah, without question. I was working nightclubs and I'd only worked three or four nightclubs, and then all of a sudden the record took off, and one of the first clubs I played was up in Winnipeg, and I played the Cave in Vancouver in '65, '66.

VG Do you remember the first time you played a night-club?

BN I was terrified, absolutely terrified. I walked out, and I had about twenty minutes, that's all. I walked out and I didn't look right or left, I just tried to repeat it as well as I could remember it, and then came off. There was some applause, and the maitre d' said, "Go back out," and I said, "Well, I don't have anything else, that's all I have. And he said, "Well you better go back out, 'cause they're applauding." So I went back out and asked them, "What would you like to hear again?"

VG Did they laugh then?

BN Oh, yeah, yeah.

VG Lucky for you, eh, kid?

BN But then, it was kind of a strange career. It never happened before that way. Still, I think the records created the demand.

VG I take it you don't do nightclubs any more.

BN I don't think I've played a nightclub in maybe, I would guess, four years. Largely because of time, I do one-nighters. I go out and do one or two nights, maybe at a university, to renew the juices. Those two nights do the same as seven nights in Vegas. I used to play five weeks in a row, with two shows a night, seven days a week. That's something you do when you're much younger.

VG When you see a guy like Eddie Murphy, who seems to be covering the waterfront and doing stand-up and doing concerts and doing everything . . .

BN You've gotta be young to do that. I did it for twenty-five years, and frankly you get a little tired of the Chagall prints in the motel rooms.

VG What about the movie business for you. You said a very funny thing about the motion pictures you've made going directly to airplanes.

BN That's right. I said my movies are going directly to inflight now, they don't even bother putting them in theatres. I had an unfortunate string of those. I just found it was one of the things that kind of pushed me back into television. I did a movie called "First Family" with Buck Henry who wrote and directed, and Madeleine Kahn and Harvey Korman and Richard Benjamin and Gilda Radner and a whole bunch of wonderful, marvellous people. It took about six months altogether, and we had just a wonderful time. The picture came out and it was not well received at all. For about two months I kind of wandered around in a fog saying, "But I thought it was good." And then I realized that when you do a weekly television show, you can do a bad show, but the next week you're doing a good one and you're back up on top again.

VG And you can redeem yourself immediately.

BN Exactly, exactly. It was devastating to devote that much time and I agree it wasn't that good a movie, but it sure felt like it when we were doing it.

VG But you know, you have managed to go through, lo, these many years of being in show business with precious few bad reviews.

BN Oh, I have some at home that I could send you. My wife insists I save those so when I'm starting to get a little big-headed she just drops it by my place and lets me know.

VG Well, you don't have a big ego problem, do you?

BN No, and justifiably so. I'm self-deprecating and have much to be self-deprecating about.

VG Do you get mobbed in the streets?

BN I don't get mobbed, no. People either think they were in the army with me, or I was their first husband.

VG That's pretty frightening! You've only been married the once?

BN Yes, just the once. The once is enough. If you do it right, once is enough.

VG Well she sounds like a stalwart girl.

BN Oh, she's lovely, she's lovely. She's really the reason I guess I've lasted this long. 'Cause she makes me toe the line. And she says, "Don't get carried away. You know, you're not all that great."

Well, there's hardly anything more Hollywood than Zsa Zsa, darling. And Zsa Zsa Gabor, the Hungarian perpetual blonde bombshell has borne the brunt of many smart cracks during her career. Oscar Levant once said that she had discovered the secret of eternal middle age. An American congressman called her the most expensive courtesan since Madame Pompadour. I guess when one is an institution, one has to accept all that as being part of the game. She certainly is not beyond making remarks about herself either. Just look at the material she's got to work with, the husbands alone. What about the diamonds and the clothes and the parties. Of the three Gabor sisters, Eva, Magda, and Zsa Zsa, she is the most wild and the most glamorous.

ZZ I don't know about that. You know it is very expensive to be glamorous. I love it though. I do have an enormous wardrobe. And right now I hate every piece I have. Usually I go through this phase. You know a wardrobe, you have to buy all the time new clothes to really like them. As a matter of fact, I'm running from here to order a new evening gown, as soon as I'm through with you.

VG Has your style changed much over the years?

ZZ Well, sweetheart, I don't know. I mean, you know those big shoulder pads which I don't even like on anybody, I don't like on me, but if you wear something without shoulder pads now, you're out of fashion. And that all goes with the profession and being in the public.

VG What about skirt length?

ZZ I like a skirt just by the knees. I happen, thank God, having good legs, so I don't mind showing them. But you know I give away quite a bit of my clothes for charity. There is a place here [Los Angeles] for homeless women and I give my clothes to them.

VG Were you born blonde or are you brunette in there somewhere?

ZZ No, I am blonde. But I was sort of reddish blonde origin-ally. And, of course, over the years I've bleached my hair out, because it photographs much much better. And you know what they say in Hollywood? "Women in Hollywood don't age, they just get blonder."

VG Tell me about your name? Is it a pet name, a childhood name?

ZZ My name is Shary, Shary Gabor. Shary was an aunt of mine. My mother always loved the name Zsa Zsa which is a pet name of Shary, so she bribed my nanny, you have to call her from now on Zsa Zsa. And it stuck.

VG When you say you give away your clothes, I take it you don't give away your jewellery?

ZZ No, the jewellery I hate to give away. I don't think anybody in their right mind would give away the jewellery.

VG How about give it back?

ZZ Well, yes I did that. I did give back more diamond rings than most women. I had once a 41-carat blue diamond. I have lived to be sorry for it, but I did give it back.

VG Why? Did you have a twinge of guilt?

ZZ I didn't want to marry the man, and I felt it was too much. But one should never think like that because it winds up on another woman's hand anyhow.

VG One of your famous quotes deals with this very subject.

ZZ I said, and it was my very first day on television and it is how I got famous . . . This girl asked me if she breaks up her engagement if she should give back the ring, and I said, "By all means. You must give back the ring. Just keep the stone." Is that the one you mean?

VG Actually, I thought the story went like this: A girl asked about all the presents her boyfriend had given her and now she wanted to break off the relationship and give the stuff back. You asked her what it all was. A ring and a fur coat and a stove and other stuff. You thought for a minute and said, "I think you give him back the stove."

ZZ Oh my. Yes, that was another one. It is good advice.

VG You are not married now, are you?

ZZ I'm not married now for the last three years, so I think I'm slipping.

VG Do you really think you'll do it again?

ZZ Oh, yes, I will. If I meet the right man, of course.

VG Well, what is required now, somebody calm?

ZZ Calm! Never! Intelligent, understanding, and a sports-
    man, definitely. I love sports. You know I ride and I was
    riding in the Olympics in 1984. Did you see me?

VG I was there but I couldn't go to the equestrian events
    because they were too far away from the studio.

ZZ Oh, what a pity. It was gorgeous. It was a demonstra-
    tion event. I rode the grand champion Tennessee Walker
    and there were thirty thousand people all screaming at
    me.

VG You fence, too, now that's a sport.

ZZ Fencing is very good for the posture and the figure, too,
    and the legs, everything. I play polo, too. It is very dan-
    gerous. Prince Philip once said, "How more glamorous
    can you die than on a polo pony?"

VG I've tried and had a terrible time. I couldn't hit the darn
    ball at all.

ZZ Do you ride? I love to, but you have to exercise and
    keep at it. Like everything.

VG How long have you lived in your house in Bel Air?

ZZ I bought it twelve years ago from the Howard Hughes
    estate. I have a disco upstairs and an exercise room, and
    I have a Hungarian village upstairs too.

VG A Hungarian village, you say.

ZZ Yeah, a Hungarian village. It's charming, with all kinds
    of Hungarian furnishings and Hungarian colours, and it
    is really very cute. I can entertain upstairs, two hun-
    dred people for a sitting-down dinner. I have a very
    large house.

VG So you might as well marry again, there is lots of room.

ZZ Well, I have a German prince who is after me now for
    four and a half years, and he calls me almost every day
    from Munich when he isn't here.

VG Well, at least he is loyal.

ZZ He is loyal and he's very sweet and he is a nice man, but
    I don't know. I'm petrified of marrying a German,
    prince or no prince. I would like maybe an American.
    Canadians are wonderful. I must say I very much ad-
    mire Canadian people.

VG You have never married a Canadian, have you?

ZZ No. That was bad luck. Well, maybe. I mean, who can

tell? Maybe a gorgeous Canadian man is going to listen to this interview and he'll think, "There's the girl for me."

[Phone rings]

VG Was it anybody good?

ZZ No. It was my agent.

Everybody loves Dolly Parton. And why not. She is a screaming success as a singer, a downright natural as an actor and she has a wit that cuts like a blade. At eighteen she left her home in the Smoky Mountains of Tennessee to find fame and fortune in Nashville. Actually I think it found her. When I talked to Dolly in the spring of 1986, she had just opened "Dollywood," a theme park dedicated to the country life which she knows so well. Although she is a shrewd businesss person, it is fairly obvious that she opened this park to employ local people and to make a contribution to the preservation of the culture and history of the place where she grew up.

VG The name of your park is too good.

DP I had the idea for the park about ten or twelve years ago, but the name came a little later. When I first went to Hollywood I saw that Hollywood sign on the side of the mountain, you know it, that huge one. Well I always thought it would be such fun if there was some way I could change the "H" to a "D" for a day. I even re-searched it. But you'd have to get helicopters and pull off some Mission Impossible scam and all that. I kept it in mind but I hadn't linked it to the park yet.

VG Has this park turned out the way you imagined in your dreams?

DP Well, it's no nightmare, so far. I wanted it to be like goin' back in time. To the 1800s, and all the people that work there are dressed like that and almost everything in the place is handmade. There is basket weaving and candle making and there is a blacksmith shop, you know, stuff like that.

VG What is the state of the culture in the Smoky Mountains? Do people still make dulcimers and so on?

DP It's still there but not as much as it used to be. They still make dulcimers and they still make a little moonshine and they still make a lot of blacksmithing things, but actually most that is now done in the park. Progress you know, everything moves along. But I wanted to do this park to preserve our mountain heritage so that people would come, especially city people—they are often afraid to go to the mountains because they have this terrible fear that everything is like the movie *Deliverance*. You know, a bunch of wild mountain men that's gonna trap you on some back street and kill you or somethin'. It's just a chance to see what mountain people are really like.

VG Guess you don't sell any moonshine?

DP No, you're not allowed to. But some people still do.

VG It's not great, is it? It just about knocks you on your behind too.

DP It does that, and it's not even good. It's like drinkin' rubbing alcohol. My daddy used to make it, and several of my kinfolks, but it is not a good drink. Oh boy. I think I prefer a little scotch over moonshine. I think I prefer Drano over moonshine.

VG You're in New York right now. Do you have to go out in a scarf or anything?

DP No, I go just as I am. It is amazing about New York. They see so many celebrities that they're immune to them. Everybody is so friendly and so nice. They'll say "Hello Dolly" just as if I know them. And I love that. They don't run you down or pull at you, they just speak. So I just go walkin' along, sometimes just by myself, all around New York.

VG How can you walk around so much, you always wear those impossibly high, high heels. No running shoes?

DP Well, I ain't got into runnin' shoes. Even my skis have five-inch heels on them. I'm so short, unless my back gives out completely, I'm gonna stay on high shoes forever.

VG Are you a good cook?

DP Yes, I'm a real good cook, but I love to cook country food. And that's in fact one of the things we have in Dollywood. We've built some really nice restaurants and there's one called Aunt Granny's Dixie Fixin's, which is a restaurant of mine, and I'm gonna have a chain of those as time goes by. But it's got a lot of my recipes and it got its name because my nieces and nephews all call me Aunt Granny because I raised several brothers and sisters, and then when they married and had kids, their kids didn't know what to call me. I seemed like their Granma, but their Granma was still alive, so I said, "Just call me Aunt Granny." We've got blackberry dumplings there and lots of things that the kids all like and that I like to cook. We have turnip greens and fried okra, potatoes, beans, fried chicken, meat loaf, and all that good stuff that's gonna put twenty pounds back on me that I worked so hard to get off lately.

VG But no Velveeta.

DP But I love Velveeta. We may have a slab or two now and then.

VG You did lose tons of weight. You know, even when you said in the paper that you had gained all this weight and everything, to me you always looked exactly the same.

DP Well, thank you. But I'm sure there's a lot of people that wouldn't agree with you—me for one. 'Cause, boy, I mean I got up to be a porker there for a while. I'm serious. I weighed about 150 pounds and I'm only five-foot-one, five-foot-two, and I got up to about 150 pounds, and boy I tell you, I was just like a little butterball. It's like "Here I Roll Again."

VG You must have looked like a fireplug.

DP Oh, I did. But you know, anyway, I've got the weight down now. But if I spend much time at Aunt Granny's Dixie Fixin's, I'm sure that'll all end.

VG Well, you don't run around? Do you exercise?

DP No, I hate to exercise. I mean, I'm tryin' to, I'm tryin' to do some, but I'm just a lazy physical person and I'm a hog at heart. So that makes for a bad combination.

VG I think that's why the world loves you.

DP You think so?

VG Yup. It's got hardly anything to do with your singing, I s'pose.

DP Probably not.

VG Do you know what's interesting about country singers? You appear to be a lot closer to your public than movie stars or rock musicians. A lot more personal contact—it's expected by the audience and it's anticipated by you people.

DP Yeah, I think a lot of that comes from the fact that country singers, or most of them, are from rural areas. We lived so far back in the mountains that we didn't see anybody comin' to see us, and it used to thrill us to death. I never got over that excitement of seein' people and likin' to be around people 'cause I always hated for company to leave when they'd come to see us. So I think a lot of it has to do with just really lovin' people.

VG But I would think that, given your enormous popularity, it must be a temptation on occasion to put up barriers because you're just so overwhelmed by the attention.

DP Well, the only barriers that I have to put up is for safety reasons, 'cause in the early days when I started out, like so many of the artists did and some of them still do, I used to sit on stage until every last person in the auditorium had an autograph, if that's what they wanted. I mean for hours we'd stay, sometimes two and three hours after a show was finished. But then it got to where, you know, the more popular you'd get, people'd start shovin', they start pushin', then it gets to be dangerous. You're too close and two or three different times like somebody'd get so excited they'd try to pull you off the stage. You know, they just want to hug you or somethin'. But as far as lovin' the people, I've always enjoyed the fans. I think that's one of the reasons I wanted to be a star, 'cause I wanted all that attention. I had a lot of love to give, and I wanted to get a lot of love back.

VG And you have.

DP Yeah, I have.

VG How do you account for your extreme boldness in rushing off to Nashville at . . . you were eighteen, I think.

DP Well, I was eighteen when I went to stay but I started rushin' off to Nashville when I was about ten, eleven, twelve. Anytime I could bug somebody or we could scrape up enough money to get a tank of gas we'd go to

Nashville. We'd sleep in the car. "We" meaning usually my Uncle Bill, my mother's brother, and me. He was also a songwriter and a singer, and we used to spend a lot of time just walkin' the streets of Nashville, and I'd just go down and try to get somebody to listen to my songs, try to get a record contract. I just figured that I'd been as poor as anybody could be, so I had everything to gain and nothin' to lose. I was used to hard times, so I just had this real good attitude about it. It was just somethin' I wanted, it was somethin' I was willing to work for, and I headed out. I was so dumb I didn't know I couldn't have it till I already had it.

VG Well, you may have been dumb, but they obviously received you with open arms at that stage.

DP Yeah. So I guess they were as dumb as I was.

VG Your old fans from the early days, does it upset them in the least that you are so popular outside the country field?

DP Well, I think the real true devoted "Dolly" fans are really happy for me and proud of me. I think there are some died-in-the-wool country music fans that don't appreciate the fact that I have tried to do other kinds of music. And, I mean, I don't want to offend anybody, but when I was just recordin' country music I wasn't makin' any money. I was one of the biggest artists of all time in country music, female artists, at the time. Me and Tammy and Loretta were like the three hottest women for several years there. Yet even the biggest records that I was havin', like "Jolene" and "I Will Always Love You," people thought I was makin' millions of dollars, and both those records only sold like a hundred thousand copies. Well that ain't enough to buy toothpaste.

VG Wait a minute. "Jolene" only sold one hundred thousand copies? But I got one.

DP You got one? Well, you're one of a hundred thousand then. And although that was a big chart record, and it's a very popular song as far as people listenin' to it on the radio, it didn't sell. And I was tryin' to do this and that, and I realized that I wasn't makin' any money, and I was just barely breakin' even, and sometimes not even doin' that. So, I just felt that I had enough talent to do a lot of things, and if I was gonna spend my life in the business, I was gonna have to be business-minded about it. And so I just headed out and decided that I could do more. I figured it was my life, I could screw it up if I wanted to, so I just went with that attitude, just like I went to Nashville. I was not afraid of failure and I was not afraid of success, and so I think it proved to be a good thing. I don't think anybody has any real resentment toward me personally just because I made the move. Some people just don't like the kind of music I'm doin'.

VG Tough luck.

DP Well that's the way I look at it.

VG Have you ever hesitated? Have you ever had a moment, let's say in the last fifteen years, when you thought of pulling out, retiring, hiding out for a while?

DP No way! I don't ever want to retire. Even when I had to take off the road for about eighteen months when I was quite ill a few years back . . . I mean I had some surgery. I had some problems with my stomach and some female problems, and just had a real bad run of luck, and I was really down physically and spiritually. My will was a bit broken there for a while, and my confidence a bit shaken, but that was good for me because when I did overcome that, I was a much better person. But while I was off work, and while I was flat on my back, I realized, although I had never thought about it until then, that the one thing in this world that I never want to do is retire. I want to just work until I fall over, and it don't feel like work to me. It's just fun.

SIX

Of a Certain Age

Over the years I have had a tendency to favour people of a certain age: advanced. Not that I am biased against up-and-comers, it is just that I think I behave better with those who have reached a milestone. With people my own age I tend to be more loose-mouthed, slightly off-colour, and occasionally lippy. This brashness does, however, seem to disappear with someone with twenty-five years on me. Respect? Maybe. It is evident that I get more from subjects by using a gentler touch, so you would think I'd learn. Even so, a gentler touch is not always a good idea, and it can be great folly to underestimate someone's sharpness on account of age. Take Milton Berle—please.

Way back in 1952-3, if you lived in North America you were likely to be among the millions who gathered around the old Philco on Tuesday night to watch Milton Berle. It is said he sold more television sets than any advertising campaign. He was called an overnight sensation, but Milton Berle has been in show business almost from the day he took his first breath. In 1983 he came to Vancouver to be part of a roast for the B.C. Lions football club and he agreed to be assaulted by me beforehand. On the same bill for the roast were Henny Youngman, Jan Murray, and Red Buttons, so when Mr Berle was booked to be interviewed he had assumed we wanted them all together. He seemed much happier when it was made clear that he was the object of our desires and that the others would get their turns singly. As it turned out, Red Buttons didn't appear in the city till much later. Henny Youngman was interviewed, but he was waiting for a call from New York because his wife had been ill and he was distracted, so that interview was never aired. Jan Murray was a swell guy and we mostly talked about the T.V. show that he used to do live, following the Friday-night fights.

Interviewing Milton Berle is a sensation akin to jumping off a cliff or leaping from a plane. Uncle Miltie has had so much practice at running jokes that no one in her right mind would try to compete. I was so polite that he was yawning and that made me mad, so I woke up.

> **VG** I have a sinking feeling that this is going to be a bit of a contest.
>
> **MB** I think you are going to be the winner, Vicki, because I'm a little tired; I've been ironing all morning. I love it here in Vancouver. I wasn't born here, but I died here many times—at the Orpheum Theatre. I was here in 19—oh my goodness, 1922. I was on the vaudeville circuit and I appeared with a little girl by the name of Elizabeth Kennedy. I was a dramatic actor then, and we did *Romeo and Juliet.*
>
> **VG** What did you play?
>
> **MB** I played Juliet. Boy, smartass, what are you talking about?
>
> **VG** You could have been Mercutio.
>
> **MB** Oh, I could have been Mercutio, but I couldn't because I was only fourteen and I would have had to grow a beard like your engineer [Gary Heald, our technician]. Pardon me for coughing.
>
> **VG** Would you like a glass of water?
>
> **MB** You're not smoking a cigarette are you?
>
> **VG** No, I'm not, but would you like a glass of water?
>
> **MB** No, I don't drink water. Yes I do.
>
> **VG** You don't drink anything?
>
> **MB** I never drank in my life. Never had a drop of liquor, which is not all that thrilling. I like other people to have a drink.
>
> **VG** You have never—not even a glass of wine?

MB No, never. Never smoked a cigarette. Never drank liquor. So I think two out of three ain't bad.

VG It was announced recently by the president of the academy for the Emmy Awards that a television hall of fame was being established.

MB About two months ago, Vick—I say "Vick" because I don't want to rub it in—I got a telegram and it said that I was to be the first to be inducted into the television hall of fame. Then the press asked me what I thought about being the first in the hall of fame. They were expecting me to say, "I think it is about time; I deserved it." I won't say it. I might think it, but I won't say it.

VG Because you are too modest?

MB No, I'm not modest. I'm honest, and I think a lot of BS is done on interviews and I don't approve of it. I approve of being truthful, honest, and provocative and of telling the truth, because if you don't tell the truth, well, it is like a divorce case; there are three sides to every story—hers, his, and the truth.

VG Do you ever take a vacation?

MB Why? Is there one missing?

VG Har, har.

MB I can't lie. Now, just let me say this: I like to go fishing, I've got a pool, I've got a tennis court. It's strictly, you know, Beverly Hills style. But a vacation to me is working. I'm a worker and I don't know if you know this, but I am the National Chairman of the ALA. Now let me explain. It is the American Longevity Association and it concerns itself with the span of life and the extension of life. And we at the ALA don't care how much money you've got; never retire. If you are incapacitated, well, maybe then, but if you're healthy then I think you've got to keep your mind busy. You have got to keep those arteries going. Somebody asked George Burns once, "George, when are you going to retire?" And George said, "To what?" What was our question again?

VG Vacations.

MB I don't like vacations. They say, "Oh Milton, let's go on a cruise." Well, I don't like boats. Number one, I can't swim. I never learned how to swim because I was too busy fighting with the drummer, asking him to give me a rimshot on a joke when I was ten years old. But I did sports—tennis.

VG Pool?

MB Yes. I play pool with Jackie Gleason all the time. He is an excellent player, so are Peter Falk and Fred Astaire, and I did play pool when I was a kid. I got locked up here in Vancouver because I was under age in a pool room.

VG They locked you up?

MB Well, no, they didn't lock me up but they threw me in a cab or something. I said, "I'm an actor, over there at the Orpheum," and they said, "Well, sonny, go over there and act and don't come in here."

VG Do you like to gamble?

MB Yeah, I used to.

VG Horses?

MB Oh, I lost a lot of money on horses, yes. There was only one problem: I followed the horses that followed other horses.

VG I've been to that racetrack. You always speak of your wife in such glowing terms.

MB She was a number-one press agent in the United States and we've been married over thirty years. She says funnier things in thirty seconds than I can say in five minutes. When we go to parties, the next day all around Beverly Hills you'll hear people say, "Did you hear what Ruth Berle said last night?" She said one of the greatest things when George Burns got hot again in *Sunshine Boys*, and we were at somebody's house sitting in a sort of circle with George. Well, I just have to drop this name—Peck—the great Peck pointed to George and he said, "Isn't it wonderful, the career that George Burns has at his age—a new career." And Ruth turned to him quickly and said, "Yeah, I can hardly wait until Milton gets old."

VG I thank you for this and I will leave you now. I am thrilled to have met you.

MB Don't leave me, Vicki. Well, I'm glad to have been on your programme. Do keep yourself in good health, because I feel wonderful. And as Henny Youngman would say, "I feel great. I was up this morning at the crack of my knuckles and took a brisk walk to my teeth." All I can say is that I hope you and your listeners and yours truly live to be as old as Henny Youngman's act. Good night.

Some of my favourites of the old guard continue to elude me. If you watched television in the fifties, then it is likely that you hold in your heart a warm place for Phil Silvers, the star of the situation comedy "You'll Never Get Rich." All the action took place in and around the barracks of a U.S. military base, in particular a motor-pool battalion that was solely occupied with gambling, with Sergeant Bilko running the show. I tried for years to book Phil Silvers on *my* show, but I was never successful. He wanted to be paid (and who could blame him) and naturally we didn't have any funds. A couple of years ago he died; I should have paid him myself.

If I never missed Phil Silvers's show, I also never missed "Love That Bob." Bob Cummings was the star, along with Rosemary De Camp, Ann B. Davis, Nancy Culp, and Dwayne Hickman (who went on to star in "Dobie Gillis"). My father didn't think "Love That Bob" was all that funny, and he and I would argue about watching it. The premise was that Bob, a photographer, was forever getting into messes with an assortment of young women. Because my father was a photographer, he found the scenario mildly unrealistic. Such cynicism.

Several decades after "Love That Bob" went off the air, I found myself in Cummings's company. He turned out to be one of the most fascinating of guests and certainly the one with the most unusual name.

BC My real name is Charles Clarence Robert Orville Cummings. At least that was my real name when I was born in 1910. My father delivered me, which is sort of in the raised-eyebrow department of the American Medical Association. The day I was born, the nurse in the delivery room was a nun named Sister Mary Alphonsus. When they wrote out the birth certificate, my dad, a doctor, by the way, put down Robert Orville Cummings, but my mother hated the name Orville. My father named me Orville after a patient of his, but she wanted me to be called after my dad, so she changed it. Apparently, someone handed my mother a pen and she drew a line through it and put a couple of arrows to the name she favoured. Then, where it said witness, Sister Mary Alphonsus signed. Well, are you following this? In around 1930 when I got my first passport, I had to get a birth certificate and found that my real name was Charles Clarence Robert Orville Sister Mary Alphonsus Cummings Junior.

VG You must have nearly fainted.

BC And I don't like to be called Sister.

VG Or Mary?

BC Or Mary or Alphonsus.

VG But Orville is not bad.

BC Well, my godfather was Orville Wright. It was an exciting thing, because he came to Joplin, Missouri, in about 1907 and became very ill and my father treated him. I had always thought that I would become an aeronautical engineer. When the depression hit in 1929 I was studying at Carnegie Tech in Pittsburgh, and there just wasn't enough money to stay in school. My roommate, Frank Crenshaw, wanted to be an actor and I thought that that was the silliest thing I had ever heard of. You can't eat acting. What does it build? It is such a nebulous pursuit. He said, "I am going to New York next week," and because I had never seen New York, I went, too. Frank had some connections at the American Academy of Dramatic Arts and he had a scholarship. While I was waiting for him to have his interview, I was looking out the window at the buildings and a man came out and said, "Are you waiting to see me, son?" And I said, "No thanks, I'm just with Mr Crenshaw here." The man said to Frank, "How about him?" Anyway, I won't go on and on, but they offered me a scholarship, too. The man said, "You have a peculiar quality and I'll tell you the problem we have: 165 girls in the April class and almost no boys." This was in 1930 and in April, there I was.

VG And that was the end of aeronautical school?

BC Well, I didn't think so. I thought I'd go back some day.

You know, in those days in New York it was impossible, absolutely impossible to get a job on Broadway or in the theatre or in movies or almost on radio, unless you were British. There were twenty-three shows running in New York at the time and nineteen of them were British. The movies were loaded with British talent and an American could hardly get a job. Soon, though, I needed a job and I saw a sign that said Waiters Wanted. Because I had waited on tables during college I got a job on a Cunard liner bound for Scotland. So before I knew it I was going to Scotland and I was on the high seas for nine days. We thought it was going to be six, but there was a storm. Finally we came up the Clyde into Glasgow.

VG Were you committed to go back on that boat?

BC Well, I thought I was, but I found out that I could stay in Britain for twenty-nine days if I had sufficient money. I think I had ninety-seven dollars. I could stay in England for the duration and leave from Southampton and so I did. Well, in the twenty-nine days I began to listen to the British people talk and I went to the theatre and then I wound up doing something that was wild and crazy and silly. I wrote letters to some New York managers, producers, and agents and told them that I was the youngest actor, author, manager, director, producer in England and the owner of the Herongate Repertory Company. I said that I was coming to America for a short visit, and I wasn't particularly interested in money, but I did want the experience of playing before American audiences. Three days after my arrival in New York I had a feature part in John Galworthy's *The Roof*, with the playwright directing. I lived in mortal terror that somebody was going to walk up and say, "You're a phony. I know you, you're Bob Cummings from the Ozark Mountains, from Joplin, Missouri." And you know what? Nobody ever did. I went for five years.

VG What name were you using?

BC Blade Stanhope Conway. I picked the name from Conway Turles. Stanhope I got from the second-act curtain, from the captain in *Journey's End*, Captain Stanhope. And Blade I got from the second act of a play I saw somewhere. So Blade Stanhope Conway I was.

VG And all this time you are speaking with an English accent?

BC I was so British that had I been any more, I couldn't have talked at all.

VG What about your friends?

BC I didn't have any. I tried to stay away. British actors would ask me what school I had gone to, and as Frank Crenshaw, my old roommate, had had a collection of books about the Raj, I said that I had gone to school in India. They were mightily impressed. I said I was tutored with the children of the maharajah and I found that almost nobody knew anything about India.

VG But one day the axe had to fall?

BC Well, eventually after playing on Broadway and then in the Ziegfeld Follies I went to California, to Hollywood, to be tested for *The Lives of the Bengal Lancers*. But I didn't make it. I went back to New York and a funny thing began to happen. The English era died. They didn't want Englishmen any more. They wanted Gary Cooper types, James Cagney types, Edward G. Robinson, Paul Muni—gangsters and big, raw-boned western types. So I thought, "I'm in a fine spot now, with a British accent and background in India." One day I met an agent who had known me in New York City. His name was Manny Frank. I asked him to be my agent and he said that there was only one problem. "Blade," he said, "they don't want Englishmen any more. They are a dime a dozen and they are all trying to get jobs. The problem is that you are too British." I said, "Come and sit in the car. I don't want anybody to hear this." I think he thought there was something wrong with me. "What if I were to tell you that I am not British, but I am Bob Cummings from Joplin, Missouri?" He said, "I wouldn't believe you. Blade, it's a good try but you'll never make it because you are so typically, definitely British and there is no way to change."

"Come with me," I said, and I took him to my apartment and showed him my passport, which had Charles Clarence Robert Orville Cummings on it, and he could not believe it. But the very next day he called to say that

Paramount was producing *So Red the Rose*, with King Vidor directing and Margaret Sullavan starring, and they said they needed a Texan. I said, "By when?" And he said, "Tomorrow morning." Well, by nine o'clock the next morning I was, ah, Bob Cummings from St Angelo, Texas. I stayed up that night and listened to Spade Cooley's Band on the radio and practised my accent.

When our interview finished about three hours after it began and I thanked him, he suggested that I had been a brick through the whole ugly mess. I loved every minute of it.

In the fall of 1983 the renowned photographer Yousuf Karsh published *Karsh, A Fifty-Year Retrospective*, a book of his favourite works. Naturally, he did a book tour of Canada and the United States. I didn't care if he had been interviewed by every living, breathing talk-show barker in the world, I was going to talk to this man. I also didn't care that there were some things about which he did not wish to speak. The man displays great discretion and that, in addition to his talent as a photographer, is what makes him so much in demand. He doesn't blab; he shoots.

Now, Yousuf Karsh is a snappy dresser: Old World charm and all that. His shirts are obviously handmade, and when I met him, he was wearing a red-and-white shirt with white collar and cuffs. Now, that may not seem so terribly out of the ordinary, but on the cuffs and just a bit of the collar were little slips of the coloured fabric, ever so beautifully worked in. I could hardly take my eyes off the shirt.

Karsh has yet to write a definitive autobiography, although in 1962 he published *In Search of Greatness*, and his fifty-year retrospective contained many anecdotal observations, but absolutely no dirt.

VG Do you think you will ever write the *real* story?

YK It is very, very much under consideration. But I don't know how I can free myself from the discipline that is part of my upbringing. If you were brought up correctly, with consideration for your fellow man, you just can't throw that off your shoulders completely and say, "I'm going to write a sensational book and tell all." It is

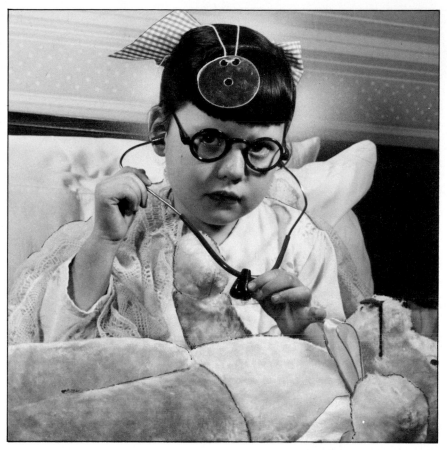

This won't hurt a bit . . .
Four-year-old Vicki with her Dr U-B-Well kit
and patient "Ross Mortimer," named after
the late Vancouver broadcaster.
CREDIT: HARRY FILION

Harry Filion goes shopping for a hat, 1963.

Veryl and Harry Filion blend
in with the locals in
Acapulco, Mexico, 1977.

Nine-year-old Vicki and her
pal Lorelei.

Vicki's sixteenth-birthday photo, 1962.
CREDIT: HARRY FILION

Candidates Rosie Sunrise and
David Crombie work the crowd
during the 1974 mayoralty race
in Toronto.
CREDIT: TORONTO STAR

Well-known pump organist
Pierre Berton in Kleinberg, 1976.
CREDIT: HARRY FILION

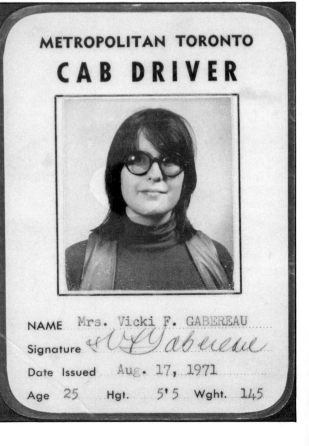

METROPOLITAN TORONTO

CAB DRIVER

NAME   Mrs. Vicki F. GABEREAU

Signature

Date Issued   Aug. 17, 1971

Age 25   Hgt. 5'5   Wght. 145

Vicki and the Berton clan at the New York World's Fair, 1965. Back row, left to right: Vicki, Penny, Pierre, Janet, Pam. Front row, left to right: Peggy Anne, Patsy, Peter, and in front of him, Paul. (Missing: Perry)

Mark Lee

Vicki

Mark Lee and co-host, Vicki, and the CBC Radio Sports crew at the Broadcast Centre for the Commonwealth Games held in Edinburgh, Scotland, 1986.

Toronto crew of "Variety Tonight," 1982.
Back row, left to right: March Thompson, Alex Barris, Kim Orchard, Helicia Glucksman, Judy Brake, Margot Crack. Front row, left to right: Janice Parker, Doug I. Jones.
CREDIT: FRED PHIPPS

Vicki and Jack Webster at his farewell party following his last show on BC-TV, 1987.
CREDIT: JOHN DENNISTON

Tom's girlfriend, Vicki, in the workplace, 1983.

Vicki's boyfriend, Tom Rowe, in the workplace, 1987. (Favourite photo of self)

Vancouver crew of "Variety Tonight," 1985.
Left to right: Susan Englebert, Doug I. Jones, Marion Gonneville, Vicki,
Elizabeth Wilson, David Wisdom, Rosemary Allenbach, Tod Elvidge, Gary Heald.

Vicki's daughter, Eve, and son, Morgan, in Toronto, 1987.

not my temperament. It is not in my nature. But this book has an autobiography, which is moving. Having been born under the oppression and tragedies of the Armenian massacres, coming to realize that at the age of fourteen I did not even know that there was a birthday in my life. My life began only then. The moment I came to Canada. Everything looked so glorious to me, whether it was cold, sunshine, or snow. I thought everything was most marvellous and I still do.

VG Had you seen snow before you arrived?

YK Very little. I remember even seeing red snow, now that you remind me for the first time. Probably the atmosphere was so bloody contaminated that even the snow was red. I don't know what to attribute that to. I just mention that for the first time in all of my life.

VG I have read that you do not have too many photographs in your household. None on the walls.

YK No, we have art. Many people I have been privileged to photograph have inscribed photographs—Sibelius, Casals, Churchill, many others—but they are not framed on the wall. I think it is because I like to move into a different environment. I like to expose my brain to many other esthetics.

VG In your new book I was fascinated by the photo of Alberto Giacometti.

YK Yes, Giacometti was rather a surprise to me. I very much wanted to photograph him, but unbeknownst to me, he was in great pain and was suffering from an advanced case of cancer. He was really very impatient, horrible, but all that time, that penetrating pain was constant. But he did not give any signal. [His habit] was to go to bed at three o'clock in the morning, yet he had made arrangements with me at twelve o'clock to photograph him. When we arrived he was still sound asleep, and then he went out to have a cup of coffee. After the photography was over, my wife and the painter Matisse's son, who was Giacometti's representative, stood for about forty-five minutes in a little alleyway off Giacometti's studio. Then we went to a familiar place [for a drink] and Giacometti came in with a lady of joy, a lady of the night. All he wanted was a companion, someone to listen to him. He came over to us and said, "I was a bad boy today, please forgive me." And we assured him that we were very pleased to have made the photographs.

VG He was not long for this world, was he?

YK Some three weeks, four weeks. I experienced the same thing with Hemingway; there was excessive pain. I experienced it with John Buchan, Lord Tweedsmuir, our own Governor General. He was always very highly sensitive, a glorious companion and host. But he came with his two sons and was very impatient. This was during the war. I said, "That is not at all like Lord Tweedsmuir." And the next day he was hospitalized for some excessive pain. I realized then and there that no more must I make any judgement on anyone until I know the facts. But now, you must tell me when I should stop.

VG Never. Will you tell me, please, how you managed to get Castro to take off his shirt?

YK Well, that was not difficult, because even though we know him as a revolutionary, I am a photographer first and foremost. After having made two or three shots I felt that his beard was blending too readily with his khaki uniform, and I merely explained that. He said, "Oh, you want me to remove it?" So he did. And he looks very much like a poet. Indeed he is probably very poetic, because he is one of the few revolutionaries who has made time to read books outside his ideology.

VG Do you have time for anything else? Tennis, golf?

YK Tennis, yes. Golf, no. I played golf once and I didn't make a hole in one, so I gave it up.

It is a rare occasion when I interview two people together. But two at a time has never been more fun than with the Adaskins. Harry and Frances Adaskin are a remarkable pair. They are equally remarkable separately, but they have been together for sixty years and even if I had been dumb enough to want to interview just one or the other, it would not have been right.

In Canada there are scattered all across the country those of us who learned to listen to music through the efforts of Harry

Adaskin. There were thousands who took his music courses at the University of British Columbia, and equal numbers who listened to him on CBC's "Tuesday Night" and the New York Philharmonic Sunday broadcasts. Since 1923 Harry the violinist and Frances the pianist have been playing together. They married in 1926.

VG I guess you can hardly remember life without each other?

FA I can't remember.

HA I really can't.

VG Did you meet each other playing?

FA Yes we did, in Toronto. It was really very funny. I had gone to Toronto to study at the conservatory at age nineteen. I had not been well taught in everything, being from the country. One of my acquaintances at the conservatory used to play in public. One night she rang me up and said, "I would like you to play for me tonight at such and such a café." And I said, "But I can't, I'm not a member of the union and I've never played in my life other than in private." So Harry was at the place with the cellist and he said, "What would you like to play?" And I said, "Well, I don't know." They thought they had some sort of dud on their hands. But he was very nice and we played some simple pieces. At the end of the three nights, which was what I was engaged for, he said, "Would you like a dish of ice-cream?" And I said, "Yes, I would love it."

HA I was dangerously advanced.

FA I know, I know.

VG You two lived for quite a while in France. Where did you live there?

HA We lived 150 miles south of Paris. Delius lived there at Fontainbleu, which was not far. We, of course, have loved his music all our lives. We played everything he wrote, and I often said then that it would be lovely to go and play his music for him and see if he approved of our way of doing it. But when the thought arose in my mind that he might not like it, I became terrified. So I never went and he died, finally. But I met a man who was sort of his amanuensis, who wrote down a lot of his things for him at the end because he was blind and paralysed and couldn't write himself. We met this man in London and we told him the story. "Oh," he said, "you have made the mistake of your life. He loved people to come and play for him. If they played badly or well it made no difference. It was his music you were playing." I tell you, I did feel badly.

VG You won't ever let yourself feel that way again?

FA We never did.

VG Were you ever part of the Lost Generation in France?

HA We are not part of any generation. We are just ourselves. We are not joiners. We do not join groups. We don't get enthusiastic about things going on. I have no interest in politics. I have no interest in world affairs. We don't really belong to the human race, generally speaking. I don't mean we are above them, it is just that our interests don't coincide with the natural interests of most people.

VG You are, however, interested in painting. You have a wonderful collection.

HA Oh, sure. Art is our life, paintings are a part of that. I look upon art, you see, as the only language of the transcendental world. This is where we differ from animals. We are the only animals in the whole of creation that are able to grasp something about the transcendental world, the eternal world, not the limited one. And I always hope, when I play the violin, that something of that will come through, and occasionally it does. Even I could tell that. But I couldn't always *do* that.

VG When you played, were there times when you would be almost off the floor, with the violin an extension of your body?

HA Yes, but it didn't happen often enough. That was the only criticism I have of it. It didn't always happen, but when it did, it was unforgettable. And if you ask me how I did it, I couldn't tell you. And that is why when it comes to teaching, we can teach any normal person to play the violin, anybody; but you cannot teach a person to be an artist. That he has to drag out of his guts, out of his own being. And if he does that, it will transfer into his playing. And what do the fingers do at that time? Well, I don't know, but when they do it you recognize it instantly. I am going to New York to be on an awards jury and I'll hear the best fiddlers living today, young people. But I will know at once those who are first-rate violinists and those who are artists. And I'll tell you, they are never in large numbers. There are a lot of wonderful players but they are not all artists. The orchestras are full of them. You know, we need them but they are not inspiring. Artists are a special breed. They are another thing altogether.

I knew a man who was a pupil of Fritz Kreisler's and I was very interested in this. He was a good fiddler, this boy. And I said, "What was Kreisler like as a teacher?" "Well," he said, "he wasn't very good." And I said, "How is this possible?" "Well, he'd say, 'Do the passage with a little more this or a little more that.' When I would do the passage with a little more this and that, 'No, no, no,' he would say. Finally he [Kreisler] would give up and say, 'Just a minute.' He would pick up his violin and say, 'Play it like this.' And then he would knock you over with the phrase." Well, what did he do to it? Kreisler couldn't even tell him. But if you have a sensitive ear, you might catch it. And it can be found at any age, some very early. Yehudi Menuhin played at twelve. He is a real artist, you know.

VG You were not that young?

HA Well, I was twelve, but I was not as formed as I later became, naturally. I do know from what happened to me and what scholarships I won and so on that I must have had something.

VG Frances, did you always know that the piano was your baby?

FA I know it now, but I had no idea that I was going to be a pianist or in the musical life, so to speak. I had no ambition but my family thought I should study, so I did. I was always an accompanist and when I retired from university teaching I was seventy something. Harry said, "Well, now you'll have lots of time to play by yourself." I said, "I'm not going to play by myself. I never have in my life." However, he nagged me into it and now I play by myself and I love it. It is so much easier than accompanying.

VG It is a particular talent. You have to be paying attention all the time.

FA I'll tell you, if you are an accompanist, there is only one thing that you have to know or have by instinct. You cannot learn it. You always need to know where they are or what they are going to do before they do it. Because if you have to hear it, you're late.

VG You've never lost your place?

FA NO, and the first time I played for Harry in public, he skipped sixteen bars of the "Symphony Espangole." I thought afterwards, "How did I do that?"

HA How did she know? How did she know where I was at that minute? Maybe I skipped thirty bars, but she hit the right spot and went on and I never found out that there was something wrong.

FA But that is what an accompanist should be able to do.

VG Tell me something. Are you ever going to outgrow this business of not having a car?

FA No.

HA They wouldn't let me have a car now, at eighty-three. I used to drive my father's car when I was a boy, but I've never owned one.

VG No driver's licence?

FA I did. I had one at one time.

VG How do you write a cheque if you don't have a driver's licence?

HA As a matter of fact, I tried to get a shopping card at Woodward's department store, and first of all the woman said, "Wasn't the dawn beautiful this morning, sir?" I said, "Well, I didn't see the dawn and actually I have never seen the dawn." "You've never seen the dawn?" "No," I said, "I haven't." "You've really never seen the dawn?" I thought for sure I wasn't going to get the card. Finally, she wrote something down and then asked for the licence number of the car. I told her I didn't have a car, so I could have no licence number. Then she said, "But you have a car?" and I said, "No, never had a car." "You've never had a car?" Well, it was such a shock to her that when finally we had arranged something and I was leaving, I turned around to give her a final wave and there she was sitting at her desk just nodding her head up and down.

Hugh Pickett was born in Vancouver. To the best of my knowledge, he still lives in the house in which he was born and has never lived for any length of time anywhere else. But you wouldn't know it by the international company he keeps. The son of a steamship magnate, he bucked the system and fell for show business. If it were not for Hugh and a handful of others, Vancouver audiences might never have seen the actors, singers, and first-rate performers that he brought to town. For forty years he and his partner ran the booking agency, Famous Artists. I would call him an impresario, but he has always maintained that there was only one impresario, the great Sol Hurok. I think Pickett is too modest.

VG How did you get the bug?

HP Lewis Stone was a great friend of my father. Stone was a very famous actor [he played the father in the Hardy family series with Mickey Rooney]. I stayed at his house in Hollywood many, many times. It was through the Stone family I met Lela Rogers, the mother of Ginger. I was fascinated by RKO Pictures and what went on. I met Katharine Hepburn, who was charming and still is, and I knew what they were all doing in pictures. Not everybody is interested in that sort of thing, or interested in listening to them *ad infinitum*. I was, so they sort of liked me and I was certainly fascinated by them.

VG You seem to remember everything.

HP That's right. Phyllis Diller said, "Why don't you write a book? Only don't write it, just write little chapters and send them to people saying, 'This is what I am going to say about you in a book. Would you like to add something?' " She said I'd get fifteen thousand dollars in the mail, in a minute.

VG Have you tried that yet?

HP No, but I will.

VG Your friendship with Marlene Dietrich is well known. She is your dear friend?

HP She really is, although she's been terribly difficult to people and to me. I love her dearly and understand her. You have to understand that these people are under a hell of a strain, doing what they do.

VG But she doesn't do anything any more.

HP Not any more, no. But when Marlene was sixty-seven years old she looked like she was thirty-five on stage. It is a strain to have to get up; just like a hockey player getting up for a game. She always got fantastic reviews. She really wasn't a good singer, it was acting she did. But it was tough on her and I understood her and I understood she wanted to yell, and she could yell at me.

VG Quite volatile?

HP Well now, Marlene has a theory: never raise your voice. If you want to get into an argument with somebody, get quieter and quieter and drive them mad. While they are screaming they have to listen to you or they don't know what you're saying. It is a good theory and I have worked it myself. She is an absolutely wonderful woman. The people who came to see her and who were at her feet were amazing. Not theatre people. One night we were at Sardi's and a man came to the table. She asked if I would speak to him for a bit while she finished a conversation with someone else. For about fifteen minutes I listened to this fascinating man and then he left. I asked who it was and it turned out to be Abba Eban. And those were the people she knew. She couldn't stand actors, although Gielgud was a great friend and Olivier and Coward. But the average actor, like Gary Cooper—she said all this nonsense about my having a romance with him—couldn't say two consecutive words that made any sense. And she couldn't stand Boyer. She didn't like actors much. She liked Laughton. She said Charles Laughton made her act in *Witness for the Prosecution*. Up to that point, everybody had just wanted to photograph her.

VG Perhaps you could give me the lowdown on Ginger and Fred. Did they get along, or what?

HP They got along professionally, but they were not best friends. They never socialized together. Ginger was never in Fred's house. They were difficult. Ginger didn't have to be difficult—her mother did it for her. You see, if there was ever a crisis, Ginger would go to her dressing room and Lela took over.

VG Well, is Fred a nice chap?

HP Yes. He's very funny. I was Ginger's escort at the tribute to her a few years ago at the Master's Club in Los Angeles. Ginger is a Christian Scientist, doesn't drink or smoke, and there were a lot of photographers. Fred arrived with Hermes Pan, the choreographer for all their numbers, and Ginger didn't expect that he would come to the thing. Well anyway, before the thing got started, Fred noticed that Ginger had a glass of gingerale and he said to the photographer, "Is that colour film?" The fellow said, "Yes." And Fred said, "Get it fast, because I'm gonna say she's drinking scotch." Just before the man took the picture, Ginger handed me the glass. She knew what he was doing.

VG You were, on occasion, on movie sets with them. Did you see the actual shooting of the "Continental," the big dance number from *The Gay Divorcee*?

HP No, but I watched the rehearsal. It was supposed to be in Venice and it was very Art Deco, all beautiful and white. They had built a canal on the sound stage. After working on the thing for three weeks, the water in the canal was never changed and it absolutely stunk. They had to scoop cigarette butts and oranges and junk out of it before they could finally shoot the thing. It still holds up, you know, it is still beautiful.

VG May we talk about some of your work, now? You have brought so many acts to this country. You have had a lot to do with introducing Canadian audiences to Soviet performers.

HP It was all very strange. One day my partner Holly Maxwell of Famous Artists got a phone call asking if she would like to present a pianist called Helena Czerny-Stefnska, whom nobody ever heard of. It was the Soviet embassy in Ottawa calling and this was to be the first Russian to come to Canada after the war. After several calls and a few letters, we presented her in the Vancouver Art Gallery. There were only about five hundred seats but it did sell out. They were all very pleased about the whole thing, except that nobody asked for the money. We didn't know what we were paying her, not a clue. We paid the expenses and the money sat in the bank and sat in the bank and finally we wrote to the embassy and said, "How are we going to pay this—to an agent, manager, or Czerny-Stefnska?" They said it was just a trial, we didn't do it for money. It was not a great deal of money, but it was a strange way to do business.

VG Things, however, did change and they smartened up?

HP They certainly did. And they started sending out the artists. We presented the Red Army Chorus. The Moiseyev Dancers, the Bolshoi and the Kirov Ballet, and a lot of individuals. Now the Russians were clever. If you wanted the Bolshoi Ballet you had to take three totally unknown violinists, pianists, cellists. One of the cellists was Rostropovich, whom no one had ever heard of. I think we paid him one thousand dollars. Now he will condescend to do a concert for sixty thousand dollars. And it has to be in a big building, too.

VG Were you ever worried about defections?

HP Well, it did happen to us. The day before the Bolshoi was to come to Vancouver, Baryshnikov defected in Toronto. But when the headlines came out that this great star had defected—we were opening the next night—a lot of idiots who bought tickets wanted refunds because the star wasn't going to be there. Believe me, they didn't even know who the star was. Anyway, it threw the company, and they did a very bad performance. They got bad reviews and they were all terribly upset about the whole thing. It was the last time the Bolshoi ever came here.

VG Have you ever lost your shirt?

HP Well, it's worked out. You have terrible losses. You've got to have something behind you to cover them. You can't just present two things, you've gotta have a series. One of the greatest singers of all time, Birgit Nilsson, sang for us and it was a disaster. We lost six thousand dollars because people in Vancouver didn't know her and they didn't go. If something was on the cover of *Time*, in those days especially, or on the cover of *Life*, you could sell it out. Here is an example. The Royal Ballet, which was the Sadler's Wells then, was brought to America by Mr Hurok, the great, only real impresario there ever was—I'm not an impresario and nobody else is either. He was. The first year he had Moira Shearer as the star; then she made a movie, *The Red Shoes*, and she didn't come the next time. So he had to build somebody. There was a little gal called Peggy Hookham who used the name Margot Fonteyn. He built Margot into a star by paying Mr Luce fifteen thousand dollars to put her on the cover of *Life*, and all across the country people were waiting at the stage doors to get her to sign copies of the magazine. He was a genius.

Hugh Pickett may not hoist himself into the same zone as Mr Hurok, but when he called to tell me he was to receive the Order of Canada in 1987 I was not surprised. In fact, I thought it was long overdue.

My interview with Vincent Price was arranged by his long-time friend Hugh Pickett. It is one thing to see Vincent Price on the screen, but it is quite another to see him in person. He has the most extraordinary hair. Does that seem a silly observation? It is partially grey, as one would expect, yet the bits that haven't turned are strawberry blond. No phoney dye job, either. His manner is continental and he has great charm. I talked to him in his hotel room in Vancouver while he was in town to perform his one-man show, *Oscar Wilde*. Granted, he is best known for the scores of horror films he has made, but he is also a world-famous art historian and connoisseur.

VG Your movies are designed to scare us, but what scares *you*?

VP Well, I have a gag answer to that one. One night, I woke up screaming, and my wife [Coral Browne] sort of hit me and asked what was the matter. I told her I had just had a terrible nightmare and that something had really scared me to death. She said, "What was it?" And I said "I dreamed I was being interviewed by Barbara Walters."

VG Har, har, har.

VP With Barbara Walters I always feel like I'm in intensive care. If they pull the apparatus out, you just collapse.

VG Gee, I thought you might say bad food or bad art or something like that.

VP No, to be honest, fire frightens me. I've been in a lot of pictures with fire, and it is frightening. Even controlled fire. I did one film called *Tomb of Ligeia*, an Edgar Allan Poe story, and it was a *very* good movie, very close to Poe. And there was this point—because Poe always has this kind of immolation in fire—when the girl and I were placed under the wreck of a building, sort of saddled down. The whole thing, all the walls, had been coated with liquid rubber, which is very flammable and gives off a gas, so nobody was supposed to smoke. Well, some joker walked on the set and lit a cigarette, and the whole thing went up. Of course, we were not ready for the camera and they weren't rolling. We got out of there in quick time, costumes and everything on fire, the whole thing. I *have* been in some dicey spots.

VG Speaking of dicey, didn't you make a film in Spain once?

VP I did make a movie in Spain once, and it shall remain nameless.

VG Oh, that's fine, but I am going to ask you to talk about it. It turned out to be a naughty little number?

VP It was dirty, yes. One day I decided to go and visit the set. I thought it would be kind of fun. It was my day off, so I went back. The scene I had done the day before, which was very innocent—well, suddenly there were all these naked ladies. And I said, "What *is* this movie they are making with a German crew?"

VG You had no idea?

VP No, we did not know. You see, they were making two versions of the picture.

VG But the German version didn't have your name on it?

VP Oh, yes, it did.

VG You could have sued.

VP Ah, no. It was such a bad picture, it didn't really matter. I don't think anybody ever saw it.

VG Is it true that Alec Guinness called you about the part he was offered in *Star Wars*? Whether or not he should take it?

VP Well, he was fascinated with the idea of doing that kind of film. You know he had always done very distinguished films and everything, and he said, "What's it like working in a science-fiction film?" And I said, "Well, it is great fun and if you're interested in the technique of movies, it's fascinating." And I think it was a good thing that he did it.

VG Rather!

VP Yes, and I think he took a percentage. But it was terrible, you know. I mean, as I understand it, the English people who got a percentage of it didn't make anything. Taxes! Something like ninety-two percent of it went to the government.

VG It *is* awful. But still, I understand that you were furious that they didn't ask you.

VP I would have given anything to be in it.

VG Really?

VP *Anything* to have been in it. Peter Cushing, this great friend of mine, was in it, too. And I asked him the other day—I did a film with him recently—"What was it like being in the biggest money-maker of all time?" He said, "It was a bore!" Because all of the things that he was working on were in front of process screen. I did a film once—*The Ten Commandments*—with Cecil B. DeMille. I played the architect of Egypt, building the great city for Seth, and I had this line, "Yonder is the city of Seth's glory." DeMille said, "Do you know what you're talking about?" I said, "It's a great big blue screen out there, and it's empty." And he said, "Well, perhaps it would do you some good if you came into the projection room and I showed you what's going to be put on the screen." So we went in there and I saw thirteen thousand people walking up the Valley of the Kings. So it did give a different reading of "*Yonder* is the city of Seth!"

VG What do you think is the best film you've done in the horror genre?

VP I think *Theatre of Blood*. It really was a funny film. It and the two *Dr Phibes* films were really nonsense. In *Theatre* *of Blood* I played eight Shakespearian roles.

VG Have you, or had you, ever done Shakespeare?

VP Yes, yes. I did *Richard III* with Jose Ferrer at the City Centre in New York. We weren't very good at it, though. The premise of *Theatre of Blood* was that a Shakespearian actor takes revenge on his critics. And the revenges were so funny. I mean, they were hysterical. Oh but I loved it, just loved it. I was with a cast of English people [Diana Rigg, Robert Morley, Ian Hendry, Harry Andrews, Coral Browne, Robert Coote, Michael Hordern, Jack Hawkins, Diana Dors, and Dennis Price, and Milo O'Shea who is Irish]. They were all laughing and chatting and carrying on and I asked what was up. "We've just been thinking that between us we've been in every play that Shakespeare ever wrote." And they had.

VG Did you ever get to wear fangs?

VP Only once, but I couldn't talk with them. So they made me take them out. The only time I did play Dracula was on a thing called *F-Troop*.

VG I loved *F-Troop*.

VP Me, too. I played a cousin of Dracula's and they kicked me out of Transylvania because I couldn't stand the sight of blood.

Seattle, Washington, the closest large American city to Vancouver, has curiously provided only two interviews in five years. (Maybe I haven't looked carefully enough.) One of these interviews was with Gary Larson, who is responsible for "The Far Side," the wildly funny cartoon that feature animals in grotesque human situations. He lives (or did then) in a small basement apartment near the zoo. His roommates seemed to be restricted to reptiles. He had in one cage a beautiful toad, so colourful that it resembled a Christmas ornament. Larson warned me, as I lunged at the beast, not to touch it; this little toad was deadly. Some sense of humour. After the piece with Larson was finished I had cause to face a less deadly but still formidable soul.

The second interview was with Stanley Kramer, who is responsible for some of the best motion pictures made in America. He produced *High Noon*, *The Caine Mutiny*, *The Wild One*, and others.

He directed *On the Beach, Ship of Fools, Guess Who's Coming to Dinner, Inherit the Wind, Judgment at Nuremberg,* and *It's a Mad, Mad, Mad, Mad World,* plus.

When Kramer and his family moved from Hollywood to Seattle in the late seventies, the house that they were building took seven months longer than expected to be finished. He, his wife, and two kids moved into rooms at the Holiday Inn down the road. When I went to interview him, we went to the hotel coffee shop, where the staff knew him—he had his own corner and was considered landed gentry and entitled to the privileges thereof. Sometimes he even got free coffee.

SK I'm really something around here.

VG Why did you come to Seattle?

SK I'd been thinking of moving away from Hollywood for quite a while because I had a feeling—undoubtedly induced by some box office falling-shorts—that where I had been half a step ahead for some part of my life, maybe I had fallen half a step behind. I thought if I came to a place like this, sat on a porch and looked out on a lake, contemplated my navel occasionally and thought, "Where am I?" and "What am I doing?" maybe I'd find something. I find myself at a time in my life when I have the ability to provide lots of questions and no answers whatsoever, after being very definite most of my life.

VG Would you say that you are content in any way?

SK This is a statement you don't dare put on the air. I am not content in any manner. Anybody who purports to be an artist—and I didn't say I was—would never be satisfied with anything that he's done, and I certainly am not. Once you are satisfied, then you are really through.

VG I think there is a difference between being satisfied and being content.

SK Well, that is a Canadian definition.

VG Is that so.

SK Look, just because we let a little acid rain go over there, don't get mean. Look, I came up here to write a book, not about film but about where film took me. Somehow, because I grew up in the Roosevelt era and latched on to social issues all the time, it led me into a lot of trouble and controversy. For a picture like *Inherit the Wind* I became the Antichrist for two years with the fundamentalists. With *The Caine Mutiny*, the navy swore there had never been a mutiny in the United States navy.

VG Did you ever lose sleep over all the controversies?

SK I never lost sleep because I had the arrogance of the profession. What is it that they say about a film director? "Fifty percent of them say they are God and the other fifty percent are sure of it." I was just about that arrogant and I sought only to please myself, which, as I say, I never did.

VG You have had occasion to visit the Soviet Union, as a guest, to shoot your movies?

SK Ya. They call me Krah-mer. I've always been the sort of ugly American who turns beautiful by being frank with them. I'll tell you a story. On two occasions I took films critical of *our* way of life, one was *West Side Story*, a musical. So David Mirish, who produced that show, went to the hotel, where you get a key that is about a foot long and weighs about three pounds, so you don't take it away. Well, Mirish got into his room with one of these big keys and he locked it from the inside and he couldn't get out. So they finally had to break the door down. He was in full pique and he wouldn't wait for the screening of *West Side Story* at the Kremlin. He went right back to London that afternoon. So I was designated to introduce the film. Well, for two previous nights they had been running the film, bicycling the print around downtown Moscow, from one theatre to another. Run reel one and then pass it to another theatre. They must have had a hundred thousand people see it in one night. Now, they turn the sound down so that the commentator and narrator who does the translation can be heard. They don't dub or use subtitles. The narrator narrates the film and he starts very factually and then he warms up to the test. Finally, he is playing all the parts.

VG Do you mean to tell me that there is a guy sitting there as if he were playing the piano to a silent movie?

SK Exactly. He's had the script in advance.

VG So you never hear the English dialogue?

SK Well, you hear it *sotto voce*. But because it was a big musical we made them turn the sound up. And the next morning *Pravda* had a big story: what are the Americans trying to hide? They bring films here that are supposedly critical of their own way of life and then they turn the sound up so you can't hear the translation. So the next night from the stage of the Kremlin palace I had an interpreter read all the lyrics of all the songs, including "America," which is of course devastating. And at the end of it I merely said, "So you see, we can do a better job of criticizing ourselves than even *Pravda* can do," which brought the house down. I was drunk with power.

VG Would you say that actors would clamour to get in on one of your pictures?

SK Nobody ever clamoured to my knowledge. Nobody.

VG Not even Spencer Tracy?

SK Well, Spencer was different. Spencer Tracy taught me a great deal and I guided him a great deal in his later life. *Inherit the Wind*, *Mad World*, *Nuremberg* and *Guess Who's Coming to Dinner*—directed and produced them all. We had a very close relationship. He didn't clamour. I sought him out all the time. I always felt that whatever I had to say or wanted to say or thought I should say, Spencer said better than anyone else I could think of. He, about William Jennings Bryan, said, "He looked for God too high up and too far away." Tracy was so remarkable.

I once made a film with an actor whom I felt was one of the greatest actors with whom I'd ever worked. Trouble, but a great actor—Oscar Werner.

VG Oh God, he is the only actor I ever loved.

SK Well, to know him is not always to love him. He was a lot of trouble. He insulted everybody. I was in a London press conference for *Ship of Fools* and I said that Oscar Werner is absolutely one of the greatest movie actors with whom I had ever worked. A week later I got a special delivery letter in Paris, from Spencer. He sent a clipping of this interview and he'd written across it in red crayon, "What the hell is this?" I got off the hook. I wired him back: "I was speaking only of mortals, Spencer."

SEVEN

Rode Hard
and
Put Away Wet

Outside the work for CBC Radio Sports, I don't often have occasion to talk to athletes or those in related professions. Mostly they are busy being athletes, and unless they write a book or in some way seek publicity, they are hard to pin down. That is OK with me, because I get rather weary of hearing hockey, football, and baseball players talking about the old team spirit—"Couldn't have done it without them" and all that.

There are exceptions. Hockey-playing lawyer Ken Dryden, when he toured for his book *The Game*, was a welcome change. Hockey player and coach Don Cherry was a laugh a minute. Bill Lee, the baseball pitcher, is guaranteed to cause a stir. And football player Mark "Jacko" Jackson was a lot of trouble, but that was his intention. Jacko Jackson was in Canada hyping Australian Rules Football, a wild and strenuous game that has to be seen to be believed. So it is with Jacko.

I first saw him on a Sunday-night sports programme on television, CBC's "Sportsline" from Vancouver. There is a phone-in segment on this show and the guests are often pretty lively. Some are more lively than others. The host, J.P. McConnell, was going through his paces one fine Sunday and when it finally came time for him to introduce his guest, it was screamingly obvious that something out of the ordinary was about to happen. As the camera pulled back for the two-shot, there was revealed in the guest chair a man of extreme proportions. His face looked like a shovel and his hair was bleached white and stood straight up, resembling a picket fence. Not only was this character loud, he was wound up like a two-dollar watch. I watched transfixed; at least he was laughing. I thought J.P. might leap from his chair at any moment to throttle the guest, but Jacko Jackson is close to six feet six inches tall and J.P. ain't. Little did I know, while I was rolling about the floor watching this hysterical piece, that I was to be his next victim. It was with shock that I noticed the following morning that some zealot had booked Jacko for me to interview. Why me? It was, however, useless to complain. (I may complain and whine about the bookings but I never win.) There was at least the outside chance that he might be polite to me, given my sex, because we all know how old-fashioned Australian men are. When you're desperate, you look for loopholes.

I had noticed—who could miss it—that on the show the night before, Jackson had been wearing a rather fancy, hand-knit sweater with a big star on it—what else? J.P. had asked about it and Jacko announced he'd knitted it himself. It seems Australian men knit. The thing that really struck me, though, was his remark that Canadians were dull in their attire.

He was scheduled to make an appearance at the studio Tuesday morning. It was still only Monday. That afternoon I took a march down a fashionable Vancouver street just to see if perhaps I could find something less than dull. Actually, I was looking for something that would make me look as if I were from outer space. The outer-space stuff cost a thousand dollars, so I settled for a sweater that was almost identical to his, only black. It had an entire cityscape knitted into it, apartment buildings and kites. I was resigned to the fact that I could not afford to look like Gort (the robot from the movie *The Day the Earth Stood Still*), but it was better than a tweed skirt, of which I have a million. The best-case scenario would be for Jacko to show up wearing his weirdo sweater, too. I prayed. I was not to be disappointed. Frankly, I think he was running out of clothes, because he had been on the road for some weeks. When the moment of reckoning arrived, I vaulted into the studio and there he stood, looking for all the world like a wall. He howled with delight. He was wearing all white, with a universe knitted into the front of his "jumper" and I was wearing all black with a slanting metropolis on mine. He was so taken aback by this (some people are easily impressed) that this man who spins like a Dervish was quite well behaved. He only yelped and carried on a bit, especially when we played his record. I forgot to tell you, he is a rock-and-roll singer, too, with a song on the charts that did well in his country. The title, "I'm an Individual, an Inda-bloody-vidual," came as a little surprise to me. It is one of the few times that I have thought, "Too bad this is radio."

In March of 1983 I interviewed Jack LaLanne, one of the first people to promote exercise and health on the television. To this day he does a daily programme. He was sixty-eight when we had this conversation and I have no reason to suspect that anything has changed as far as his state of extreme good health is concerned. This man's chest defies gravity still.

VG What have you done so far today?

JL Well, I was up at four o'clock and I worked out with the weights for an hour and a half and then I swam two miles. That is my daily schedule. I work out and I take my vitamins and I also take my high-protein drink.

VG I find it hard to believe that in a recent magazine article you said you were a bit lazy.

JL Everybody's lazy. You don't like to work out. You don't like to do a lot of things, but you do them out of survival and it is something one has to do. I've developed this pride and discipline and willpower and I just do it. It is one of those things. I want to feel well, I want to look well, and I do not want to have any diseases. So that is why I do it.

VG Have you ever been sick?

JL Never. Not since I was fifteen. Up till fifteen I was sick all the time. Then I entered this health regime, started exercising, eating natural food and no processed food, and my whole life changed dramatically in just a few weeks.

VG You were ahead of your time.

JL Well, somebody had to be there and I just happened to be in the right spot at the right time. But when I started I didn't think I was in the right spot, because it was really tough to motivate and stimulate people, especially in the thirties. People thought that exercise was strictly for a few muscle-bound wrestlers and boxers. And trying to get women to exercise and to get athletes to eat normally was a difficult thing, because nobody was interested. The doctor's weren't into it and the educators—everybody was against it. Everybody talked about Jack LaLanne as "that crackpot, that muscle-bound ass trying to get people to exercise and eat properly." I was considered some kind of a charlatan in those days.

VG Considered vulgar, was it?

JL Well, that kind of thing was supposed to be for people with no brains. That is as far as it went. When I tried to expound on the validity of the idea that every one of the 640 muscles in your body is important, and if you don't exercise them you're not efficient, nobody gave a hoot.

VG But your television show was a big hit. Is it still?

JL Well, we're on every day.

VG You used to have two German shepherds with you on the set, Walter and Happy.

JL Happy I had to put away, finally. He was suffering and he couldn't handle himself well. He had so much pride, I couldn't stand to see him suffer.

VG Will you get another?

JL Oh yes, absolutely. I'm going to import one from Germany. Ever since I was a young boy I have loved German shepherds. You know, they are working dogs and they're so loyal. They will do things for you and they are easily trained. I like people and animals that are trained and disciplined.

VG What about your kids? Are they in as good shape as you?

JL I have terrific kids. I have three children. I live in Hollywood, have one of each—just kidding. My daughter is a social psychologist and she is going to get a Ph.D. in nutrition. My older son is a professional photographer, and my other son is the captain of the surfing team at college. He is twenty-one. But I have never preached to my kids or anybody. I do it by example. And if they are smart enough to see what is happening and they want what you have, then they go along with it. They are all in good shape, although they have not gone into it like I have. They keep a good balance.

VG You have quite a reputation for doing—well, "stunts" is not really the right word—extravaganzas on your birthdays.

JL Well, it started way back when. I had to prove that you could have a Mr America physique and still move. That used to be the thing—if you had a Mr America physique you were not supposed to be able to move or do this and that. I had to prove you could look like that and still be a terrific athlete. So when I had my thirtieth and fortieth birthdays, when people really think you're over the hill, I started doing these feats. I swam from Alcatraz Prison to San Francisco, handcuffed.

VG Handcuffed, you say?

JL Yup. From Alcatraz to San Francisco, handcuffed.

VG I thought there were sharks in there.

JL Well, there are. But I had deputy sheriffs with rifles riding beside me. What I wanted to prove was that anything is possible and I wanted to give those prisoners hope.

VG Bet you were popular with the management.

JL That was one of the things. The warden was really mad because he used to tell all the guys, "Don't try to escape. The sharks will get you, and the water is too cold. The prison is escape-proof."

VG Wrong-o.

JL Yeah. He was really mad. Then I broke the world record in push-ups. I did 1,033 push-ups in twenty-three and a half minutes on a U.S. sports show. Then another year I broke the world record. I did a thousand chins and a thousand push-ups in an hour and twenty minutes. Then another year I swam from Alcatraz to San Francisco handcuffed and shackled, while towing a thousand-pound boat.

VG I'll tell you, you have an active imagination.

JL Again, I just wanted to call attention to my profession. So after all these stunts people say, "My God, that guy, at his age, sixty-five or sixty-six, is doing these feats. I am ashamed of myself. I've got to start working out, got to get with it. There must be something to all this." And it also gave me a psychological boost to prove that as the years go by, you don't have to sit in a rocking chair and think about the good old days. You see, anything the mind can conceive, the body can go along with. Look at all the records today in sports, the weight-lifting, the speed of the women athletes. Just look at what they are doing now. If they can do it, then I can do it. That's the idea. Just make up your mind.

VG Do you think that you can live to be a hundred?

JL Boy, oh, boy. I'm telling you. I'm going to give it the best shot I can.

If Jack LaLanne has done everything a person can do to keep himself in a condition that will allow him to live to a ripe old age, Stirling Moss spent his prime in a profession that nearly took his life a thousand times. At nineteen Stirling Moss won his first major auto race and was ever after taken with the sensation of speed. He was the first Englishman to win the prestigious Italian Mille Miglia. He was second on two occasions at Le Mans and he missed, again on two occasions, being the World Grand Prix champion. He lost once to the great Argentinian driver Juan Fangio (a four-time winner) and once to fellow Englishman Mike Hawthorne by only one point. Stirling Moss was a great competi-tor and if he hadn't racked himself up at Goodwood Race Course in England in 1962, he might have achieved that ultimate title, the World Grand Prix championship. I spoke to Moss in London in 1985. He arrived at the studio, wearing a helmet, riding a little Honda scooter; not what I might have expected. Practicality and caution have taken over, but not completely, from bravado.

VG When you began racing, were you required to wear a helmet?

SM No, funnily enough when I started racing, you didn't have to wear a helmet. My father made me, so I always did. I said to my father, "I'm going to be a real sissy." I mean, the fast drivers like Farina and Ascari and so on just wore the cloth helmet.

VG Like the old flyers?

SM Yeah, literally, and a pair of goggles, and we used to race in short sleeves. Of course, now you have to wear crash hats and you've got a life-support system that gives you air to breathe, and fireproof overalls. It is a lot safer for them now.

VG They are also going perhaps a hundred miles an hour faster, too.

SM Yeah, but anything over fifty and you can kill yourself. Well, even below fifty. But really, very few accidents in racing happen at very high speeds; they usually happen at, shall we say, 60 to 120.

VG It is remarkable now, when you watch car races, the way in which the machine brakes up into great chunks. It's ingenious.

SM Oh, that is done on purpose, you know. There is a cell, which the driver is in. In other words, it's the centre part, and normally that doesn't break up. You'll see the wheels fall off and you'll see all sorts of things come off and it doesn't matter. A few weeks ago, on television, did you see that enormous shunt, when the driver went end over end and he was quite all right? It was absolutely stunning. It says a lot for the actual tub, which is what that cocoon thing is called.

VG No such thing in your day?

SM Oh, good Lord, no. No, in my day they were all lightweight tubs with thin aluminium over them. They were not very strong, and they would fold up. In fact, we didn't wear belts. In case of fire you wanted to get the hell out. I've been known to jump out of the car. Now they have rubber tanks for fuel—we used aluminium— and in my day we used alcohol, which was the worst because you couldn't see it burning. Now they have rubber bladders and therefore spillage of fuel is not that common.

VG Thank God for these innovations because that endless injury and death was not encouraging. But I guess there will always be a breed of cat—

SM Oh, there is always some idiot like myself who'll say, "Well, damn the danger, let's have a go." It is part of the thrill and the attraction of motor racing. I don't mean we want to die, because that is the last thing I wanted to do. I like life too much. But it's that knowledge—that if you overstep the limit, you might face the ultimate thing—that attracts us.

VG Are you sure you fellows don't do this for the attention paid to you by adoring fans, especially female?

SM Oh, good Lord, yes. I mean there is no doubt that motor racing is the greatest sport for the crumpet.

VG Tell me about camaraderie with other race drivers.

SM Twenty years ago I think we were much closer than most drivers today. It is very much a business, now. These guys come in on their planes and they go off after the race and have their debriefings in these great big trucks, and they take off to the next place. When I was married, my ushers were racing drivers. But you know, if you are going to race against a man in a sort of life-and-death deal, an it's him-or-it's-you kind of thing, then I think it is very difficult to do that to your very best friend. But there is still that great, great comrade-ship, especially with two drivers on the same team.

VG What are you aware of when you're flying around a course?

SM Well, an awful lot, really. Firstly you are aware of your instruments, especially the changes in your instruments. Take the water gauge; you may not be aware of the degrees but you are aware if it has gone a little higher than it was last lap, or lower, too. Oil pressure, that kind of thing. You're very aware of people around the circuit. There are certain things you can spot: a photographer in a certain place, or if you know there is a pretty girl, you might blow her a kiss—that sort of thing.

VG Oh, come on. At 175 miles per hour?

SM Well, at 175 it is a bit much, that would be on a straight. But on a corner, you can see a girl at 60. I'll tell you what, you are certainly aware of where the other cars are, the relevant cars. In other words, your pit gives you a minus sign on the car ahead and plus on the one behind, and so you can see the gap diminishing or getting greater. You are aware of how long there is to go.

VG How were you signalled? Now they have radios.

SM They would put a signal out with numbers and letters, plus and minus signs. If there were ten laps to go, you'd get a 10L signal maybe. Your position would be shown as 5 if you were fifth; -16 would mean you were sixteen seconds behind. Now they have the radio. But with radio it is quite interesting. It has been proven that a man who is really concentrating can't hear, so they have to make sure when they do break silence, when they give the information, the driver is in a position where he'll be able to accept the input.

VG What about this new business of mounting a camera in the car. How can they stand it?

SM Well, it is show biz, isn't it?

VG Would you have submitted to it?

SM Oh, absolutely yes, I'd love it. But then I am a bit of an exhibitionist, you know. I think it is terrific. There are some people, I must admit, who wouldn't like it, who wouldn't want this kind of intrusion. Personally, I would rather have enjoyed it.

VG What is involved in the emotional preparation for a race? Were you antsy, lippy with your family, did you prefer to be alone?

SM I was always able to relax, and frankly I enjoyed messing around and upsetting other people.

VG Well, that was a charming thing to do.

SM It's one-upmanship. Graham Hill was the best example of a person who liked to be alone. Phil Hill, the American world champion, was very nervous. You could really tease him and he would get so upset. It's part of it.

VG Do you want to play a piece of music now?

SM I think it should be "That's Life" with Frank Sinatra. The reason I want to play it is that I had a very bad crash once, and Sinatra called up, and the girls at the hospital went absolutely mad. I wasn't well enough to talk to him. I was lying there half-dead

VG The accident, was that the big one—the last one—at Goodwood?

SM Yes, at the beginning of 1962. You know, I don't know what happened even now. I was unconscious for a month and paralyzed for six months. That was the end of my racing career.

VG You have seen the footage of that accident many times.

SM Yes, but it's only from an eight-millimetre camera that some enthusiast was using. It is taken from the wrong side of the car, so you can't really see what happened. And I have no memory. I still have amnesia there. But it seems to be coming back.

VG This last accident was the end for you for a lot of reasons, apart from your tremendous injury. By the time you had recovered completely, the game had changed.

SM Oh, yes, that is true. Unfortunately, by the time my concentration, which is the most important commodity, came back [five years later], the whole concept of motor-car racing had changed, entirely new formula cars, slick tires. It just wasn't viable, really, for me to go back into the sport that I had lived. So I knew I had to leave it. Which I did until I got much older and a bit more stupid, and now I play around doing the odd race, but not Formula One. I race mainly in Europe in super sports cars in what they call showroom stock in America. They are on an amateur basis and mostly it costs me money. Which is quite different from being paid by somebody to drive their car.

VG Prices have gone up, haven't they?

SM Oh, good Lord, yes. In my best year [1961] I grossed £32,000. Now if I were racing I would be signing up for over £1 million. I didn't do it for the money anyway. I was lucky enough to be paid to do it.

VG I would like to talk just a bit about the other part of your life. You live in a house that is full of gadgets.

SM Well, I have 196 different electrical operations, but it isn't as elaborate as it sounds.

VG A hundred and ninety-six is more than most.

SM It is more than most, I'll accept that. I do have an electro-hydraulic table that is quite unusual. It's in the room where I watch television and I can push a button and the table comes down from the ceiling. When I was a bachelor, the housekeeper would tell me on the intercom that the dinner was ready and then I would push a button and the tray-table would come down from the ceiling.

VG Sort of like a dumbwaiter.

SM Yeah, then you push the button and it goes back up. It has access to the kitchen, you see. It was a great ploy when I was a bachelor.

VG You were such a smooth operator.

SM Oh, I was. But now my wife cooks the dinner, then she loads up the table and if she runs like hell, she can be downstairs before the table arrives.

VG What else have you got there?

SM I can run the bath from anywhere in the house, at least from any floor. It automatically fills to the right height and the right temperature and then stops, which takes about five minutes and twenty seconds. It's a two-seater bath sunk in the floor, with a triple water-jet system that is also rather good. I have a television in the ceiling and sauna, stuff like that. Oh yeah, I forgot, I have a heated "loo" seat.

VG You did this all yourself?

SM Yes, oh yes. It was a bomb site I bought after the war. I built the house twenty-two years ago and just keep working on it.

VG Say, do you have a back-scratcher? I think that would be the ticket.

SM Yes, I do. I married one.

At about the same time that Stirling Moss was retiring from the sport he so loved, Canadian boxer George Chuvalo was reaching his prime. In 1965, *Ring* magazine rated him number three behind the all-time great heavyweight Muhammad Ali. George Chuvalo fought professionally for twenty years and he was never knocked off his feet once.

When I talked to George in 1986 he said he was soon to write a book about his life. I haven't seen it yet; maybe seeing his words in print will encourage him to do it. How could he lose?

VG Do you think if you had been born twenty years later you might have chosen another sport?

GC Well, you never know; we are all products of our environment. I do think, though, that kids today who have a certain degree of sports talent, if they were in high school they would navigate towards hockey or football or baseball. But in my day, anybody with any kind of physical talent who didn't go to school would have a tendency to drop into a gym, thereby giving themselves an opportunity to fight. And see, I always loved the fights. I remember the first time I saw *Ring* magazine in a cigar store. I was so intrigued by it I opened it up, and from that moment on, I fell in love with boxing. I just wanted to be a fighter. I even remember the name of the store: Morgan's Cigar Store in Toronto. It is no more.

VG Going back to the choice of sport here, you could have been a football player, given your size.

GC Yes, and I liked football. First of all it is a body-contact sport and I like that. But the thing with boxing is that it is one-on-one. You have no one to blame or no one else to give credit to if you win or if you lose. You take it all.

VG Is it true you drove your mother crazy, with all your exercising?

GC Yeah, I would do push-ups on chairs. I'd have three chairs, and put my feet on one chair and I'd dip my body between the two chairs ahead of me. And of course I made all kinds of noises, grunting and groaning. It was hard to do. My dad had to get up at 4:30 to go to work at Canada Packers, and I'd be up in the middle of the night doing all these push-ups. He did not take too kindly to it. My mother would get upset and say, "Hey what are you doing up there?" And I would say, "I'm trying to get somewhere."

VG Who was the first fighter of some magnitude that you saw live?

GC I guess that would have to be Earl Walls. He wasn't the champion of the world, but he was highly ranked. He was the Canadian heavyweight champion [1952–55] and he was also number three or four in the world at the time. I saw him fight a fella named Tommy Harris. It was a big thrill. And when I was about twelve years old I saw Solly Kenner, who I think became the British Empire champion. He was an outstanding professional.

VG Who was your hero?

GC I didn't have heroes as such, but I admired many. I think the big three were Sugar Ray Robinson, Willie Pep, and Joe Louis. I think Robinson was the greatest fighter that I have ever seen, pound for pound, because he could do everything so well. He was a good boxer, a good puncher. He had all the attributes needed to make a good fighter. He had good reflexes and a sort of sixth sense about boxing. He had a feel for the ring, and he could anticipate well, just like Gretzky is around the goal. He had a tremendous reach and he was a good combination puncher. He was flawless, really, in every respect.

VG And he was good for the sport, too.

GC He was a good fighter and was around a long time, too, till he was about forty-five. And he always conducted himself with a certain grace. I don't think anybody ever said anything bad about Sugar Ray Robinson, except maybe a couple fellas that fought him.

VG Forty-five, that's a fair vintage.

GC A little long in the tooth.

VG Archie Moore lasted even longer.

GC Yeah, he went till about forty-nine. I think his last fight was against Muhammad Ali.

VG You have such an extraordinary memory. Why do you not write a book, George?

GC Well, I am going to this year. Wanna know what it's called?

VG You bet.

GC *And Still Standing.*

VG Well, that really surprises me, because you used to get irritated when reporters referred to you as still standing, as someone who could take any punch, a human punching bag. Nothing short of a Sherman tank could knock you over.

GC A lot of that had to do with the fact that I pride myself with having a lot better reflexes than I was given credit for. I took exception to those remarks, because once you get stuck with a label it's hard to shake. And as a matter of fact, if I had been hit with as many punches as I was reported to have been hit with, I don't think I'd be on your show today.

VG Do you think you were underestimated by sports writers and fans? They didn't give you credit for any finesse?

GC I wouldn't go so far as to say finesse, but I was a much better fighter technically, than I was given credit for.

VG Are you, or were you, superstitious?

GC Yeah, most fighters are superstitious, I think. You always figure that there are some gods out there trying to mess you up and you don't want to get any of those gods upset. I think that *all* athletes are a bit like that. I know a hockey player who won't wash his underwear till they lose.

VG What about in the days leading up to a fight?

GC You have to remember that you are preparing for war, if you will. And there is another thing: A lot of fighters are gym fighters. What I mean is that without the pressure they can function extremely well. I've seen fighters in the gym, Vick, and they really look like champions of the world. But once it's for real, once the pressure is on, they can't function. On the other hand, you'll find individuals who aren't that good in the gym. They need the excitement and the pressure to operate at full capacity. And other guys like Robinson and Leonard or Louis can function well no matter what, whether sparring or for real.

VG What was your routine in advance of a fight, then?

GC The routine is the same really as training. I used to run and then chop wood.

VG Chop wood?

GC Just like the old-time fighters. I think it helps your punching muscles, especially if you're chopping a tree down, not just logs. It gets your oblique muscles in good shape, and it gets your twisting muscles, too. Any time you are throwing a punch, in order to maximize your power and leverage, you have to be able to twist from the hips. And I would imagine that anybody who can really hit a ball out of the park, a good home-run hitter, let's say, is using the same muscles as a good knock-out puncher. But as for a routine before a fight, everybody has their own way. I used to play records or tapes or go to a movie just to get my mind off it. Of course, you're always aware of the fight, but I didn't like to be consumed by it. I tried to keep it in perspective, if you know what I mean. You can't go to any excesses, food or anything else, and you must rest as much as possible, and be with people you like.

VG How do you think things have changed in the way that young fighters are handled, as opposed to when you started out?

GC In those days they'd throw young guys in there no matter what. The best man wins and that was that. Whereas today I think there is a lot more guidance. You will see fighters today, and basically there aren't that many around, who don't get a crack at the title until after ten or even fifteen fights. Even Leon Spinks only had eight fights before he fought Ali for the title. But you have to bear in mind that he was also an Olympic champion and he was very high-profile. But basically, years ago there were so many fighters around that it was tough to get to the top. A lot of fighters who might have had a lot of potential were knocked off early, because their managers didn't know or care or were not really astute. For instance, even Sugar Ray Leonard, as great a fighter as he was, when you saw him fight at the Olympics and then in his first two or three pro fights, you realized he was a kid with tremendous potential. But if his manager had not been a cautious individual, if he had thrown him in with somebody from the top ten right away, it is a good bet that Sugar Ray Leonard would have been knocked out, and perhaps knocked out of boxing. He might never have been around long enough to realize his full potential.

VG Do you think you realized your full potential?

GC No, I don't think so. Everyone looks back and thinks that. I certainly wouldn't make the same mistakes again, but I just would have made new ones.

VG Why did you not go the Olympic route?

GC Actually, I'm embarrassed to tell you why. At the age of seventeen I *was* picked to go on the Olympic team. I fought a fellow named Peter Piper on May 7, 1955 in Regina and I knocked him out in the second round. There were ten divisions then, starting from flyweight all the way up to heavyweight. Canada decided to send four of their best fighters, four of the best hopes, to Melbourne, Australia, and I was one of the four. When I first heard about it, I was flattered, but it was almost a year and a half away.

VG And it seemed like forever?

GC Yes. Their summer is our winter, so it was going to be late in the year, you see. And the people looking after my interests thought, "Hey, if he goes out there and wins the title, maybe some other guy'll get a hold of him and wave some green bucks in front of his face and lure the kid away." I was only seventeen, so I couldn't have signed a contract anyway. I was pretty well talked into turning pro at too early an age. By the same token, the Olympics were not the big deal they are today. I mean, they were a big deal, but they did not have the exposure that they do today. In retrospect, it was a terrible mistake on my part. It would have been a great honour to represent my country at the Olympics.

VG Professional boxing gets bad press, very mixed reviews. I happen to be partial to the sport, but it does seem to me that those who scream the loudest about loathing the fight business are those who know little and care less about it.

GC Well, there is no question about that. I think to get a true grip on boxing you have to know the game. You don't hear the fighters hollering about abolition of boxing. For most of these guys, like Roberto Duran, Thomas Hearns, Willie Pep, Sugar Ray Robinson, Joe Louis, and a host of others, they never, ever would have got the chance to be anything else than what they were— champions. They realized that their destiny could have been something quite different, if they were not fighters. What else could they have been? I mean, garbage workers, construction workers. None of them would have got far because of their lack of education. They would have done menial work. And this way they had a chance to do something in life. They had gifts dropped on them and they became great fighters. That, coupled with the right mental attitude and a lot of luck. They made it all the way.

VG Do you think that was the case with you?

GC Well, I don't know. If I hadn't been so in love in boxing I might have stayed in school. Perhaps if I hadn't been so enthralled I would have devoted my energies in other directions and I would have furthered my education. That is something I am sorry I didn't do. I quit school in grade eleven and you know, if I woulda quit school and not become a fighter, I don't know what I would have done with just grade eleven. I would not really have been qualified to do much.

VG How is your eye now?

GC Oh, it has been good for quite a while now. You wanna know the story on that one, don't you? It started as a result of a fight in Montana with a fella called Archie Ray. He threw a jab, I slipped, although a lot of fight folks wouldn't believe that, and I did slip the punch. I hit him with a hook to the body, but the moment I hit him, he jerked his body forward, basically because I took his breath away. His forehead struck me on the right cheekbone. I knocked him out, but it was clear that my eye was quite swollen after the fight. It wasn't split open, just swollen. Anyway, I took treatment and the swelling was reduced. But I had to go right back into the gym because I had another fight, almost right away. Usually you take a week or so off before you go back in the gym. And my eye kept blowing up. I used a lot of ice and took the enzyme treatment for this kind of thing, but in that fight with Joe Frazier, just one month after the Montana one, I got hit with a good left hook in the second round. It shut the eye tight and by the fourth round the blood welled up and my eye was sticking out about three-quarters of an inch. Then one more left hook and that punch drove it south of the border. They practically picked my eye up. It really looked as if my career was over, but I came back. They put a plastic silicone piece in there to hold my eyeball up.

VG You talked about this silicone piece before, in *The Globe and Mail* I think. Do you remember what you said?

GC I'll have to think ... If I'm not cremated and I'm lying in a grave, when all the tendons and ligaments have worn away, that little piece of plastic silicone—I'm lying on my back, see—all of a sudden the silicone will pop and hit the back of my skull. And it will make a little noise, a little tinkle. Maybe the termites that are around or the insects will hear it, just a little clunk.

VG Oh, George, you're a poet. I do hope you write that book.

GC I am gonna write it. I think it will be fun and I do think I have a story to tell.

When major-league pitcher Bill Lee published his hilarious auto-biography, *The Wrong Stuff*, it caused quite a stir. In addition to his wickedly funny observations of the sport, and indeed the world, he was candid with a capital C. And even a non-afficianado like me found a new interest in the game.

Also known as the Spaceman, a term he doesn't care for much, Bill Lee is one of the few baseball players to go to university on an academic scholarship, as opposed to an athletic one. A fat lot of good it did him when it came to his chosen career. He was a pitcher with the Boston Red Sox and the Montreal Expos and he performed well, even brilliantly sometimes.

Pitching well was not his problem. The problem, as management seemed to think, was with his outrageous behaviour. He once appeared on the mound in a real space suit. He said he spread marijuana on his pancakes. He called one manager a gerbil. He said and says anything that occurs to him. What occurs to him generally is inventive and very funny, but major-league ball clubs got fed up with his antics. No sense of humour, these guys. Bill Lee lives and works in New Brunswick now. He pitches for the Moncton Mets. This conversation is from May 3, 1985.

VG I get the impression that you would like nothing more in this life than to have your own baseball team. What would it be like?

BL Well, we would play in the ancient town of Baghdad, Hammurabi would be the king and we'd have this little garden, hanging gardens, and there would be a bar underneath, a piano bar. And we would be the Utopia League. We would play anywhere and the winner and the loser would get free meals, just play and play for your own individual well-being. A nomadic life. I like being a nomad; I like not having any permanent roots.

VG You remember Hammurabi's code, don't you? An eye for an eye.

BL An eye for an eye, a tooth for a tooth, and I've lost six teeth, so I'm up by six already.

VG Didn't you leave some of those teeth in the cement after a street altercation in Puerto Rico?

BL I left them in a steel pole, or at least next to a steel pole. But that was only two of them. They were fake, anyway. I left the originals in the back of my brother's head.

VG Why did you not take your father's advice when you left home to play major-league ball? He said, "Son, if you pitch like we both know you can, and you can keep your mouth shut, you'll end up playing for a long time."

BL Who knows. I do think, however, that I got a lot of mileage out of a mediocre arm. I think I'm a good pitcher; I don't think I was a great thrower. I was tenacious. I'm kinda like a Gila Monster; you know, I bite you and you can cut off my body, but my head will stay intact, until you die. I am tenacious and I speak loudly, but I did the job on the field. But baseball managers don't want that, they want people who are squeaky clean off the field, and I've never been squeaky clean off the field.

VG I have always thought that you were a lot squeakier and a lot cleaner than some of them.

BL Well, I was. I never even chewed tobacco. I don't spit, dip, or chew. That is probably why they got rid of me. I'm not a good ol' boy.

VG You seem to have some old-fashioned ideas about baseball.

BL My grandfather was old-fashioned; he played second base in L.A. He used to cut the centre of his glove out, the leather part, in order to feel the ball really smack into his hand, so he knew if he had it. He was a traditionalist. He used to hone his bats all the time and make 'em real hard so he could hit the ball further.

VG In all the years you pitched in the majors, who was your favourite catcher? And what is it that those catchers say, anyway, then they come out to the mound?

BL Well, Carlton Fisk was my favourite receiver; he was soft and cuddly. But Gary Carter was better in that he was quicker and stronger-armed and you just felt invincible with him behind, catchin' ya. Carlton was like an easy chair, Carter like an immovable wall. Carlton used to come out and say to me, "Bill, you've got to start gettin' the ball down. If you're gonna start pitching like that, we're going to be out of here really fast." And I'd say, "No, Carlton, I keep pitching like that and we're gonna be here for another two hours and twenty minutes." We'd argue, then I'd get mad, he'd get mad, and then he'd go back and sit down and I'd throw the ball down. And it was just great. We had a way of agitating each other. We were just like two washing machines bangin' against each other.

VG You said you felt invincible with Carter? Is that the key?

BL I think it helps. I think when you throw the ball and you know wherever you throw it—let's say I'm gonna waste a curve ball in the dirt and I've got a runner on third— you don't ever have to worry about it getting by him, because Carter is going to stop it. So you have the luxury of throwing bad pitches when you're ahead of the count, and getting people to go fishin'. And there ain't nothin' better than when the fish're biting, and it's a good day to fish.

VG Do you recall the longest game you ever played?

BL I pitched one time during three rain delays against Baltimore. I started the game at 2:10 on national T.V. and I got the last out at 9:15 that night. I must say, that was amazing. You're hallucinating at the end, because you've got the lights and the stars in the tops of your eyes. You don't realize it, but you're just running on intuition and guts, really.

VG And then you collapse in a heap and drink beer with the guys.

BL Yeah, that is exactly right. And then you get up and do it again.

VG What are you going to do if and when the day arrives that you can't play baseball any more, anywhere?

BL Oh, I'll be fishing. Coachin' kids, farming, you know, things. Practising the French double-digging tech- nique—

VG Oh, what's that, pray tell?

BL That is where you take the soil and you till it with your own hands instead of using the horse and plow. You get better root production. You turn it over in such a way that you dig down an extra foot under the topsoil, and then you plant hexagonally and you use your own compost and manure and recycle everything, and your crops grow twice as big. You get twice as much per acre.

VG Did you have such a farm?

BL Well, I'm going to. I was raised on my grandfather's farm down in the San Joaquin River Valley, but all my relatives more or less took that place over while I was out playin' baseball. So I'm going to settle down and get a little place in Canada out in the Maritimes, maybe the Annapolis Valley, and have two acres and a plow. Hook my wife up to the harness—

VG Oh, I'm sure she'll go for that in a big way.

BL I know what you mean. She is not exactly the Jeremiah Johnson type. But I'll teach her it's best for her health.

VG Good luck to you. Say, do you think that you have been misrepresented by the press? Do you think that your reputation has been slightly overblown over the years?

BL Not really. I think they've done a pretty good job on me. I think I've been so open and out front that they have to have got me cold by now. I guess the bartender in Minneapolis summed it up. He said, "Bill, they ain't gonna take you back. You have too much fun." And that is basically it, in a nutshell. Don't you know it's detrimental to the youth of today to see a guy like me, a grown man, runnin' out there and having a good time? You're supposed to be in agony and sitting back in your Mercedes-Benz with your walkie-talkie and sellin' short on the Dow. And that ain't me.

VG But you know that this attitude has probably cost you your fortune?

BL Oh, fortunes come and go. You remember this: It's easier to pass a camel through the eye of a needle than it is for a rich man to gain entry to the gates of heaven. So I'm not gettin' through the eye of a needle, and I'm a long way from purgatory, even.

VG Since *The Wrong Stuff* did so well, would you try another book?

BL I had to work with Dick Lalley on that one, you know. He pushed me and the publisher pushed me. But me and William Kinsella think we'll get together and do the definitive baseball book about being blackballed, and how this guy, this poor dirt farmer, tried to get back into baseball after he'd been reincarnated. Kinsella slays me. His stuff is the greatest.

Bill Lee's last music choice was "The Needle and Damage Done" by Neil Young. And just for interest's sake, the other two were "Ball of Confusion" by the Temptations and "It's a Long Way Home" by Supertramp. Telling, don't you think?

Don Cherry, former coach of the Boston Bruins, says in his funny book *Grapes* that he died on May 10, 1979, the day he parted company with the team that he so loved. I have never met Cherry in person, but brother I've seen him in action. I love everything about him, especially his clothes. I am fairly crazy for his dog, Blue, although I've never met her, either. She is a raving beauty— bull-terriers always are. The man has undeniably good taste. When we invited him to be on "Variety Tonight" his book was just out, so he was a willing victim. He thought we ran a pretty high-toned show:

DC Hey, listen Vick!

VG Hey?

DC Every time I hear your programme you have on a lovely writer, and I'm surprised—you know—I'm surprised I'm on.

VG What *are* you talking about?

DC Well, I remember the last time you had on a guy playing Verdi (pronounced like "birdie") or something. I was at a banquet and I was introduced as an author. And a guy says, "An author?" and I said, "Yeah. Three years ago, I couldn't spell author and now I are one." But I had help from Stan Fischler, he did a pretty good job. He did what I told him.

VG I was talking to a fellow and I said I was interviewing Don Cherry and he said, "Who, the golfer?"

DC Oh yeah, well there are people who don't know me, ya know.

VG I am sure that absolutely everyone who has interviewed you on your book tour has mentioned the fact that you start your book with a date.

DC I do?

VG Yes, you do. That is your first line. "I died on May 10, 1979." And you know, there is another historic coach, Imlach, who also starts his book with a date. You professional sports types seem to peg everything to dates.

DC Well, I'll tell ya, that is the only thing you can work on. Everything is run by schedules when you're in pro sports. You have to be at the bus at a certain time and you have to go out on your shift at a certain time, everything like clockwork. Or it is supposed to be.

VG Are ulcers a problem in your business?

DC I never had ulcers—maybe heart attacks or something—but I used to let it out and break sticks and yell and holler, and the doctor told me that was the best thing to do.

VG Would you consider yourself an eccentric?

DC Nah, an eccentric is a person that's rich and a guy that's poor is nuts. But I'd say that Harry Sinden, general manager of the Boston Bruins, thought I was. Wanna hear a Harry Sinden story?

VG You bet.

DC I consider myself to be Lord Nelson, and the ship is the team and the sailors are the players, and this is the English Navy, and you have to get out there. So one night, after a particularly brilliant move on my part, we won the game. I said to Harry, "You know, out there I *was* Lord Nelson." At the time I didn't know Harry was up knifing me in the back with the president of the team. He went out and says, "You know, Cherry has really flipped this time. He really thinks he's Lord Nelson. He's got brain damage." So maybe I am a little eccentric. I just don't know.

VG I must say you are a lively individual. Frankly, I've never seen such outfits in my life. Who *is* your tailor?

DC Well, I have it done right and I get it all custom made and I think they look pretty sharp.

VG Are you still wearing those big plaid pants?

DC Nah, they're out. That was years ago. No, I've got pin stripes now. I'm a businessman. Yeah.

Vancouver sprinter Harry Jerome was for a time the world's fastest human. He was the co-holder of world records for the hundred-yard dash and hundred-metre sprint (9.1 and 10.0 flat, respectively) in the sixties. He won a gold medal in the Commonwealth Games in Jamaica in 1966 and again in the Pan-American Games in 1967. But despite his remarkable speed and ability, he was not the darling of the sports writers and they were not a big favourite of his, either. Ultimately things got straightened out when Harry overcame an injury that should have ended his career, but he came back and won the bronze medal at the 1964 Tokyo Olympics. Harry retired from competition at age twenty-eight, gained a degree in Physical Education from the University of Oregon, and worked all his life in the promotion of programmes to develop physical education in the schools. When Harry Jerome died of a blood clot in his brain in November 1982 at the age of forty-two, he had only just begun. This interview took place three weeks before he died. He was a childhood hero of mine and an inspiration to thousands.

All through the introduction, which I had so carefully prepared, listing off his score of accomplishments, Harry sat across from me, his head buried in the newspaper.

VG What is it that you are reading there?

HJ Oh, something by Jim Taylor [a Vancouver columnist].

VG Here I am railing on about you. Most people pay attention, you know, when people are talking about them. You don't care?

HJ Well, I hope not. I'm interested in some other things besides myself or what I accomplished in the past. I kinda look forward to what I'm doing on a daily basis, or what I can do in the future.

VG Do you mind talking about what a speedy individual you were?

HJ Oh, no, and I'll tell you, some days when I go out and look at a track meet, and I see how fast these people run, it seems unbelievable. I say to myself, "Geez, did I really run that fast? And how did I do it?" I do think that now the tracks are in better shape. With the all-weather tracks, they have more opportunities to run the faster times. But the important thing about running, or about just plain competition, isn't necessarily always the times. It is often just surviving the competition. In other words, how many races did you win against whom? How well did you do in the major meets?

VJ I said at the beginning that the press was hard on you; they called you a choker.

HJ Well, I think in a number of situations I probably didn't really understand the press, nor did they really understand me. First of all, since that time I've run into a heck of a lot of nice people in the media, but when you go back to the beginning, to 1960, that was only my second year in track and field. I didn't even get started until I was in grade eleven.

VG So you were really a novice?

HJ Really. Mentally and physically. So when I first competed, in the Pan-American Games in 1959 in Chicago, some of the characters there had a few weeks previously run against the Russians—Ray Norton and Bobby Pointer and Woodhouse, all those characters. All of a sudden I was competing against them and that was a heck of a shock. And I hadn't come up through any system. As my old principal in North Van said, I was "a bit of a freak at the time." I had the times, but I didn't have any sort of mental background. A couple of little incidents happened along the way, too. In 1960 I met a hero of mine, a sports writer—a good one, too. And here I was facing him! One morning we were in a nice room in Rome [during the 1960 Olympics] after I had just completed the first run of the hundred metre. He turned to me and asked me how I had run, or what I had done that morning. I was really surprised because I thought he'd be out at the track. There were only a couple of Canadians who had a chance to do well. I was one and I think Irene MacDonald was another, and of course the rowers were always up there. Anyway, I told him to go and look it up in the press box. Well, the next morning I ended up with a pulled muscle, so I was fair game and I came across as a bad character. And then in 1962, in the Commonwealth Games [Perth, Australia], I pulled a muscle again. So that was two bad experiences in competing for Canada, and the press questioned my durability or my inability in international competition.

VG What exactly happened at Rome in 1960?

HJ As I look back on my Olympic participation, if I was going to win a gold, I think that was the race where I should have been close or even in there. But a number of things happened. You know that in the race I didn't start very well. Basically I just never got to the track on time, and I didn't have time to warm up long enough. I'm sure that if you talked to Hal Brown, who was the coach at the time, he would confirm that. We got out there and I was a little pushed for time and I didn't do a good warm-up. In the race there was a lot of pressure and under the circumstances I probably tightened up and pulled the old hamstring. It is a very painful injury and there is really not very much you can do about it.

VG But then in 1964, all was redeemed?

HJ Well, yes. It was a very interesting competition for me, because I was sort of coming back after two flops in international competition, competing for Canada. I had had that injury in 1962, where they operated and put my ligaments and muscle back together, so it *was* a challenge. And I was running against Bob Hayes [U.S.A.] and a few other characters. The competition was keen. I ended up just missing the silver medal to Figuerola [Cuba], who just nipped me at the wire. But I also competed in the two-hundred metre and I was the only sprinter to make both finals. I was fourth in that event. So, I must tell you that it was a very, very satisfying competition.

VG The fact is that all these years later, we can still make a story of it.

HJ Well, that is true.

VG The hundred metre doesn't last very long. It's over so fast. Does anything go through your mind at all?

HJ Well, first you *have* to—and obviously I didn't do it in Rome—relax. You don't want to tighten up. Now, some sprinters can run better not knowing where they're at, in other words, running on the side. I think the same goes for swimmers too, where there is a lane. But I like to run in the middle, where I could sort of judge where everybody is. And I think, particularly in the hundred metre, that if you are in the middle of the pack beside the better guys, other sprinters who are supposed to be the best; then they'll draw you along. You should also know where the finish line is.

VG Do you ever run any more?

HJ I'm a graduate of the University of Oregon, and that is supposedly where the jogging craze started. So I'm used to the joggers and the physical-fitness aspects of sports. But personally I have never been a long-distance runner. In fact, my high-school coach got very upset one time when I ran. He entered me in the mile-and-a-half cross-country course in Stanley Park in Vancouver, and I ran it in twenty-nine minutes, which is a terrible time. I got lost a couple of times, and I embarrassed him, so he wouldn't allow me to do it any longer. But to answer your question, I am basically now just a hobbyist at sport.

As Jeffrey Archer, author, sprinter, and former British MP, said of Harry Jerome, "He was fast, that one."

EIGHT

The Dreaded Book Tour

I couldn't possibly have left William Golding out of this book because he taught me two things: never to pre-judge a prospective guest and never to assume that you have an interview all sewn up just because you've been a good dog and have done all your homework. William Golding's reputation preceded him: I was convinced that Golding was a dour and humourless man. I suppose the poor soul has been saddled with these labels because his very first published novel, *Lord of the Flies* (1954), was such a grim parable about a group of wretched school boys who revert to savagery when the chips are down. In the spring of 1986, William Golding was in Canada to take part in the International Festival of Authors in Toronto. It was just my luck that his itinerary, on the lecture tour that followed, included Vancouver. That is, *now* I consider myself lucky; but when I was faced with the prospect of interviewing the Nobel Prize winner himself, I was concerned (in truth, I was panic-stricken).

What would you do if you had to face Golding as an inquisitor three days hence? You'd read everything the man ever wrote. Right? Naturally, that is what I set out to do. Well, of course you can't; that is, you can, but you certainly can't absorb it all. The process is not unlike cramming for an exam.

When Mr Golding entered the studio, I was armed. I had heard from assorted members of the Harbourfront festival audience in

Toronto that he had had them in convulsions of laughter. Could this be the man I was expecting? Turns out it was.

VG I hear that you read bits from "Billy the Kid" and the place went nuts. Is that your party piece?

WG I tend to kick off with that one, because it gets everyone in a good humour and we can go on from there. "Party piece" is about the right description.

VG It occurs to me that members of the audience would think that you were an extremely serious man. They likely did not come thinking they would be laughing in the aisles.

WG I'm very pleased, I must say. It is the sort of miserable image that I would like to get rid of. But I suppose I got stuck with it early on. Say, I suppose we've got to talk about books, do we?

VG Oh, no. (What follows is the sound of twenty pages of notes and questions about books being thrown out.)

WG Oh, good. One parting word for books would be that if you look hard enough you can find funny things in all of my books, and occasionally they rise even to black humour. In fact, the last one, or not the last one but nearly the last one, *The Paper Man*, I think is a black comedy; it was intended that way. However, enough of books.

VG How about your play *The Brass Butterfly*?

WG Oh, that one, that wasn't any good. I don't think it could even be rescued. I wrote it as a long story, which is quite amusing in a kind of snooty way, and they turned it into a play, for Alistair Sim, of all people.

VG He directed it too, did he not?

WG Yes, he did. But I don't think Alistair and I really were on quite the same wavelength, so we fell between many, many stools, flat on whatever one does fall on. No, not a success, that one.

VG Did that make you quit? It seems to me that that play was the one and only .

WG It more or less made me quit. I thought, "I know how to write novels, or I think I know how to write." I can, in fact, tell a story on paper, and I must be able to tell a story dramatically because I've done a number of things on radio that came over, but somehow I never got it right, that play, and I think people were probably glad to see the back of me in the theatre. And besides, you need an idea for a play, and I just don't seem to have any ideas for plays.

VG Let's try hobbies.

WG My hobby, I think, always has been music because I can't be a professional. I just haven't got any talent. I was working it out the other day: I'm seventy-four now and I think it is literally true that I have spent a year sitting on a piano stool. It sounds mad, doesn't it? But it is literally true. It is one of my big pastimes. You add it up—I've been playing the piano ever since I was knee-high to the curb, as they say in the adjoining country—and the total number of hours is massive; appalling, really. I think, "A *year* sitting on a piano stool and I still can't play the damned instrument!" You know, it just defeats me. There it is. I have lived cheek by jowl with professional musicians, and this is all very humiliating.

VG And you didn't pick up any pointers?

WG Oh, I picked up masses of pointers, but what is the good of a pointer, if you haven't anything to point with?

VG Well, where do you think the problem is?

WG There is one basic problem, and that is that I am left-handed. No matter what you say, music is written with the assumption, more or less, that your right hand can do more than your left. And if it's the other way around, I suppose it is possible that you could practise enough to get ambidextrous, in the musical sense. I don't believe it, but I suppose it is possible.

VG I guess the accordion is out, too. Actually, I don't much care for the accordion.

WG You don't? I'm so glad. I think the saxophone runs a close second.

VG You don't care for the saxophone?

WG No, I don't. I hate it. It's not that I don't care for it, I hate it! It has a faintly vulgar tone as far as I'm concerned. But there you are, I speak from the heart. I'm not going to hide anything from you. I used to think, when I knew nothing about it, that I would like to be a concert pianist. I thought that a concert pianist would play music very loud and very fast to an admiring audience, who would burst into applause at the drop of a hat or the drop of a note. I thought concert pianists lived a kind of lofty, god-like life. Now I realize, or I began to realize as I grew up, that these poor soloists spend most of their time in aeroplanes, when they are not bashing a practice piano, and then they play the same dreary programme time after time and time.

VG I know you don't want to talk about books, but the fact is that it's got to be the same thing with very well known writers such as yourself. It all seems too, too glamorous. There you are, spending a year or two slugging away, and then you reap all of this great praise and everyone says, "Aren't you wonderful!"

WG Oh no, they don't. People who don't write books and would like to are perhaps a bit naïve about it to say that. But people who do write books say, "Why aren't *I* writing your books?" Look, I'll tell you, a friend of mine, who shall remain nameless, and who won the Nobel Prize for literature, said that the first thing you discover when you win the Nobel Prize is how many people dislike you. And there is something in that. It's a nasty thought, but it's true.

VG It happened to you, didn't it?

WG Oh, yeah, but it is how things are.

VG I had no idea that people would say rude things about you after you'd won such a prize.

WG Well, they do for a little while and then things die down, because you've won the prize. It's rather like a medal pinned on your chest. They may hate your guts and they may think you're a nasty person, but there's the medal, you see.

VG They don't have it and you do.

WG And they don't have it, and you do, yes. Aren't we being disgusting?

VG Shall we move along to the riding, then?

WG I *was* willing to stay with the music as long as you like. As I say, having spent this year at the piano stool, it's a pity not to get something—what the heck, it's only a radio programme. Yes, riding if you like. That, you know, only turned up when I was seventy. When I got to be seventy I thought to myself, "This is a hell of an age to be. There is only one way to cope with this and that is to learn to do something new or something entirely different." As I'd sailed a boat a lot, and had given it up for various reasons—

VG You got run over by a freighter.

WG Yeah, I got run over by a freighter.

VG That was a decent enough reason.

WG It was a hint, I thought. So I thought, "I'll learn to ride a horse." So since the age of seventy I've been riding around the countryside of England and enjoying every moment of it.

VG You really have a cob?

WG Yes, I have an Australian cob and he's all right. He carries me around. He's not going to win the Grand National or anything, but occasionally I urge him along. It's interesting, anyway, to meet someone less intelligent than one's self. I think that's probably the reason people go riding. The view is good and no intellectual friends, unless they are on horses, too. And they seldom are. I should add a proviso, whatever that may be. We've just changed from living where we were to living somewhere else, and I have left the horse behind me. Now my great problem is how to get the horse from A to B, or whether to buy another horse in B and sell the horse in A.

VG But aren't we loyal to horse A?

WG Oh, I don't think we are, provided it has a good home and nice people looking after it. And that is the case. I think I'll get a larger, faster model.

VG A new streamlined edition?

WG Yes, a new streamlined model.

VG Oh, you men are all alike.

WG I know we are, it's terrible.

VG Well, where is it that you live?

WG I moved from a county called Wiltshire. Do you know England?

VG Vaguely, I've been around a bit.

WG Well, there is a sticking-out bit down in the bottom left-hand corner, Cornwall.

VG The sticking-out bit, yeah, I know that part.

WG I was born there and I've gone back to it because in English terms, although not in Canadian, you can't get from London to Cornwall and back in one day. So that means anybody who comes looking for me has got to book himself into a hotel.

VG Pilgrims, you mean?

WG Yes, something like that. There was, I remember, one very nice French boy who really caught me out when I was living in Wiltshire. The phone rang and I picked it up and this boy said, "I'm XYZ, can I come and see you?" I thought, "Oh, God," and wondered how to fend him off. I said, "Well, where are you?" And he said, "I'm standing in the phone box at the bottom of your garden." So there it was. He won that contest.

VG You were hoping he'd be in Brussels or someplace.

WG Oh, indeed. I thought he would say, "I can be with you next Thursday," and I'd say, "Alas, I shall be in Canada." But now I've disappeared into the woodwork.

VG I hope we haven't given it away, but you haven't said the name of the village.

WG No, no, no. That little bit of sticking-out land has quite a lot of corners in it.

Separately they are forces to be reckoned with and together they are worse. Canadian writers Morley and Barry Callaghan, father and son, are the funniest act since Eric and Frac. They answer each other's questions and they practise the same art with the ends of sentences.

Author of a dozen novels, Morley Callaghan made a great big name for himself, especially in the thirties and forties, as a short-story writer of the first rank. He was a frequent contributor to *The New Yorker* magazine, among others, and his work was read all over the world. In 1951 he published *The Loved and the Lost*, for which he received the Governor General's Award. Now in his eighties he continues to live and work in Toronto. He is still a scream, and hasn't got one bolt loose.

Son Barry, writer, poet, and journalist, is the editor of *Exile* magazine and a professor at York University in Toronto. The one and only time I ever met Barry in person was some years ago, the day after he won the triactor at the racetrack. He was weighted down by the huge wad of bills he had yet to deposit. My kinda guy.

The story behind this interview with the two of them is fairly standard, in that they were made available to us via a line link (a studio-to-studio broadcast line with good sound quality) because of the publication of Morley's new book in the fall of 1985. Except that the book wasn't exactly new. Legend has it that Barry, after having had dinner one night at Morley's, became restless and decided to plough through the attic. While searching around for some lost picture he came across an old manuscript, one he had never seen before. This find whetted both their appetites and soon the two of them had discovered boxes of forgotten stuff. The resulting volume, a collection of twenty-six short stores that had never been published or hadn't seen the light for forty years, was titled *The Lost and Found Stories of Morley Callaghan*.

> **VG** I don't have much of a clue as to how I'm going to keep you guys in tow here.
>
> **BC** Just throw us a rope.
>
> **VG** Perhaps we ought to talk about this new book. I think it is a grand revelation. Are you as thrilled, Morley, as the rest of us?
>
> **MC** No.
>
> **VG** I see.
>
> **BC** Well, that is the end of that interview.
>
> **MC** Look, there is a point here. How could I be? It's like asking a painter who hasn't looked at twenty-six of his paintings for forty years, and maybe he has even forgotten that he even painted some of them. Now if he walked in there and was thrilled, he'd be rather surprised at himself, wouldn't he?
>
> **VG** I suppose.
>
> **MC** But on the other hand, without sounding too egotistical about it, I had written so many stories and they had appeared all over the world, so I had to come to the honest, and you will say absolutely sensible, conclusion

that those stories were first-rate. When Barry first started collecting them, I found it very painful looking at them. Then I was astonished to find that they read as if I'd just written them yesterday. So I guess I was on the right track as far as story-writing was concerned.

BC You see, none of this was planned. Morley had mentioned to me casually one day that he had two or three stories he thought were lying around somewhere. And we decided to go on a little search of the house to see what we could find. So this was kind of a discovery, half-hour by half-hour, as we went through old boxes up in the linen closet. We'd discover a story that he couldn't even remember the title of, let alone what the story was about, because at the time he was writing them, there were so many.

VG This search followed your initial find of the longer manuscript?

BC It was actually a short story that had never been published. To tell you the truth, I thought I had found a complete book. That was the night that I got a little bored with the conversation and decided to go upstairs and see if I could fine one of the George Grosz drawings that had been done for the stories in *Esquire* magazine back in the late thirties. As I went through the boxes, I found this story, "A Couple of Million Dollars." It was in my mother's typing, as my mother used to do all Morley's typing. He looked at it and said he had only a vague recollection. Well, it's a terrific story, still ten years ahead of its time. So this whole experience has been a surprise, but it was not an exercise in nostalgia for me. It was like discovering something of the moment. It just happened to be in these dirty old boxes.

VG Were the papers crumbling or were they in good shape?

MC The thing about "A Couple of Million Dollars" is that he must have fished it out of a pile of papers and there it was, perfectly typed and perfectly fresh. I know this is hard to believe, Vicki, but I had written so many stories that I honest to heaven didn't know why that story was sitting there or why it had never been published or why it was just left there, all beautifully typed out. To this day I don't know. I probably just put the thing aside.

Perhaps it was from the beginning of the fifties and I had become enormously interested in the long story or the novel. But I was a fool to set it aside. Why didn't I send it to my agent?

BC Can I tell you the one thing that I do remember feeling? It came with a certain astonishment. You have to say about Morley, damn it all, that he's just a natural story-teller. There are a lot of people who work at a story. Publishing *Exile* magazine as I do, I get all sorts of manuscripts from young writers across the country, and you can see that there are writers who are trying to perfect a little story and you can see them building a sheaf of stories that will be the monument of their lives. Well, this sucker has just produced story after story after story after story. And there are still more. I've discovered at least another twenty-five. He doesn't re-member them, but we know the titles are there. It is just an endless outflow. And he tells me that, during the period he just mentioned when he started writing long stories and novels, he had just got bored with the form. Just think of the writers in this country who would love to be able to say, "Oh well, I've written a hundred stories. Now I'm bored. I'll go on to something else."

MC Well, let me tell you about this business of being a story writer, Vicki.

VG Yes, sir!

BC It does help to pay attention.

VG I'm paying so much attention. I'm doing exactly as I'm told.

MC I'm going to set you on the way to fortune right now.

VG Thank you.

MC All right. The thing is, it helps if you like telling stories. And I've always had a peculiar suspicion that a good story is one you can tell. You can dress it up and do all kinds of weird things on the page and you can get profound admiration from your literary fellows, but at the root of the matter is the story. I was earning my living writing stories and that, as you know, is a precar-ious business; but also I was a Canadian. Remember also that I had written forty-five stories in *The New Yorker*. Now, a strange thing happened. These stories of mine were not called commercial stories, at all. You know what I mean by that? They were not formula stories that went into the big slicks. The big slicks of the day were *Cosmopolitan, Saturday Evening Post, Redbook, Good Housekeeping.* Down on my level was *Esquire, Harper's Bazaar, The New Yorker,* say, *The Atlantic Monthly,* or even *The Yale Review.*

There was an editor at this big slick magazine called *Redbook* who had always read my stories in *The New Yorker.* He said to my agent, "It would be so easy for this guy, meaning me, to make a lot of money. I'll tell him how to twist the stories and in short, give him the formula." My agent said he'd talk to me, and then I left town or he left, whatever. But what I knew was this: there are guys who can write those machine stories who are really wonderful. That is how they earn their living, and they are good at it. I couldn't compete with them. I can't write stories like that. However, the editor suggested to the agent that my stories keep being offered and sent to him anyway, even though they weren't the right thing for his magazine. Then one day, much to my astonishment, he printed my story, but he did it in a very neat way. He put a little note in the magazine saying that an editor sometimes feels he ought to have the right to print what he called an editor's story. So in that way he could warn the readers that this wasn't one of the *regular* stories.

VG And it might just be art.

MC Yeah. It might even be art. And of course he found out, much to his shock, that his artless readers liked the art. Then *Good Housekeeping* started publishing my stories. The same ones might easily have gone in *The New Yorker,* except that I was getting a lot more money, do you see? I'll tell you something. I remember I ran into a girl on the street once, a rather intellectual lady, an old friend of mine, and she knew that my stories were practically appearing all over America in all these magazines, very high-paying magazines. And as her lip curled with profound academic disgust she said to me, "Well, I suppose the next thing, Morley, you'll be writing for is *Collier's* magazine." Why she picked *Collier's* as the pits I do not know. So I looked at her and said, "I'll tell you what. I'm bringing out my collected stories very shortly and I will give you twenty-five dollars for every one you can pick out as having appeared in the big slicks as opposed to the ones that have appeared in *The New Yorker* or *The Yale Review*.

VG Did she ever make any money?

MC She never made a nickel.

VG Say, Barry, do you spend a lot of time listening to the master here?

BC I think that our relationship in that regard is a roller coaster. I've mastered his trick. One thing about Morley is that although he is a man who can obviously talk, he's also a terrific listener. He has this wonderful habit, if you are telling him a story, of cocking his head kind of back and it will appear that he is staring at the ceiling and has gone into a slightly spaced-out trance. My young son—young, he's twenty-one now—does a wonderful imitation of Morley doing this. Now, what Morley is doing is half-thinking and half-listening. And I have noticed in recent years that I have developed the same capacity, although my head does not cock back. It cocks slightly to the left.

VG Do you think that your son is lying in wait to go through your linen closet, some years from now?

BC No. I think that my son is going through exactly the same stage that I went through at his age. I remember the first novel of Morley's that I read. I was on the train to college. I studiously ignored his work till about the age of twenty-one. I don't think my son has read my collection. I know that even though he thinks himself something of a painter, and even though his painting is on the cover of one of my books of poems, that that is about as close as we have come. He's busy, you know. I was busy. So he may get around to my linen closet when he is about forty-five.

MC Barry being an editor and, I suppose, a professor—

BC My dean has the same view of it, I want you to know. Every now and then he says, "I suppose he's a professor."

MC Well, no, he does an honourable job in an honourable university. But, you see, he is trained to keep things in order. Barry has copies of everything and Barry actually owns a steel filing case.

BC Do you know where it is? Look, you've got to get this straight. You see, he will mislead you wonderfully. I own a steel filing case, that is true. But the drawers to the steel filing cabinet are in my basement and the actual frame of the steel filing cabinet is in Morley's house.

MC But you see how cunning he is! The drawers are in his basement, and that is where the stuff is and I'm left with the empty steel case.

BC No, it is not where the stuff is.

VG What is the matter with you two? Can't you get anything organized? Who drives whom crazier?

BC I'll tell you. I used to watch Morley work all the time. He'd just sit down. I might even have been in the library with him when I was sixteen or seventeen. That was where the record player was. And I was an early enthusiast of rhythm and blues. I would stand there in the library, hammering away on the wall, listening to rhythm and blues, and Morley would be six feet away writing a perfect little story.

VG The man is a saint. I don't know how he endured it.

BC Well, in later years, my dear, I don't know how I endure him. Because now he comes around and hammers on my head.

MC I remember Barry used to be in his room and at that time he was fascinated with Shostakovich's "Leningrad Symphony." Do you know it at all?

VG Hum me a few bars.

BC Have you got an hour?

MC It's kind of slow and monotonous at the beginning.

BC That's right. It's supposed to describe the Nazis slowly moving in on Leningrad.

MC And then it's followed by the bombardment. I'd be downstairs in my library, sitting writing, and I'd pause for a moment's thought and I'd hear this damn symphony and this slow pounding. Then I'd get interested in the thing, you know. Then I'd finally get back to what I was doing. But it went on night after night. It was the same thing with Ray Charles. You were crazy about him, too.

BC He's still around, Dad.

MC Yes, I know.

BC You'll get to learn about him yet. Do you see what I've had to struggle with all my life? It's been an uphill struggle to bring this man into contemporary life.

VG Really and truly?

BC It's not that his stories were lost and not found. It's that he's been lost.

MC No, I haven't been lost at all.

BC I have to try and find him all the time.

VG Say, you fellas don't really need me here. All you need is a microphone and you two together in a room and you've got the interview.

MC Look, you could prove my whole point about every-thing I have been saying here if you would simply take one of the little stories in this book, *Lost and Found Stories of Morley Callaghan*, to illustrate what I think about things.

BC In case you forgot.

MC In case you've forgotten what we are talking about.

VG How about "Just Like Her Mother"?

MC The funny thing about it was, Vicki, honest to God, I had all my life forgotten I'd written it. But if you would take it and read it you'd get the whole point of every-thing I'm saying.

VG I will. Well, thank you, gentlemen.

BC That's the nicest thing anyone has said to us in years.

An actor read the story "Just Like Her Mother" from Morley's latest book. Do you remember the title? *The Lost and Found Stories of Morley Callaghan*. How could you forget?

You may have noticed throughout this book that I have a tenden-cy to repeat myself in interviews. Some things just have to be asked, regardless of their frequency. The point of this great confession is to tell you that there is in existence a list of things I'm no longer permitted to ask or say. These things are not exactly written in stone, but generally any producer or technician who might hear me making one of these forbidden remarks has licence to throttle me, even in front of a guest. Some of these oft-repeated phrases are as follows:

Have you ever had a real job?

Are you mobbed in the streets?

I'll bet that really made your socks roll up and down.

Did it come to you in a blinding flash?

Actually, they sound pretty good to me.

I do, however, think I have asked two good questions. One was aimed at Laurens van der Post, the philosopher, writer, conservationist, and godfather to Prince William. Sir Laurens was a great pal of Carl Jung's and what I wanted to know more than almost anything else was: When they were together, who got the beer? The second good one was directed to Leonard Cohen. I had the cheek to ask him, "Oh, Leonard, what does it all mean?" I am sorry to report that I didn't really get much of an answer to either question. (Carl did.) So even a swell question can get you nowhere.

Much to my horror, it is the really bone-stupid questions that very often get the response that is most intriguing. This suits me rather well, given that I am quite adept at thinking up all manner of stupid questions. Witness the following, offered to Leonard Cohen: "Gee, I've often wondered if you really existed." How's that? Pretty awful. At least I didn't say "Golly gee," but by God I was close. I could not relax at all. So seized with fear was I that if you could hear the tape, you would hear a bird-like voice, almost unrecognizable. I wish he'd give me another chance. He came to the studio on September 6, 1984. That fall Cohen was on tour promoting his latest work, *A Book of Mercy*, a collection of fifty prayers and psalms.

VG This book of yours is so personal. Reviewers have said that it was extremely bold of you to do this.

LC I'm sometimes worried about the indiscretion of the thing. First of all, there is a very good book of psalms that we already have. And there is no urgency to produce another one. But it was the only form I could use that confers a certain legitimacy. It was an attempt to speak from the deepest place, and I think they could be useful to one or two people here and there.

VG I think they are uplifting.

LC Yes? Well, one is driven to the kind of words that are unfashionable, but they saved me.

VG From what?

LC From despair. I don't think you approach this subject unless you are driven to it. Unless all other avenues of expression are blocked.

VG Were there more than fifty?

LC Yes. But some of them weren't as true. And on assembling them it became very, very clear. Some of them just didn't ring true.

VG Could they have been reworked, in the conventional sense?

LC I don't think I would rework these. I was ready to stay in this landscape as long as it was necessary. I don't think it's one you want to return to. As soon as the deliverance came, the inspiration went.

VG Where are all your papers? Have you given them to a university?

LC Well, actually the University of Toronto bailed me out of poverty about twelve years ago by buying a bunch of my papers and laundry and old napkins and things I'd kept around. That was a wonderful moment. And now I have a whole bunch of new stuff. Perhaps I can sell it to them again. But a lot of it is in Montreal or Greece and in various suitcases here and there. People are holding them for me.

VG Are you a pack rat?

LC I tend to keep everything. I tend to keep all the letters I'm going to answer any minute now.

VG It is probably a good idea for a person like you to keep everything, even the light bill. Posterity and all that. Which brings me to how you might consider yourself historically. How will the world view you in a hundred years, say?

LC Oh that's a good one. You go from very inflated views of yourself all the way down to the other side. Sometimes I feel that those papers are more important than anything else I put out. They could be looked at, not from the point of view of literature or excellence, but just from the point of view of somebody who has kept a careful record of their thoughts and experiences. I think in that way they might be useful.

VG Do you keep a diary?

LC Well, in a sense it's one big diary, set to guitar music.

VG When was the first time you did a concert tour?

LC It was with my last record, 1979 to 1980. I did about a hundred concerts in Europe and Australia and I guess I'll do it again soon.

VG Does it throw you when you have such a long time between performances?

LC I think that is why I always have a band. Otherwise I'd do the whole thing with my own guitar. But in the first two or three concerts my fingers wouldn't work and I was very nervous.

VG Were you nervous when you worked with Phil Spector (American record producer of "wall of sound" fame)?

LC I was very, very nervous, very nervous that one of his guns would go off.

VG He's got guns?

LC In the recording studio it looked like an arsenal. He was carrying a gun and three or four of his bodyguards were carrying them. There were bullets falling on the floor. And as the evening wore on and the Manischewitz was consumed, it got very loose and things got a little bit dangerous.

VG When was this?

LC Nineteen seventy-seven.

VG He has all but disappeared. Is he a total recluse?

LC He stays in his big house that he keeps at about thirty-two degrees.

VG Fahrenheit?

LC Yes. It's very cold. After you get to know Phil a while you take a fur coat to go and visit.

VG Didn't you ask him why he kept it so cold?

LC No, I don't know. He really is a magnificent eccentric. And to work with him just by himself is a real delight. We wrote some songs for an album over a space of a few months. When I visited him we'd have really good times and work till late in the morning. But when he got into the studio he moved into a different gear; he became very exhibitionist and very mad. I lost a handle on the record completely. He would take the tapes away every night under armed guard. Then he mixed the sound in secret. He wouldn't let me in.

VG Did you kick, scream, beg?

LC He disappeared. I couldn't find him. I was stuck with the option, after a lot of work over a year, either of saying no or just letting it go out as it was. I thought it was good enough to let go but it wasn't what I thought it could have been. The instinct was right to work together and I think the songs are good, but I think that my voice is lost in the mix.

VG Maybe he wanted you to disappear.

LC I think he wanted me to disappear. One time he came over about four in the morning with a bottle of Manischewitz in one hand and a .45 in the other. He put his arm around my shoulder and shoved the nozzle of the .45 into my neck and cocked it and said, "I love you, Leonard."

VG My God. Have there ever been any moments in your life when you thought you could get that mad?

LC His madness has a kind of theatrical expression. Mine tends to get very silent.

VG Have you ever contemplated ending it all?

LC No. I've been taught somehow or acquired the notion that it is not the right thing to do.

VG Are you afraid to die?

LC No. And I think Layton put it all very nicely. He has a poem addressed to Sir Mortimer on his death. Mortimer said, "I don't mind the dying, it's the preliminaries that I'm worried about."

VG Have you ever noticed that in stories about you what you are wearing is always mentioned?

LC Yeah, they review my suit. I've been wearing the same suit for years. And I usually wear a suit because I emerged before blue jeans and I was never very comfortable in them and I like a slightly formal cast to things. A double-breasted suit I have always felt good in. I put on a grey shirt this morning, but it didn't go with the rain.

Irving Layton is Canada's raging bull of letters. When I talked to this man who has published over fifty books of poetry and received world acclaim, he had just released his memoir, *Waiting for the Messiah*. Rather than go on here, I'll let Irving speak for himself.

VG You seem to have this great elixir of life. What is it?

IL Dominate reality. Imagination is one way, love another. And that is my gospel, and it has worked for me. I have never been bored and I've had wonderful experiences of affection, of love, and of creativity. I believe that creativity is what distinguishes the human animal from everything else on this planet. I am much more impressed by a little girl or boy who figures that two and two make five. That's being creative. Somebody who's not creative might say that two and two make four.

VG Or a banker.

IL Or a banker.

VG You say that you have never been bored. You do seem, however, to be constantly restless.

IL I don't know what you mean by restless, quite. Because there is a kind of nervous restlessness, which is a waste of energy. But there is a kind of creative restlessness, which is not a waste of energy, it's a gathering, an explosion. I have that kind of restlessness. I am not restless with people, for example, or when I was teaching. I was known to be a very good teacher because of my tremendous patience. I wasn't restless at all.

VG Do you have a restless spirit, then?

IL Yes, I am a restless spirit in the sense that I am dissatisfied with something which I can do, or dissatisfied with things as they are because I can always think of improvements.

VG And as a child?

IL I certainly was a very restless child. Let's say exuberant and happy. I enjoyed my activities and what I was doing, new sights, new smells, going with my mother to the marketplace, seeing her bargain for boxes of tomatoes and bags of potatoes. These were great sights. I loved the noises and the confusion. And that is what gave me my first idea of poetry. To be vital, poetry has to exhibit the same kind of chaos and the same wonderful, colourful confusion. I have one brother, Hyman, who is older, who manifested the same restlessness. We were cut from the same cloth.

VG You were the baby. Were you treated with kid gloves?

IL There was no such thing as kid gloves. My mother might have shown somewhat more affection for me only because the pressures had been somewhat lessened. Things, by the time I appeared, were not as tough as they had been after they arrived from Rumania in 1912. By 1924 they had electricity instead of lamps and candles, coal in the stove instead of wood. Things like that. Just a little more comfortable.

VG Is that what allowed you to be able to carry on in school?

IL Well, yes. My mother was able to pay the fees. But I would not have gone to high school if I hadn't been born circumcised, you see. When I was born without a foreskin, naturally it was taken as a Messianic sign. It is folklore, that is all that it is. Legend. Moses was born this way.

VG And you were treated differently because of this?

IL Yes. In part, yes. My mother treated me differently, but my father realized very early that despite the *sign*, I didn't show any other great evidence of piety or orthodoxy. All that didn't count much with my mother. They were totally unlike one another. She had a certain viscerality. My father, on the other hand, was shy, introverted, scholarly, and a very pious, orthodox Jew. Anyway, my mother still felt that maybe I was the Messiah, or maybe I was gonna be somebody special. So if I was going to be the Messiah, I'd better be able to speak English properly and know a couple of things, right?

VG The Messiah absolutely must speak English.

IL Certainly, what else? He wasn't going to break into Aramaic, that's for sure.

VG Have you ever met anyone else in this condition, or I should say, not in this condition?

IL Well, probably, but they were probably more discreet than myself.

VG I guess if you have one big item to flog, you might as well do it.

IL Absolutely, right.

When asked about his musical choice, it came as no surprise that Layton wanted a piece by Leonard Cohen, "Bird on a Wire."

VG Do you remember your first encounter with Leonard Cohen?

IL Yes, I remember it very distinctly. At that time he was the president of his fraternity at McGill, and I'd just brought out a book called *The Long Pea-Shooter* [1954]. Since he was writing poetry, and he had heard of me and the book, he invited me to give a reading for his fraternity. He didn't show me any of his poems then. I didn't even know that he wrote poems, not until later. But my first impression of him was that this man is an artist. This man is going to be somebody important.

VG How did you read that?

IL Ah. There is a great silence in his soul. And he's got two eyes. One eye has death and the other eye has sexuality. And that is the signature of any poet. I can tell someone who is a poet by simply looking at that person, because every person who is a poet has these eyes. Death and sexuality.

VG I'm peering at you now, of course, Irving. Which is which in your case?

IL They change places.

VG Both you and he have spent time in Greece, a lot of time.

IL It wouldn't be a bad idea if more Canadians could do that. The sunshine, the sensuousness, a different kind of life. The Greeks are not uptight the way Canadians are, especially Anglo-Canadians. French-speaking Canadians are not uptight in that way. But Anglo-Canadians are really very, very uptight, or so I have found them.

VG Oh come on, you always go on about that. Aren't we getting better yet?

IL If you want me to encourage you, I'll say that it has got better.

VG Please. I've got one eye French and one eye English. You tell me which is which.

IL Just give me time.

VG But don't you think that things are slightly more flamboyant in this country than, let's say, in the forties and the fifties?

IL I'd come back to the word that you used before, restlessness. Excitation rather than excitement. It isn't so much that they [Canadians] are going after anything exciting; it's as if they're being prodded by God knows what satanic force into a strange dance. They don't impress me.

VG Have you been married more times than Pope Innocent II?

IL Well, I'm glad you know your history.

VG But you have had long-term relationships with at least five women.

IL Is that many?

VG Well, it is more than some.

IL If you consider my age—I am seventy-three—do you suppose it would cast a different colour on it if I told you that my first marriage—not my first marriage, because it was hardly a marriage, but my second marriage—lasted for about eighteen years, and it produced two wonderful children. And the marriage after that lasted twenty-five years. Now, if you take that into account, along with the fact that the first marriage was not a marriage at all, it was a marriage done out of compassion and foolishness and idealism and so on—

VG And youth?

IL And youth. But those first two were very real.

VG Where do you think you got this reputation, then, of being the Tommy Mansville (a much-married American) of the north?

IL I think the press plays an important part in these things. They generally pick out one thing and they focus on that, you know. It generally saves any original or fresh thinking on the part of the journalist, because the truth of the matter is that I am a furiously mono-erotic person.

VG If we are in fact such a WASPy little nation, maybe we

need a person like you to have or at least appear to have
such a romantic or wild life, because we want to have it.

IL I believe that you've really put your finger on this. I
became Canada's exotica? Well, I accept my position.

VG You wanted one more piece of music: Bob Dylan, "The
Times They Are A-Changing."

IL A more suitable record we couldn't find.

It started out to be an interview with a painter of wildflowers,
and Joan Ward Harris is certainly that. At the time of this conversation she had just published a book, *More Than Meets the Eye: The
Life and Lore of Western Wildflowers*. The prospect of an interview
with this refined woman from Victoria, B.C. did not have me in a
state; in fact, I thought the process would be charming. What can
happen, after all, when one talks about wildflowers?

Joan Ward Harris's appearance caused a sensation, the proportions of which are still being measured. Hardly a week goes by
that someone doesn't mention "that woman who painted wildflowers." It really is a wonder that anyone remembers the part of
the conversation dealing with the flowers, because I was so taken
with the stories from her youth that I hardly let the poor woman
speak about her book. I guess I can be forgiven for wanting to
find out about her career as an exhibition ballroom dancer, high-
diver, knife-thrower's target, and professional associate of Leslie
Howard and Laurence Olivier—to say nothing of her close brush
with the white-slave trade.

VG It seems that you took chances in your youth that most
young ladies would never have thought of. Hardly any
of them would become knife-throwing targets, for
instance.

JH No, but you have to put it into the context of its time.
My father lost all his very considerable fortune in the
1929 crash. I was in Paris, on holiday with some elderly
people, when it happened. The news came to me that
my father's money had all gone. Well, far from this being
an appalling shock, which it would have been had I
been ten years older, it came as an enormous bonus.
Surprise! Here I am in Paris, the most glamorous city on
earth, especially at that time, and I'm all alone. Whoo-

pee! Free! Can't go home. There is no money. The home is broken up. They have sold everything, including my Steinway.

VG All this happened during your three-week vacation?

JH Oh, yes. In 1929 it all went overnight, and it happened to thousands of people. I was in no way unique. I didn't have to go back to the boarding school, that dreary uniform, the cold water, and the chilblains. And so I got jobs and I started teaching English and I stayed in Paris.

VG That was a respectable job.

JH Very respectable. Except that the people I was teaching for were a couple of old women. One was English, the other French, and they were exploiters almost to the point of slavery. I worked terribly hard, all over Paris, and ended up almost with TB. One cold after another, living in a garret. Ice on the bed in the morning and only cold water.

VG So much for the wild Bohemian life.

JH So much for the Bohemian life and nothing to eat but lentils, except on Friday, when you got a bit of fish. So I was taken to the doctor and then fired because I was a threat to the children. It was suggested that I go to a warmer climate. Switzerland was too expensive. The doctor pointed to a map, "Would you like to go down here?" He had pointed to the Mediterranean coast and, of course, I hadn't a clue. I was just out of school but I didn't know very much about the Mediterranean. I saw Monte Carlo and said, "That's a lovely name. Please could I go there?" The following day I was escorted to a train with my little luggage. I had forty francs in my pocket. I left Paris when it was cold and miserable and ended up in this paradise of flowers and balmy air and palm trees. Everybody was leisurely and beautifully dressed. But I had only forty francs.

VG Did you have an address?

JH Only the address of an English pastor whom I decided to avoid like the plague, if I could. They all wanted to send me home, you see. I stayed one night in a hotel, and it took the whole of my forty francs. I then spent the next four nights on the beach.

VG And not a soul took pity on you?

JH Nobody. Nobody did. Nobody would. Why would they? I was a total stranger and completely alone. Nobody to supervise me, and delighted to be that way.

VG And consumptive. How nice.

JH Oh yes, consumptive. Well, eventually I had to find the English pastor. I was getting very hungry. They took me in at the church and fed me for a week and I more or less got back on my feet. They decided that Monte Carlo was too hilly so I moved over to Menton, nine kilometres away. And that is where I got my first job. There were lots of ways of making a dishonest living. They were thrown at me daily. Anyway, I found this little bar/café/restaurant. It was very attractive and had a dance floor. I remember I said to the owner, "Look, you've got nothing here, nothing lively. I'm a good dancer. How about me?" So with the sheer brashness of extreme youth I got myself a job on commission with a small salary.

VG Ten cents a dance?

JH Ten cents a dance, yes. Sort of, but not quite. And it was from that place that I did get briefly, fortunately not tragically, involved with white-slave traffic. I don't tell this story any more because frankly it is so unbelievable today, but it is all true. My drink was doped at the café and I was put into the back of a car and taken down to Marseilles, to the docks beside a big Argentinian boat. There was a big crowd on the quayside and when I got over the effects of the dope—it couldn't have been terribly strong and you are pretty resilient at that age—I signalled to a man in the crowd.

VG Was someone holding on to you?

JH Yes. This man was there with me and he had my passport. I managed to catch the eye of this man in the crowd who was almost ludicrously English. I was able to speak with him and I said, "Look, I think this is the white-slave trade. In fact, I know. Can you possibly help?" So with great aplomb and presence of mind he took me by the arm, gave the other man a bit of a shove—he, of course, could not resist for fear of being arrested—and the Englishman simply frog-marched me out into the crowd. He gave me ten francs, which was quite a bit, and put me on the train back to Menton. He wouldn't tell me who he was and to this day I don't know.

VG Was it fairly common for young English girls to disappear?

JH Yes, personally I knew of three. Two of them were companions and one of them was a maid. They were all English and blonde and blue-eyed and attractive.

VG Taken to Argentina and made into prostitutes?

JH Oh, yes, to a bordello. And that is death. You don't come out.

VG How about the knife-throwing job?

JH Well, I took a little time from the dancing and I ran into some Russian circus people. They were great fun and to me it was glamorous. Actually, they were living in tents on the outskirts of town and I don't suppose today it would seem glamorous at all. I hooked up with these people; I loved their animals and I got interested in their whole operation. I watched their knife-throwing act many times. A girl stands in front of the board and the knife-thrower has to be good. There is no fakeroo about it. I was frightfully broke, as was everybody, and somebody, a friend from home, bet me that I wouldn't get a job, even for twenty-four hours, as a stand-in for that knife-thrower's target.

VG That is all you needed?

JH That was all I needed. The bet was for five hundred francs and that was a lot of money. Of course, the bettor was a man, so I said, "Right you are." I talked with the Russians and made it understood that I didn't want to replace the regular girl and that it was for a bet. I did a day's practice standing still and was scared out of my wits. After a few days we all set off for Corsica. It was September and the Mediterranean can be quite choppy then. Because I was just an extra, I was required to sleep in the hold with the horses, and they were sick, all six of them. It was awful. The next day we got to Corsica and we did our act in the local square. I stood still and the thrower did his act. I was surrounded by knives and there was due applause.

VG And where was the guy with the five hundred francs?

JH He was there when I got back, and it paid my rent for months.

VG Shall we move along to the high-diving act?

JH Now, that was a glamorous job. It really was. It was at a hotel on the beach at Monte Carlo, which apparently hasn't changed at all: a horseshoe-shaped hotel with a beautiful pool. And as I was a good swimmer and diver I got the job.

VG Is there anything at all that you can't do?

JH Oh, lots of things. Arithmetic. Can't balance a cheque-book to this day. Anyway, I had this job. A paying job. It was a double job, because I was diving by day and dancing at night. When you're sixteen you can do anything; a couple of hours' sleep and you're back on your feet. We had beautiful costumes with sequins and things on them. We did afternoon performances and everything was going exceedingly well, until one day we did a practice session with a new dive. It was called a swallow dive or maybe a swan—anyway, the arms were out. I was required to climb on this fellow's shoulders and grasp his ears with my feet from the fifteen-metre board, which then put me a bit higher than that. Unbeknownst to me and forgetful himself, he had put suntan oil on his shoulders. We took off and my feet slipped. We separated and I went in the water sideways and I was out for the count. They hauled me out and I never dived again from that moment on. I lost my nerve totally. To this day I wear a very hard brace around my neck, a souvenir of Monte Carlo.

VG Shall we move along to the movie business? How did you get the job with Leslie Howard?

JH I answered an ad. I read it in the paper when I was down in the south of England This is wartime now, and I read this ad for a job in London: somebody with very fast shorthand who spoke French and some Italian. I simply applied for it in the normal way. I then found myself hired as Leslie Howard's London secretary for Two Cities Films. He dictated at about 250 words a minute, non-stop. He would think nothing of dictating all day long, until one had writer's cramp.

VG What was he dictating?

JH Plays, synopses, ideas, notes—it just bubbled out of him. He'd walk up and down the room all day long, forget about his lunch and of course forget about mine, too. It was very great fun.

VG How long did you work for him?

JH About a year and a half. And then my seat was booked on his plane to go to Lisbon. Thank heaven, I was pulled off at the very last minute. You have to remember that in wartime you couldn't get on civilian planes. I was not necessary to his well-being so my seat was cancelled and it was taken by a man called Alfred Chennels, who was Leslie's accountant and the accountant for Two Cities Films. He also happened to be the spitting image of Churchill, complete with cigar, Homburg hat, and the whole bit. Right size, right face.

   The plane was shot down over Lisbon. Now, there are three theories about that currently; nobody will ever know for sure. One theory has it that with Chennels on board and I believe Churchill in Gibraltar at the time, and Lisbon being a neutral port, perhaps the Germans thought they'd got him, Churchill, that is; it seems to me a bit unlikely. Another theory is that when he came to power, Hitler sent a telegram to Leslie, congratulating him on being the perfect Aryan type. Hitler loved to watch Leslie's films, especially *The Scarlet Pimpernel*. Well Leslie, with his nice, dry, quiet sense of humour, sent him a reply telegram signed with his real name, which was Stainer. You see, his father was Jewish. It was thought that Hitler was totally enraged at having been duped. The third theory, and possibly the most likely, is that Leslie was acting as a courier. Who knows?

VG You had no idea that he was a courier?

JH Oh, no idea. I didn't know that until I read *A Man Called Intrepid*.

VG What happened to you after Leslie died?

JH Everybody ambled around that film company in shock for several days. We couldn't believe it, but it was so. I was then switched to *Henry V*, which was just beginning to be made. And of course, Larry Olivier was a totally different type. Where Leslie had been an introvert, Larry was extrovert. I worked for him on and off; in between I was a production secretary and I did some casting. One thing was awfully amusing on that partic-ular film. I was down at the studio on a cold, miserable March morning. There was a huge lot, about five or six acres, with a huge field as flat as a pancake, and in the middle of this field was a mock-up of Henry's ship. All the extras were strolling around in chainmail boots—of course, they were knitted—and they were wearing modern overcoats over their shoulders to keep them warm. They were all smoking cigarettes. A funny sight, it was.

VG What made you come to Canada in 1952?

JH A dachshund.

VG I'd come to Canada for a dachshund.

JH We were going to go to New Zealand and travel all over the place. We had a million ideas. But there was a dog quarantine all the way along the line, except in Canada. It was a hilarious trip across the Atlantic with the dog in a grip.

I'm going to leave this right here. In the actual on-air piece we did talk about her wildflower painting, her books, her animal sanctuary, and more. We talked so much that the interview had to be run over two evenings. Joan Ward Harris is bound to write her autobiography soon, so I'll leave her to finish the tale. This was nothing compared to what she'll tell you.

NINE

Their Own Way of Going

This is an odd chapter. It contains five interviews: two musicians, one primatologist, an historian, and Quentin Crisp. All of them give new meaning to the word eccentric. Quentin Crisp is the author of several books: *How To Become a Virgin* is one; others are *How To Have a Lifestyle*, which he certainly knows all about, and *The Naked Civil Servant*, for which he is famous; a television play based on it starred John Hurt.

Quentin Crisp was born in Sutton, England, in 1908 to a family that was puzzled by everything about him. It was obvious from the start that "our Denis," as he was then called, was unusual, to say the least. He was always dressing up in peculiar outfits and swanning around. He still does. He has been brutalized in the streets over the years, very often because he was dressed in such weird costumes. But nothing seems to have ever stopped him for being exactly what he is—theatrical in every way.

Although I did not meet Mr Crisp in person at the time of the interview, I had witnessed his arrival in Toronto for an appearance on "Morningside," when Don Harron was the host. He was quite a sight. I tried to keep my eyes off him; but if you are a man in your seventies with quite a bit of pancake make-up and mascara, you are courting the gawking hordes. Yet so quiet a soul is he, calm and devastatingly funny in conversation and in his one-man theatrical presentation. His initials alone provide him with a rather good monogram.

VG Would you describe to me your act? Is it a lecture of sorts?

QC Yes. It is sort of a lecture. But lecture is rather a grand word that implies that I say something about which you could take notes, and with which you could pass an exam. This is not quite so. The only thing I understand is happiness, so I explain to the audience how to be happy. And that takes about an hour. Then we have an interval. In some theatres I sign books or records and then we have another half, which is about the same length, in which members of the audience have been allowed to write some questions. I read them out and answer them. Sometimes I try to get them to speak from where they sit.

VG It must break the ice to have the first few questions written down.

QC Then they know it doesn't have to be anything profound and it needn't be witty. Just any old question.

VG There must be recurring questions?

QC The questions divide themselves into three groups. There are questions about my past, then about the television play about my past, and then there are questions in which the audience tries to apply what I've said to itself. But of course there are any number of questions, including what sign of the zodiac I was born under.

VG What do you wear?

QC I wear perfectly ordinary clothes. In some audiences I come straight off the street, through the audience and up onto the stage. Before a recent performance I had been given a very kinky suit, consisting of black velvet with green lurex threads. It was quite startling, so I decided to wear that.

VG It sounds splendid. What about hats? On the jacket of your book, *How To Become a Virgin*, you are wearing the all-time great hat.

QC I think that hat in particular is now extinct, but I do have two hats that are like it. I do wear hats, often. When I come on the stage I take the hat off, and then I put it on again when I'm coming to an end. It's a sign, you see. "Oh, he's putting on his hat, this must be the end."

VG You are quite partial to wearing recycled clothing.

QC I wear recycled clothing almost all the time, almost from head to foot.

VG What about shoes? I have read that you prefer shoes that are somewhat too small for you. Do you still do that?

QC Well, I now wear whatever shoes I can get, but as they have all been worn by other people, I have to wear what shoes are available. It is true that some of them are too small, and you just have to wait for them to get big enough. Sometimes they are too big and you have to curl up your toes in order to try and keep them on.

VG When did you decide to change your name to Quentin Crisp from Denis Pratt?

QC My name changed over the years, but I should think at least forty-five or fifty years ago. When I came out into the world, people said I couldn't go on being called by my name, so first of all my surname was changed to Crisp. And then somebody, I can't remember who or the circumstances, changed my name from Denis to Quentin. I accepted this, the way I have accepted almost everything.

VG Would members of your family still call you Denis?

QC They do, yes. They do unless they remember. That is to say, if we were in a public place, they would introduce me as Quentin, because that is what the world would expect. But their letters refer to me as Denis. They are my nieces. You see, my brothers and my sister and parents, they are all dead. I am the only one left of that generation, because I was the youngest.

VG Now, despite your flamboyance and your love of public life, it seems to me that you are quite a private person. Do you still live alone?

QC I live alone, yes. I wouldn't, however, regard myself as a private person, but I do live alone because I don't know how to recharge my batteries otherwise. I've asked other people who have been pleased to have been married for fifty years, "How did you manage to remain wise, witty, kind, and beautiful for twenty-four hours a day?"

VG And what would the answer to that be, pray?

QC They never answer. They just laugh nervously. How do you refrain for a lifetime from saying to someone, "Oh, do shut up," or "Oh, do sit down?"

VG I don't think there is a living soul that hasn't said to the other, "Shut up," "Do sit down," or "Do leave."

QC You see, how do you go on? I don't think you can do anything but join the Foreign Legion once you've said that!

VG Speaking of the Foreign Legion, did you ever have the inclination to run away, let's say to Europe, Africa, somewhere else other than England?

QC Not really. I don't believe in abroad. I believe in it more now, because I have actually seen great hunks of the world. But originally, if you lived in England, you didn't have to believe in anything else. It appears to be a self-contained unit. You didn't see any other way of life than the English life and certainly there were no foreigners. So quite a number of people of my age never really believed in abroad. If they were forced to go abroad, they would never learn the language of another country, they just spoke louder.

VG But you are at home in New York, and the American people seem to have taken to you.

QC Oh, they are marvellous. Everybody in New York seems to be your friend. And everyone talks to you.

VG I think Americans love an eccentric. Are you an eccentric?

QC To a very mild extent now, because eccentricity is sort of nearer at hand, it's more universal. In fact, in King's Road, Chelsea, London, you could say fancy dress is the national costume. I mean, there is nothing you could wear on King's Road which would cause you to be remarkable. People say to me, "You dye your hair." Well, on King's Road, people dye their hair green in the back and pink in the front, so I think that you'd have to work fairly hard to be an eccentric now.

VG I guess when you were young, and odd looking by comparison, you never would have thought that perhaps a quarter of the people in the city of London would turn out to be odd looking in the streets?

QC That's quite true. Oddity then was very noticeable. If

you looked down from a window onto any big street in London, the street would have looked grey. I don't think any woman, certainly no "nice" woman ever would wear a scarlet coat when I was young.

VG You are a slight person, but I have read that you used to consume enormous quantities of food, much to the horror of your father. What do you eat, if I may ask?

QC Oh, I eat whatever I am given. And, as New York is very expensive to live in, you have to try and find ways of not having to buy food. So the best thing is to arrive at other people's houses at about half past six in the evening and say, "Oh! I seem to have arrived at an awkward time. You are just making your evening meal," in the hope that they will say, "Oh, do stay."

VG And no doubt they do.

QC And quite often they do. So I tend to eat what I am given. But for preference, I like simple food. I am frightened by kinky food. I don't really want the goats' eyes or live fish and all those other funny things.

VG Is it true that you rarely, if ever, smile?

QC Well, I suppose I don't laugh "ha-ha" very much. But I have been informed that I smile a little more or less perpetually. I think that is because I live in a world where now everybody speaks to me. I feel it's up to me to try and look as though I welcome people speaking to me. I never, for instance, wear dark glasses, for fear people may think I'm hiding. So, actually I would have thought that I smiled a little, more or less all the time.

VG Say, how are things in the house-cleaning department? Have you learned to conquer that one?

QC I still don't clean my room, but of course I shall be about 112 before I've got my room in New York to the same state that my room in England was in when I left it.

VG When you say "room" in England, is it truly just a room?

QC I've only ever lived in one room. I lived in one room in Chelsea in a rooming house, and now I live in one room on Third Street in New York.

VG I don't suppose you could be a pack rat and have a collection of things when you live in a room.

QC I am not a collector of knick-knacks or ornaments or

what I would call nuisance things. And I certainly don't decorate my room. I would never bring pictures and hang them on the wall. Any ornaments I might have I would just put on the mantelpiece.

VG Not a picture?

QC There are no pictures. People are always saying to me, "What have you got against pictures?" And I say, "What have you got against walls?"

VG Are the walls an interesting colour, then? Or are they any colour at all?

QC It is a funny sort of peachy colour, the room. But it is a matter of absolute indifference to me what colour it is. I would *never* alter it even if it were scarlet. I would just say, "Well, that's the way it is," and leave it.

VG They say that living in a scarlet room can drive you mad.

QC Oh, well, that might be nice.

VG At one time or another you have addressed many of the "great" issues, in your books especially. One issue is homosexuality, yours and others. I wonder how you feel about being in a city [New York] where you're sitting right alongside a Tony Award-winning play, *Torch Song Trilogy*, and the huge extravagant musical, *La Cage aux Folles*. Does that cause a reaction at all?

QC It all happened very gradually, otherwise I would be amazed! When I was quite young I saw a play called *The Green Bay Tree*. Although, of course, homosexuality was never mentioned, it was quite obvious what the subject was. Everyone went in a sort of spirit of secret interest, feverish excitement, that that sort of thing should ever have got onto the stage. I did see *Torch Song* and I loved it. It worries me a little that people will say, "A great triumph for gay theatre." I see it just as a good play. If it is a triumph for anybody, it is a triumph for the playwright. If you wrote a play about florists, it wouldn't be a "great triumph" for florists, it would just be a play *about* florists. I hardly ever go to the theatre. I go to see shows if people I know are in them, or if I know the writer, or I am invited. The best shows in New York are shows about shows. This is inevitable because Americans really believe in show business. New York is a city given over to the idea of the Big Time. A wonderful expression it is, too.

VG You are definitely in the Big Time.

QC I suppose I'm in the Little Big Time. But I'm very glad to be there. Very glad indeed.

VG You must get a great number of invitations to all manner of social situations?

QC You do get invitations to all the strange clubs, which are all pitch dark and so loud you can't converse with anybody. I would love to go to them, but I can't because I really don't have the energy. I can't claim I haven't the time, but I haven't the energy to go to something which doesn't really get interesting until one in the morning. They are so dark and noisy and I can't cope, which is sad. But I am pleased to have the invitation.

VG Would you care to play a piece of music?

QC Well, yes. I have never understood music. I never know what it is for. There are certain vocalists whose voices I find appealing, like Lena Horne; there is some very appealing quality in her voice. But of course, I have at the same time to admit that if she were to sing the wrong note, I wouldn't know, because I'm so totally unmusical.

Sometimes you have to wonder what it is that scientists do, research scientists especially. I haven't talked to a great many and I guess there is an obvious reason for that. Often their fields are beyond my comprehension. Not so with Jane Goodall. It doesn't matter if we don't understand all the implications and intricate details of a primatologist's work, because we all love stories about chimpanzees. Jane Goodall is a science star, which is dandy for her, because she had been able to raise funds for continued work at her encampment at Gombe in Tanzania. Mind you, there can never be enough money, and there is a foundation that works full-time to keep her projects going, the Jane Goodall Institute in San Francisco. I spoke to her in person in May 1984.

VG Your last "National Geographic" special had an outrageous number of people viewing it.

JG It was 17.9 million. Isn't that staggering?

VG People don't seem to be able to get enough of it.

JG It is interesting, isn't it? I sometimes wonder why it is. I think it's partly because chimps are so like us and I also think that there is a strange myth around me because I was the first person to do this sort of thing.

VG At a time when it was odd for a young girl to do such a thing. Did you have this life in mind from childhood, that you would eventually rush off to the jungle?

JG Apparently, when I was two I began watching animals and when I was four I disappeared. I was staying with my mother's family in the English countryside and I was gone so long that my mother called the police. After four and a half hours I appeared and I was so happy. I can still remember the moment. I'd been hiding in a hot, stuffy, little, dark henhouse because I could not understand where there was a hole big enough in the chicken for the egg to come out. So I waited. I waited for the chicken to come in and settle down in her nest and I can still see that egg coming out.

VG Well, there's the basis of all your research—great patience.

JG Exactly.

VG The patience has been the key. You actually sat in that jungle for nearly two years before you could really get next to those chimps.

JG That's right, it did take patience. But as I loved the life and I loved the forest—and I just loved being there—it didn't require as much patience as you might think. I didn't have to rush out and get a Ph.D. and earn my living, you know.

VG But how did you keep up your enthusiasm and interest when there appeared to be no breakthroughs?

JG Well, there were, because all the time I was sitting there I could see those chimps from a distance and little pieces of the puzzle began to fit together. But I've always liked being alone. It doesn't mean I'm antisocial; I'm not. I love being with people, too.

VG How alone were you?

JG All day, from the time I got up to the time I got back to the camp in the evening, when the authorities said I had to be with somebody. But even then I would climb

up to some point and say, "You wait here, and I'll go
over there."

VG   You are a rare breed, aren't you? Not too many do this
kind of thing.

JG   There are far more now, let me tell you. I get so many
letters from children and young people saying, "What
do I do to get to do what you do?" This is a big
responsibility, because these days it's getting very difficult to do what I did. The economic situation has
changed and the political situation, too. More and more
field stations are being closed down.

VG   You said that the Tanzanian officials didn't want you to
be alone out there. Were they scratching their heads
about you?

JG   They surely thought it was peculiar. Louis Leakey, who
got the money for me to start off, was accused of being
amoral. Sending a young girl off into the bush like that,
it just wasn't done in those days.

VG   How did you get to Leakey in the first place? You didn't
just march up to him, a legendary anthropologist and
all.

JG   It wasn't quite that easy. I think when I was about
eighteen my desire to be with animals really crystal-
lized and I wanted to go to Africa. Eventually I began to
save enough money; in fact, I worked as a waitress to
save up my fare. I had to get a return fare, you see.
Finally I got to Africa. I had a temporary job, so I wasn't
dependent on anyone. And I had heard about Dr
Leakey. People told me, "If you are interested in animals, you should go to see him." So I did.

VG   Was he thrilled to meet you or did he think you a bit
odd?

JG   Oh, no. Almost immediately he offered me a job as his
assistant. While I was working with him at the Olduvai
Gorge where Zinjanthropus [the ancient human skele-
ton] was found, he started to talk to me about this little
group of chimps on a wild lake shore. I thought he was
teasing, but one day he said, "Why do you think I'm
talking to you about this? That is what I want you to do,
to study those chimps there." It really was fantastic. But
then he had to wait a whole year before he could find

any money for me to go. Because it was so unique, nobody wanted to give any money, and I had no qualifications. At least no academic qualifications.

VG Did he want you to have or get a degree?

JG No, he didn't want me to. He wanted me to have an unbiased mind. He wanted me to go because I wanted to find out.

VG Do you remember the arrival at your camp in the bush?

JG I certainly remember the moment I arrived and looked up at that rugged country, thinking, "It is going to be difficult, but how exciting. And I'm jolly well going to do it."

VG Who was with you?

JG My mother. This was the amazing thing. She is fantastic and an adventuress and she wanted to come. She lives in England, but when I was working with Dr Leakey in Nairobi she came for a short visit. When it came time for me to go in, and I told you I had to be with somebody, I chose her. She stayed for three months and she set up this clinic with the local fisherman, which put me in such a good position with them.

VG Is she a doctor or nurse?

JG No, neither, but we have a medical family and my uncle was a surgeon. He gave us masses of medicine and instructions as to how to use it. Do you know it is nearly a quarter of a century ago?

VG And I suppose some of the chimps that you encountered originally are still alive?

JG Oh, sure they are, they live till they are fifty. And I am still working and now I have ten Tanzanian field assistants and they are there all the time collecting data, even as I talk to you.

VG Throughout your studies there, it seems to me that the only encroachment you made upon them was the institution of the banana station. Apart from that, you introduced nothing into the chimps' lives that would be foreign to them.

JG That's right. But we did it very badly at one time, right at the beginning before I had any idea that this research could carry on in the way it has been. I wanted to find out as much as I could. I kept thinking, "Golly, this is the end, I have to go back and write my thesis and write my degree." So we gave bananas every day and this had the most dramatic effect on the social structure, on the levels of aggression. When I realized that I could continue the study and have students, then we had to change the feeding altogether.

VG From bananas to what?

JG We still feed bananas, but, say, six every ten days, whereas a chimp can eat fifty at one sitting. So six is a very tiny amount. We only give bananas if a chimp comes by himself or in a small group.

VG So as to not create a party atmosphere?

JG Just enough so that if they're in the neighbourhood, they'll drop by to see if there's anything going.

VG At the local pub?

JG That's right.

VG Are they gluttonous? Will they eat till they burst?

JG They'll eat till they really can't eat any more. They will stuff themselves. They do enjoy their food, and they make these lovely oo-oo-ah chimp noises. They're happy when they get food.

VG It must be a temptation to try and communicate, but you don't?

JG Oh, I don't. It is very important not to try and interact. One could. You could be right in there, part of the group. But we specifically don't.

VG What is your reaction to people who do the reverse to what you do—make attempts to communicate through sign language or whatever?

JG It certainly doesn't upset me. It's not so much another world as it is the other side of the coin. It is an attempt to find out about the chimp intellect in a way that I can't do in the wild. It could make for a very good collaborative attempt to understand this very complex creature. In fact, I was just visiting the original chimp who learned sign language. That chimp has now adopted a baby and she's teaching the baby sign language, in the lab.

VG Isn't that a remarkable thing, that what she learned, she is now teaching?

JG In the wild, although a young one learns from the

mother by observing and imitating and practising, we now find that if a chimp is taught by humans, then she is capable of teaching. That is fascinating.

VG Has any one of them ever become aggressive with you?

JG Yes. The worst are the adolescent males, because they are out to intimidate the females of the community. And they can "sex" humans into males and females, too. These adolescent males will treat me rather as they treat the females of the community. In other words, I must be intimidated. I don't think they'd ever really hurt one, but they jump up and they pound on you and hit you, and it does hurt. But once they've intimidated all the females, they work their way through the male hierarchy. Then they finally sort of grow up, as it were. They don't bother the females any more, and they don't bother with me.

VG In your opinion, do you think that they think about you in any way?

JG I don't think I could ever answer that. They basically pay very little attention to us, which is nice. It is the young ones who watch more carefully, though. The most intelligent female there today once watched me drinking a cup of coffee, and then I set it down. I didn't even know what she was doing, but she came over and picked up that cup and tried to drink it as we would. But of course it was hot, and she didn't put her lip touching the cup, but she poured it just as we would. That is pretty incredible for a wild animal. And that is the only example I have ever seen of a chimp trying to imitate something we've done. They imitate each other, but not us, fortunately. Otherwise we would really have trouble.

VG What are your living circumstances in Gombe?

JG Well, in 1975 I had a large research station with many foreign students, that is, non-Tanzanian students, mostly Americans. I lived there all the year round with my son, except when I was teaching over here. Then four of those students were kidnapped by a rebel group from Zaire. And although they were safely returned to their families in the end, unharmed, this area was then considered a sensitive one and it was deemed not wise to have foreign students there any more. So today I actually live in Dar es Salaam, the capital of Tanzania, and I visit Gombe for about three weeks every two months.

VG Would you say you are living a city life?

JG I wouldn't exactly call it that. I am outside the city, and the house is on the beach. I seldom see people. It is a beautiful place for working, and I have so much analysis to do, so much writing.

VG And on occasion the "National Geographic" specials. It must be wonderful to have all those photos and the film footage of you romping around with these creatures.

JG Yes, it is a bit like watching your family grow up, isn't it?

VG Do the chimps rejoice in any way when you visit?

JG No, thank goodness. But sometimes you feel a bit hurt. After all, I am so pleased to see them. Fifi, let's say, doesn't even look at me. But that is what I have been striving for, that is what I wanted, and that's what I've got.

VG And what of your son? He goes to school in England. Does he have a similar passion to yours?

JG No, he dislikes chimps intensely. And it is not really surprising, because chimps are hunters, and most of their prey is other primates, and this does include human infants. So when he was very tiny we had a cage made so that he'd be really safe. I think he probably resents the time that I've spent with the chimps, even though until he was nine he had one-half of every single day of my life, and when he was smaller he had the whole day virtually. But anyway, it turns out that very quietly, and unknown to anyone, he's been observing the behaviour of the boys at his school. And he has come up with some shrewd insights. So, to answer your question: sort of. I think he may share a passion, but it will be human psychology.

VG What are his observations?

JG They are to do with why boys are aggressive to each other, and why some of them can turn the aggression off more easily than others, and why some are picked on and others are not. I've only just learned about this

in the last few weeks and I think they are super insights. I would love it if he went into human psychology. If you are interested in the chimp because it's the
most complex of creatures, then there is only one creature that is more fascinating, and that is us.

In the early stages of preparing this book, it was not my intention
to include passages from the Frank Zappa interview, although I
did then and still think Mr Zappa is one of the most curious and
intriguing of American performers. I guess he could be classed as
a pop musician and singer, but he is considerably more than that.
He is his own kind of genius. He has won the guitar category in
the *Downbeat* magazine poll on a couple of occasions and his
orchestral works have been recorded by the Royal Philharmonic
and the London Symphony Orchestra. Curiously there was not a
tremendous reaction to this interview. We received only a few
letters from dyed-in-the-wool fans who thought I should have
pursued this or that, but absolutely no one was outraged. Maybe
Frank is less controversial nowadays. He's probably just resting.

I changed my mind about including this piece when I met a
woman of sixty or so who said that she had found the Frank
Zappa interview from two years past terribly interesting. I was
fairly shocked, given that she bore hardly any resemblance to
what one would imagine to be a Zappa devotee. This unlikely
enthusiast pointed out that her sons, in their youth, had looked
quite a lot like Zappa for a time. They had also played his records
incessantly. She had always wondered at their fascination.

> **VG** Interesting name, Zappa. What about this great and
> ancient musical ancestor of yours, a contemporary of
> Mozart, Francesco Zappa?
> **FZ** He is ancient but not great, because nobody ever heard
> his music before. In fact, the recording session I'm
> working on today is the finishing-off of an album of
> Francesco Zappa music, which is going to be distrib-
> uted in the States.
> **VG** How did you come upon this ancestor?
> **FZ** My wife found him. I had never seen Groves [*the* musi-
> cal dictionary and reference book]. She was at the
> library and she decided to find out whether or not I was

in the book. I wasn't, but Francesco was. Some months later I was in Europe doing a recording session with Pierre Boulez, the French composer and conductor. Afterwards in London, I was talking with some executives of the record company and I happened to mention Francesco. They all laughed, and one of them got up and brought in the Groves. Actually, I hadn't seen it myself, so we looked together. He was amazed. He asked his secretary to look up some of the abbreviations in the book to find out where the music would have been stored. So starting with that and a computer programmer, we got in touch with the Berkeley Library and Library of Congress and a couple of libraries in Europe, one in The Hague and another in London. And we got as many scores as we could.

VG How many would that be?

FZ I think there were probably about six string trios, one piano piece and so on. And they are good. They are real fun to listen to because they are real happy. They don't sound anything like the music I write. They are very Italian sounding and there's nothing disturbing about them. As with most music from that period, you already know how it is going to resolve in the end.

VG You mean it's balanced and symmetrical?

FZ It's freeze-dried. But there are people who like to know that the music starts here and goes to there and to know that it is coming home again at the end.

VG It says here about Francesco, in the article in Groves: His style tends towards seriousness of manner, in which the gallant elements are tempered by a classical dignity and sometimes by harmonic richness of a pre-romantic sort.

FZ Let me translate. I really don't know what that guy is talking about. But the harmonic richness of the pre-romantic sort is interesting because there are harmonic devices in his music which are not necessarily customary for the music of the period in which he was composing. In other words, let's say the boy was a little ahead of his time, in terms of some of the chords he was using. It could also be the reason why he wasn't so popular. Because, as with most music of the period, the people who wrote had to write it for the amusement of kings, queens, and in this case the Duke of York. Also, one of the pieces we have, his *Opus I*, is dedicated to a count who was the *plenipotenziario* of Sicily at the time. So all these guys had to go around kissing the butts of royalty in order to earn a living. And if the guy that you wrote it for didn't like your chord progressions, you were in big trouble.

VG Out!

FZ In some cases you were dead. Other places, you merely starved to death. If the church got a hold of you, you might not have any fingernails by the end of the day.

VG Well, things have picked up.

FZ No, they haven't, because then, with classical music, the guy who had the unfortunate job of writing this stuff for the royalty, who determined the taste of the rest of the people in the community, knew what the employer liked and that was that. So the composer had this problem of making them happy, otherwise he was out of business or dead or tortured. And today it is the same way with rock-and-roll musicians or people who do popular music. You can't write what you like because it won't get played on the air or you won't get a record contract. It's the same thing, except that the characters have changed. Their motives are just as mysterious and their taste is just as bad, so nothing has really evolved.

VG Will you tell me about your work habits?

FZ Well, I like to work when I'm awake.

VG That helps.

FZ I do try to work when I'm sleeping, too. I get a lot of things done while I'm asleep because when I get up I always know what I'm supposed to do. I don't think that it really stops because I'm on my back. It's not going to change because of cycles around the clock Every two or three weeks, my waking hours change from day to night. It just seems to work that way. Every day I work an hour later and it just keeps moving around the clock.

VG You know, you really ought to write essays. Do you ever?

FZ I wrote one. I sent it to *Time* or *Newsweek*, whichever one has the little column, "My Turn," where the average Joe Blow on the street can write something that will go in a national magazine. It has to be a thousand words. So I wrote one and they refused to run it because they said it was too idiosyncratic. It became the liner notes for the album I released in 1980, "You Are What You Is."

VG You have some very odd rules for members of your band. No touch football, for instance.

FZ The reason why that is forbidden in the band is because of what happened on a tour in 1974. We had a bass player named Tom Fowler. That was when we had this band with George Duke *et al*. We were playing very complicated arrangements and the bass parts were not something that could be picked up by somebody who walked in off the street. We had ten more shows left to do on this tour and they were all sold out. Tom got involved in a game of touch football with the crew and he broke his hand. Well, Tom spent the rest of the tour standing on stage with one of those glow-in-the-dark sticks. He had twelve pieces of paper with the names of the twelve chromatic pitches of the scale written on them, and we had another player playing Tom's parts. Tom stood there pointing to the name of the note. He had to do that for ten shows.

VG The end of the sporting activities?

FZ And I don't like them to ski. I don't care what they do with girls or whatever they do that is recreational, as long as there is no way in which their bodies are going to be harmed. The livelihood of everybody in the band is dependent on other members being healthy, on time, and interested in what they are doing. They have to be serious about it because not only will they let down the other guys in the band, but you're also talking about a few hundred thousand people on the tour who want to see the show done right. Right?

VG Right.

FZ And you can get very angry if you've paid big money to see a show and some guy is standing there on stage with a green thing, pointing to pieces of paper.

The second time I saw the world-famous violinist Sir Yehudi Menuhin was at the 1986 Commonwealth Games in Edinburgh. He was a featured part of the opening ceremonies. The organizing committee had the clever idea of providing Menuhin with a kilt made to order. It was mostly purple—the McMenuhin tartan, I suppose. He played some Scottish airs and dances with a mob of local fiddlers, and they all appeared to have a grand old time. That's the thing about Menuhin—he always does have a grand old time. He just loves to play that fiddle. He admits he can't or doesn't improvise like his pal Stéphane Grappelli, but their record together proves that he has his own way of wailing.

My first encounter with Sir Yehudi was not in performance, but in his hotel room. He was making a guest appearance with the Vancouver Symphony, hence the interview. He had a little suite with a parlour and glass doors that led to the sleeping department. The doors were open. On the bed, propped up on the pillow, was his violin. When were all set to roll the tape, the publicist from the symphony asked if she might use the phone. He suggested she use the one in the bedroom, for privacy, but cautioned, "Please try not to sit on the violin." I can assure you that it had never crossed her mind to go anywhere near that priceless thing. He said, "That was a joke." The desk in his suite was covered with bottles of vitamins. Menuhin is a health nut. Whatever it is he does, it is working.

Ever since his debut at age seven he has not stopped playing. Most child prodigies don't do so well. They either exhibit hornet-like behaviour or fade away. Neither of these things has happened to Yehudi Menuhin. Perhaps it is because he married a sane person when they were both very young. His wife has written an account of their life entitled *Fiddler's Moll*, suggesting a healthy sense of humour. They also have three children, always a great leveller. Whatever the reason for his balanced outlook, it is apparent that he has not only exceptional talent but also a wonderful intellect.

> **VG** Would you say that you are wildly disciplined?
>
> **YM** No, I am not wildly disciplined. I do everything that I love doing, which happens to be considered, in other people's minds very often, a disciplined way of life. I mean, if I don't eat sugar it's not because I'm disciplined, it's because I feel that I'll be healthier and possi-

bly live longer and have fewer aches and pains, touch wood. On the other hand, if you offer me, once a year, some particularly exquisite chocolate, then I will take it. So you see my discipline is only skin deep. Oscar Wilde said, "I can resist everything except temptation." That's me.

VG Your parents were extraordinary people.

YM They were totally different to the conventional way of parental behaviour, that is true. For one thing, when they saw that their children were not particularly suited to school and they didn't like it, they accepted it.

VG As far as regular school went, you lasted only one day.

YM You are quite right. I think there must have been a predisposition to keeping the children at home to educate them, but nonetheless they did the right conventional thing by sending us to school. When they found that the children somehow didn't "take," that was that. My sisters lasted more than one day. They were there several days—five, I think. The superintendent of the school, a very good woman, wrote to my mother or spoke with her and said that she thought that my sister Hepzibah was not quite normal; in fact, subnormal. So I think that was reason enough to take that child out of school, especially when they knew perfectly well that she was, how shall I say—

VG Extraordinary?

YM Yes, exactly. So it was very fortunate that my parents could educate us, my sisters and me, at home. Also, I had to have a different set-up once I started playing music. The dangers were of exploitation from wealthy people who would invite me to play or journalistic exploitation, with all due respect.

VG But you did not experience a child's life really, or have the opportunity to play with other children.

YM That's true. But my parents did their best. There were a few friends. There was Max, another young boy who was from one of my father's schools [he was the head of Hebrew schools in San Francisco] and there were a few who came to the house to play. I was always awkward at playing games, in the sense that my mind was a very funny one, a little bit formal. I seemed to lack the ability to recognize beginnings and ends and the continuity of a game. That was an aspect of all my life. When we would take a train to go down to the peninsula or up beyond Sausalito, or if we drove, I was always interested in where the town stopped and where the country began. I couldn't figure it out. Sometimes one went into the other. So when it came to games I was bothered with the idea of when the game started or ended and how it all differed from "the other," being the more regular or serious pursuits. I do remember distinctly the awkwardness with other children.

VG What about your teenage years? Did you turn hateful for a time, argumentative and irritable?

YM Oh yes, very much so. And now that we are parents, my wife and I, we recognize that in our own children. Fortunately, our children are coming out of that period.

VG How did your rebellion manifest itself? You were already in a curious situation.

YM The time factor was different in my case. Normally children get over that when they are in their teens, and by the time they are of marriageable age, shall we say, they are beginning to emerge. Well, I didn't really emerge until I was married, and it took a little while. It's not really that I had anything but admiration and love for my parents, but I was probably too courteous and too grateful within the family to assert myself until I had a home of my own.

VG You come from a family of odd names, and even your children have unusual handles. There are not too many Menuhins, either, are there? Do you look in telephone books when you go to a new city to see if there are any Menuhins?

YM No, I don't look for Menuhins, but once in a while I marvel, especially in New York City, at the names beginning with Z. They of course are largely Polish names.

VG When you and your sister played together, something I never saw, it is said that you and she never looked at each other.

YM No. Our contact was mainly, as it is with any musical partners, or when I am conducting, through the ears. It was wonderful playing with Hepzibah. She was very close to me in all matters both emotional and intellectual. I now have the same satisfaction playing with Jeremy, my son.

VG Do you think that your sister was overshadowed by you? That her brilliance at the piano was not observed as readily as was yours?

YM I really don't know. I know that she deserved to do more with her talent. The point with her was that music was not a career, shall we say. Music she loved, but as a career, she did not pursue it. The time when she played the most was when she was first married in Australia during the war, when no one was able to travel and no artists came to Australia, and she was *the* Australian pianist. I went there once during the war.

VG Will you tell me the story of the day you met Elgar?

YM Yes, sure. I was very impressed to meet a living composer. I'd met my first living composer in San Francisco, Ernest Bloch, who was very kindly. I was only seven or eight years old. He came by with a piece he had just written and dedicated it to me. I was inordinately proud to receive a work dedicated to me by a very great composer. And then I had met, in Paris, a few composers, Ravel for instance. But Elgar was the first great contemporary composer who had written a violin concerto, which I had prepared and was about to record. It was the record company that suggested that we meet. And Elgar agreed; curiously enough I've always been trusted. People didn't necessarily know me, but all the good things and opportunities have come to me in this most welcome way. Of course, I had been to England, so I was already liked and known there. But I didn't know that Elgar himself had ever heard of me. I prepared the piece and went to England with my father. We arrived at the Grosvenor Hotel and there was a piano in the room. The pianist was waiting to accompany me, to accompany the work. Elgar came and I, of course, was terribly impressed with this gentleman. Very tall, dignified, good-humoured, gentle, warm-hearted. And at the same time I was aware of this great responsibility. I had worked on the concerto alone. I had played it for Enesco, my teacher. I had never played the whole thing, I'd just played little bits.

VG And what did Elgar have to say?

YM I had hoped that he'd give me all kinds of hints and suggestions. But instead, I hadn't even arrived at the second subject [portion of the work] when he said, "It's going to be lovely, and I have no worries at all. It's a beautiful day and so I'm off to the races."

VG Were you shocked?

YM I was a little. Because I'd never encountered a musician who was so casual. I guess he thought that he'd written the work, he was going to conduct it, he liked the violinist, and he felt I was going to do it well. He didn't see why he shouldn't go to the races on that lovely day. Why stay indoors? There was no point. I took it seriously, so why should he? He took it seriously when he composed it. It was a kind of economy of the use of time and effort and emotion; it was this English way of letting things happen.

VG Do you wish you had gone to the races with Elgar?

YM Ah, yes. I'm sorry I didn't. I'd love to. I should have, if I had had any kind of initiative; if I hadn't been so worried about the piece and I wanted probably to practise; if I hadn't felt obligated to remain. If I'd suggested it, I know my father would have come along and he would have been delighted.

VG How old were you then?

YM Oh look, if only you'd been there! I had not thought of it until you suggested it now. It was a terrible oversight. Now I recognize it.

VG Oh dear!

YM Oh terrible!

VG You are not going to worry about this are you, not all day?

YM I am sorry. I should have done that, shouldn't I?

VG Well, do you think that there have been times when you have passed up things because of your extreme dedication to your work? Obviously you have had to pass on plenty, but were there times when you could have been more full of abandon?

YM Yes. I suppose you're right, I suppose you're right. But you know, you can't have everything in life, can you? And I have had great abandon, moments of abandon. I can hardly say that I didn't reap the benefit of whatever I may have foregone, over time.

VG Do you still stand on your head?

YM Yes, I stood on my head this morning. I don't do it for more than a minute or so, but when I had my yoga teacher I could do it for ten minutes. Some people do it longer but I don't want to exaggerate these things. You lie down afterwards for a few minutes and it's really very refreshing. I think that anybody who stands a great deal—saleswomen, nurses, police officers—if they don't do this headstand they should at least be given these little contraptions where you can lie back and then hang from your feet.

VG Those things look like tools from the Spanish Inquisition.

YM No. They are so good, and require no effort at all. It really would help everybody.

You may not believe this, but certain rivalries have been known to develop between shows on CBC Radio. If, for example, you are booked to make an appearance on my programme with your latest best-seller, the chances of you then getting an airing on another network show, let's say out of Toronto, become very slim indeed. Most people doing book tours or touting a stage show or film start their promotion in Toronto, for good reason. It leaves us poor suckers in Vancouver with quite a few second-hand roses. Not that we mind; we're accustomed to interviewing exhausted tourees.

What this situation causes, however, is an enthusiasm on the part of researchers and producers on the west coast that borders on the obsessive. All manner of obscure publications are subscribed to, in hopes that an unheard-of guest can be found. Local newspapers and magazines printed in languages unknown to most of us often reveal the best stuff.

For ten years I have worked on and off with Doug Jones. He is without doubt the master at finding unusual guests. Jones specializes in collectors of anything, animal enthusiasts, train nuts, the obscure. Jones also has a fondness for historians, which I share. In June 1985 the Icelandic National League brought writer, broadcaster, and Icelandic historian Magnus Magnusson to Vancouver to lecture on—what else—Iceland. Doug Jones snapped him up for us.

VG You are in this country at the invitation of the Icelandic National League to talk about what in particular?

MM To celebrate the independence of Iceland and its cultural independence as well. And to talk about the Iceland sagas, which I am addicted to. But I have been discovering the Icelandic settlement here 110 years ago, too.

VG At Gimli, Manitoba?

MM Gimli, New Iceland. And I find extraordinary parallels between that settlement and the original settlement of Iceland itself eleven hundred years ago by the Norsemen from Norway. They had the same kind of challenge to overcome. The same appalling obstacles. How they survived, I'll never know.

VG In both cases—the Norsemen going to settle Iceland and the Icelanders coming to Canada—I can't figure why they might not find the south more appealing. Is it that they understood the cold?

MM Yes. But also the south was kind of crowded. The Norsemen went to Iceland because it was so empty, totally empty at the time. So they were able to found a community which didn't exist anywhere in the world. They founded a republic. In the Middle Ages, the idea of kingship was absolutely paramount, and the thought of people saying, "Right, we don't like kings, and we're going to elect our own parliament," was a little out of step. So the first parliament in Europe was founded in Iceland.

VG Gee, I thought it was the Isle of Man.

MM Ah, the Isle of Man. Well, they had a millennium or something in 1979. It was a date plucked out of the empty air, because they felt like having a millennium. Well, good luck to them, say I.

VG So you're telling me the whole thing started in Iceland with these forward-thinking Norse types.

MM Yes. And they did precisely the same thing when the Icelanders came here a thousand years later. Because for the first dozen years or so, in which they were at Gimli in New Iceland, they were in fact a republic, even though they wanted to be totally Canadian. They were not part of Manitoba then, it was much farther south.

VG It was just a little square—the postage-stamp province.

MM That's right. They founded their own kind of commonwealth, based on the original Viking laws of the Icelandic Commonwealth. That is, until Canada was ready to subsume them into the greater entity.

VG Was all of this done painlessly?

MM Yes, it was. When they came they were rather curious creatures. Nobody had heard of Iceland, any more than they had when I came through Toronto the other day, through immigration. "Gee, Iceland, what a funny passport!" I'll tell you that the best friends the Icelanders had on arrival were the Native Indians. The Icelanders had never encountered such winters. For the first two or three years the situation was quite appalling. It was the Indians who saved them. It was the Indian population who taught them how to fish under the ice, for instance. Believe me, the winter temperatures in Manitoba were far worse than anything in Iceland.

VG Oh, come on, Iceland must be fairly grim in the winter? Mind you, I haven't been there.

MM Iceland is not nearly as cold as the name sounds. The interior of the island is immensely volcanic and sterile, really just a mountain wilderness. But around the outsides it has marvellously fertile valleys. The winter temperatures—okay, you get snow a little bit in the south, and in the north quite a lot of snow—are nothing like the forty or fifty below that you get here.

VG Well, if it's so all-fired glorious there, why did they leave?

MM Because it is a lot more glorious now, in the same way Canada is a lot more glorious than it was a hundred years ago. You see, in the 1870s Iceland had a terrible period that had lasted for four or five centuries of really bad weather. The Little Ice Age gripped Europe, and it made Iceland almost uninhabitable. It started to break in the late nineteenth century, but it came too late for some of them. The ones that lived in the northeast were on the edge of starvation. And besides, Icelanders have always wanted to see what's on the far side of the horizon. That's why Icelanders discovered Canada in the first place, round about the year 1,000. Iceland via Greenland. But in the 1870s, things were just getting to be too much in Iceland. Everybody wants to do better for themselves and their families and so they took the opportunity to pull up stakes and go west once again, as their forefathers had done. But of course they, like other immigrants to Canada, had no idea of what they were coming to. Lord Dufferin, who was Governor General, was a great Iceland lover; he had been to Iceland. In 1877 he came to Gimli. When he addressed the assembled, he made a marvellous speech in which he said, "You have some disadvantages coming here, because the three paramount things that settlers require in Canada are: to be able to fell trees, to be able to construct highways, and to be able to plough fields. Unfortunately, you people come from a country where there are no trees, where there isn't a single road, and where you've never seen a ploughed field." So, as you can see, they really had to start from scratch. It gets worse. In the first two years they had a smallpox epidemic and one-third of the settlement caught it. They were quarantined for about eight months and they practically died of starvation, never mind the pox. And yet they overcame it.

VG What is it about this Iceland wanderlust? They've had it since time began.

MM There is a word, *utprá*, that means "a longing to get out." It's not because we want to get away, it's because we feel that we need to have *been* away. The word for "stupid" in Icelandic is *heimskur*, "one who remains at home." So it is as if you've not been stretched, your mind hasn't really had a chance to grow to maturity, unless you've seen what is on the other side of the horizon. And this has always been part of the Viking make-up. To find a place in the sun for yourself, elsewhere. Taking up your roots and then putting them down in the new country. The Vikings were enormous assimilators.

VG Not just rapers and pillagers?

MM No. I think they might have done a bit of that on the side, and occasionally they found stuff that had fallen off the back of somebody else's long ship. But for the most part, they were rather more constructive than the popular image of horned helmets and rapists. Mind you, I don't want to overplay this revisionism, because I don't want to ruin the tourist trade in Scandinavia. What I find even more interesting is that Britain, where I live, is particularly interested in looking towards the Viking age as a sort of model for the future. You see, in the nineteenth century when archaeology began, the British were interested in two basic areas. One was the Roman period, because they saw themselves as the inheritors of the Roman Empire, and the other was their Biblical heritage, because they were Victorian patriarchs. Well, the empire is gone and the wretched feminists have ruined the patriarchs—

VG Oh, do hold on to your hat there now, laddie!

MM All that is left now is to look for the entrepreneurs. And who were they? The Vikings. They extended trade in a way that hadn't been known in the world till then. They were *the* traders.

VG Did they do as well as the Phoenicians?

MM They weren't so much the middle men as the Phoenicians were. But the Phoenicians were marvellous seamen. And this is what the Vikings had, above all: Everything came right for them at the right moment. They had been evolving a kind of ship, which, once they mastered how to put a mast into it, was in fact the perfect ship of its time. It was the fastest thing on the seas, and it was also the lightest. They could carry the ships overland, which gave them the enormous element of surprise. The draught was so shallow that they could go up rivers that no ships had been up before. And they could go at about twelve knots. Now, the effect was, when they worked as an army, the same as having paratroopers dropping behind lines. They'd go up the Seine past Paris, and then attack it from behind.

And there was a lot of iron being found in Scandinavia. So if you had a better kind of iron it meant that you had better weapons. But you also had better ploughshares, so you could develop farmland better. It follows that there was less infant mortality in the place. So suddenly, in Norway and Sweden and Denmark, you had quiverfuls of sons growing up. Big, strong, strapping boys who didn't die in childhood, who all wanted a place in the sun, because only the oldest son inherited. They had the ships, they had the nerve, they had the courage, and they had the wanderlust. It all came together and the Viking Age sprang to life.

VG Those ships were long, lean, and predatory, with great speed.

MM Replicas have been made and when they've been tried out, they've had a snake-like effect. They could bend, like sinuous things. They went *with* the sea, they didn't fight it. The poets called them "the bisons of the sea," all sorts of lovely images.

VG What of the people? Were they long and lean or were they short and stub-like?

MM I think they probably were a bit taller than the average for Europe at the time, which is possibly not as tall as the average person today. Then you've got somebody really tall, like Harald Hardrade, the king of Norway, who invaded England in 1066. Do you know that famous reply that was made when he met the king of England? He asked how much land the king of England would give him. And the king of England, another Harold, replied, "Seven feet of land, or as much more as he is taller than other men." So clearly Harald was a big man, presumably six feet six inches.

VG Seven feet, just enough for a coffin. In 1066 you say. Well, was England being invaded at every corner?

MM Yes, ma'am. It was a very crucial year in history for western Europe, because England was invaded from two directions; by the Norwegians in September and then a few days later, eighteen actually, by the Normans, who were in fact Norsemen as well. Normandy was Norse-mandy. It was a country that had been given to the Vikings by the king of France. They invaded from the south. Harold, king of England, had just fought off the Norwegians; he had beaten them in Yorkshire, and then suddenly he hears that the Normans have invaded the south. He then does a forced march down south with the remains of his mauled army. And in that weakened condition they were no match for the Normans. *Now* if the Norwegians had won—

VG Ah, things would be different!

MM Oh, I love these historical what-if's! What if the Norwegian king had won at Stamford? I think he would have made mincemeat of the Normans. I really do.

VG I take it that the Norwegians were less than organized?

MM Well, they certainly were not organized on the day they were beaten. They were sunbathing. It was such a lovely day and they had no idea that the English army was advancing.

VG The only nice day since they got there, probably.

MM It's *always* sunny in the north of England. It so happened that they had no idea that the English were so near. It says in the accounts that they had laid their weapons aside and they were sunning themselves and suddenly in the distance they saw what appeared to be a moving ice field. It was the sun glinting on untold numbers of spears and swords and shields. They rushed to arms, but they didn't manage to hold the one bridge that would have kept them safe. One chap did a marvellous, heroic thing, single-handedly holding off the bridge until a sneaky Englishman went under the bridge and speared him, up through the floorboards.

VG Not that it matters, but my friend has an office here in Vancouver, and the address is 1066 West Hastings. What do you think of that?

MM I think it is very nice indeed. I just love these attempts at making the past stay alive. Not just bringing it back to life, but making sure it stays alive. I see history all around me. For instance, one of my ancestors married the king of Norway. And as you know, the British throne is descended from the Norwegian throne. So every time I go past Buckingham Palace, I raise my cap. I say to myself, "How nice that my cousins are doing so well abroad." And listen to this: If the Vikings had only stayed in North America, because I am also descended from the first white child born in North America, who was the son of the first settler, one of my relatives would have at least been in the White House, and I could have gone to visit there as well.

VG I am glad to see that you and your family have made their mark, sir. Say, you are a sir, aren't you? You have an Icelandic knighthood, the Order of the Falcon [Fálkaorda]. Should I address you appropriately?

MM They don't have titles, actually. I do prefer *lord* but *sir* will do.

TEN

Sometimes You Just Can't Lose

I've won three things in my life—the pink radio and two ACTRA awards. The first Nellie came as the result of an interview with Jack Webster. I think it is fair to say that he is the world's greatest living radio personality. He has deserted radio for T.V., but he can be forgiven for that. He announced his retirement in the spring of 1987, but I'll believe it when I see it. The second award was for an interview with Margaret Atwood, a woman whose work is praised by all who read her. She was a finalist for the 1986 Booker Prize, which was won by Kingsley Amis. But for Atwood it is just a matter of time.

I've always been bowled over by the poetry, fiction, and essays of Margaret Atwood, but I fought interviewing her for many years. I guess I was just plain intimidated, her intuition and powers of observation being so keen. Finally the day of reckoning arrived, just after the publication of *The Handmaid's Tale* in 1985. I could resist no longer. Until the moment she arrived at the studio we had never met; I'd only seen her from afar. I was so nervous when she came through the door that I immediately blurted out, "My God, you're so short!" A gracious remark, I'm sure you'll agree. I could not believe my own mouth had betrayed me so. We agreed on tea and the interview began:

VG How do you do?
MA I must say, it's a great pleasure to be on this show. I

often listen to it while I'm in the kitchen of an evening.

VG Dear, dear. I think of you not as doing domestic chores, but slaving away at the typewriter. But in fact you begin work in longhand, don't you?

MA I do, yes. I slave over the old pen.

VG Do you have a big lump on your finger?

MA I still have that big lump.

VG I say, it is cheery news that *The Handmaid's Tale* is doing so well, as opposed to the less than cheery news you discuss in your cautionary tale.

MA On the other hand, it's not all raving morbid invention on the part of the author. It's right out of the news-papers. All I did was gather together some elements that are now a little bit dispersed in space and time and put them in together.

VG Did you keep a scrapbook of pertinent items?

MA I did keep a scrapbook while I was writing the book. In fact just this morning, lo and behold, there is an article on a group that wanted to overthrow the United States government and set up a religious dictatorship. And strangely enough, all the people that you would now consider to be the Moral Majority would probably be eliminated by the regime I depict in the book. They'd probably stick at the polygamy, for one thing. For another, any group that is out for power and takes over a government is going to want to eliminate the compe-tition. You know, get rid of competing sects.

VG Which is almost everybody.

MA Yeah, that's right. And that has always been true, when you think of the great social upheavals like the French Revolution. A lot of guys who got their heads chopped off were originally initiators of the revolution. There is always some sort of purge. So I figure Jerry Falwell would probably be strung up by his regime, as would anybody else heading any kind of religious organiza-tion that presented an alternate power source. They certainly wouldn't like the polygamy. And anyway, *my* regime wants to utilize all fertile women and that would include some nuns, so they'd hi-ho off to the nunneries and get the nuns out.

VG That would exclude us, mercifully.

MA Why, because we'd be too old?

VG Yeah, well, I've had those parts thrown out.

MA Well, I am afraid you'd go off to the colonies to clean up the radioactive spillage.

VG Well, not for long.

MA Not for long because you wouldn't last long there, but that is what would become of *you*.

VG You have covered all the bases.

MA You could always be an Aunt, one of the women in charge of the other women [Breeders]. They are allowed certain perks. You could be that. I'd opt for that if I were you.

VG I don't want to be a Martha, that is for sure. You really must have had a swell time naming the groups within the group.

MA I did. I chose Marthas, they are the ones that get the food and bustle about the household, from the New Testament, the story of Martha and Mary.

VG Now, the story that unfolds seems to have taken place in that area in and around Harvard. Canada seems to have escaped the whole thing. Britain seems to be the last bastion. God knows, you haven't told me what happens to Europe.

MA No, I don't tell what happens in Europe. I fudge on that one, don't I? We can't put in everything. Canada, as you know, is always less extreme than the U.S. in its trendiness or lack thereof. And you know what people say about politics here, that you have to seize the extreme centre in order to succeed in Canada. So Canadians do not all rush to embrace this new faith. Canada is fifty percent Catholic, unlike the United States, so you have a lot more elimination to do if you were going to go about eliminating people. You'd have to kill fifty percent of the people. So it was for those reasons and also for the reason that extremes like this seem to happen there first. I had Canada take its traditional role, namely as the place where people escape *to*. It was the top of the Underground Railroad, as we know, and in this book it's the top of the underground *female road*.

VG Well, I did laugh when I saw that.

MA They are smuggled out and the Quakers help them.

There are a lot of groups in opposition to this regime.

VG I wonder what people at *MS* magazine make of this scenario?

MA They bite their fingernails down to the nubs. In fact, women in the United States tend to find this more chilling and more possible and closer to them than women in Canada do, for obvious reasons.

VG When I was in England recently, and was talking to Doris Lessing—bit of a name-dropper, me—she was very concerned that people are taking their freedom for granted, perhaps especially in Canada, where we might feel too safe. Particularly you and I, who missed the Second World War.

MA Well, I don't know about you, Vicki, but I didn't miss it.

VG Oh, sorry. It's just that you look twenty-eight.

MA Oh, sure.

VG But you were just a child?

MA I was a child, but I remember perfectly well the black-outs, the air-raid sirens, Winston Churchill on the radio. Children's games then were very concerned with the war. It was "Burn the Nazis," and I had an older brother, so he was playing war games all the time, collecting airplane cards. You probably don't remember airplane cards.

VG I do remember seeing ration cards. However, they were in my grandmother's trunk.

MA Well, we actually had ration tickets. In fact, a friend my age got into terrible trouble once when he glued all the ration tickets out of his mother's ration book onto the kitchen wall. So that is how childhood memory is made.

VG But don't you think that Canadians especially, because no battle has been fought on our land in living memory, ought to keep vigil, with the notion that things can go quickly—very quickly, overnight in fact?

MA Yes, they can go overnight and they go literally over-night in my book because I postulate that we do away with liquid cash. We get into a situation where dollar bills are antiques and we paste them in our scrapbooks. Everything is done on computers and on credit. When you get into that kind of situation, any power group that gets hold of the apparatus can, of course, freeze the assets of any group at any time, making it impossible to get the next plane out. And there you are. You can't buy anything.

VG You go to the bank machine and it won't cough up. And you can't beat a machine over the head.

MA You cannot.

VG You wrote part of this book in England? When? Where were you?

MA I was in England, let's see now, from about September to March. It must have been in 1983 and 1984. I was working on another book, but the other book didn't work out. So I wrote this book because I didn't want to finish a book that wasn't working. I had my first chilblains there, didn't even know what they were at first. My toes swelled up.

VG Charming. How did it happen?

MA I was working—see, I had two houses in this Norfolk village in winter, which was off-season, and that was how I was able to do this. One of them was a large haunted house, where we lived, and the other was a small fisherman's cottage—an ex-fisherman—and that is where I wrote. The fisherman's cottage had stone floors, so I would sit there all day with my feet on the floor, typing away, and they would get cold without me noticing. I would then go back to the large haunted house, which had coal fireplaces, and put my feet up.

VG You can't do that.

MA Obviously not.

VG You can't say haunted twice and get away with it.

MA No, no, I can't.

VG Any spectres?

MA No. But we heard lots of stories about them. Locals said that in our house there were some nuns in the upstairs passage, because it was a very old house, dating back to the thirteenth century. It was called the friary because it used to be the hospital unit of the White Friars. So we had nuns in the upstairs passage and we had a jolly cavalier who stood by the dining-room door and we had a headless woman in the kitchen.

VG But you saw nothing?

MA No, I didn't. But I said to the man who owned the

house, a nice Anglican clergyman, "What about these ghosts?" He said, "Ha, ha, ha, ghosts." Then he said, "Seen any?" He discounted the headless woman. He said the only person who'd ever seen her was an American woman over there in search of her roots.

VG Maybe she was drinking the vanilla extract. Well, I'd love to see one. Show me a ghost, show me a UFO, I am prepared to be convinced by anything.

MA Maybe you don't have a receptive mind, Vicki.

VG Well, maybe you don't either. I guess that's it. You'd think that you would.

MA There was a jolly cavalier standing by the dining-room door once and it turned out to be a man who had wandered in from a nearby inn and was looking for the bar.

VG Did you give him a drink, poor lad?

MA No, alas, we just said, "It's not in here."

VG What about your child? She had to go to school.

MA She went to the local school and she picked up the accent in three weeks and then she started correcting ours.

VG Oh, nice.

MA And correcting also our vocabulary and worrying about the way her daddy dressed. The other daddies don't dress like that.

VG What about the driving? Did you have a car?

MA We bought a second-hand car, which lasted about one month, and then we bought another one. But they were both on their last legs.

VG But don't you plummet into things, what with the left hand drive?

MA Well, I don't drive a car there because I know I would crash into something.

VG Why did you go there, anyway?

MA It is a lot easier for me to write when I'm not in Canada. We wanted to find a place that was isolated and where there was frankly not a lot else to do, so that we would then *have* to write these books.

VG Do you have to gear down when you come from Toronto or Harvard or Berlin?

MA I became quite sluggish in fact.

VG How can this be?

MA I have a hidden sluggishness about me.

VG What about Berlin?

MA I went to Berlin for three months. Berlin is where in fact I started this particular book, on a German typewriter, which has a different keyboard. But I have to look, so it doesn't matter much. I'm a four-finger typist. I once started learning to type. I got a book that said "Teach Yourself To Type" and I covered up the keys and went at it for a couple of days. I got blisters on my little fingers from doing asdf fgfgfgfgf. I decided that really I could do just as well the other way. And anyway, I couldn't afford the time.

VG You need to do it when you're fifteen and there is some woman up there barking at you.

MA We had those classes in my high school but people worried that if they took typing they would have to pluck their eyebrows and become typists for life. I took Home Economics. Not that it did me much good.

VG Not much of a cook, eh?

MA Well, my methods are different than the ones I learned in Home Ec.

VG Can you still make blancmange, though?

MA I could make blancmange at a pinch. I could also make stewed apples and Harvard beets.

VG Not a big call for Harvard beets.

MA They're not bad, actually. Meat loaf we learned. In fact, you may not believe this: I was one of the entrants in the Miss Consumer Gas Contest.

VG Hold me back.

MA Miss Homemaker, it was. I didn't win, but we made meat loaf and peas. We had to iron a shirt and I forget what else. Probably dusted or something.

VG Just like Brownies. Were you a Brownie?

MA Oh, I was.

VG Did you fly up to Guides and get your Golden Hand and all that stuff?

MA I got my Golden—what do you get next? Golden Bar?

VG The Golden Handshake is what I got. I actually failed in my first attempt. Do you remember making blanc-mange with fruit, and sock-folding?

MA How could you have failed socks, really.

VG I don't know. But I failed. My mother was quite puzzled.

MA What did you do wrong? You had them inside out, or what?

VG I guess I tried to do it too quickly. I tried to throw everything in the suitcase. I just flung the stuff in. But I'll bet you have never failed anything, have you?

MA Let's see. I once failed—I once *almost* failed algebra. It was pretty close.

VG Yeah, well, almost is not as close as I was. Do you want to play a piece of music here? Algebra to Offenbach.

MA It all fits, I'll tell you. This particular song, which is the barcarole from *The Tales Of Hoffman*, was one of the songs we used in one of my first pieces of writing. It was, in fact, a Home Economics opera. It was a ploy to get out of making stuffed animals, as I recall, because we were allowed to do a special project and we could vote on it. You know, one of the hazards of democracy. So we did and I diverted the whole class and got them to vote for this Home Ec. opera. We then wrote, designed, and produced it. It had to be on a Home Economics subject, which it was. It was all about three fabrics called Orlon, Nylon, and Dacron, who lived in a castle with their father, Old King Coal. C-O-A-L, get it? Because they are all derivatives.

VG Does she ever stop?

MA Never. And the plot interest was when Sir William Willey came along, and he had a terrible problem in that he shrank from washing. And the resolution was that he married Orlon and produced a new synthetic blend. This particular tune that we will play now was the one that we used for one of the songs. And the words went something like: "Fabrics need a swim in the suds, makes them feel like new." And when you hear this tune, that is what I want you to think of.

VG I shall.

MA During the last bit we held up the nicely washed socks, speaking of socks.

VG Did the teacher go mad with delight?

MA I don't think so. I think she went mad with bemusement. But since it was a democratic vote, she had to go through with it.

VG It occurs to me, although it's perhaps wishful thinking, that you could write a dandy gothic novel.

MA Let me put it to you this way, Vicki. How do you know I haven't?

VG Next question.

MA Should I say I'm not going to tell you?

VG Lie to me, mama.

MA In fact, I haven't.

VG This leads me to believe you could be lying.

MA I could be. Yes. Well, it's like politics, you know. You just *never* know.

VG Do you still paint a bit?

MA I do. I paint rather primitively with watercolours. I used to be a poster designer. It was one of my other careers. But it was my own little business in the basement. I designed and printed them. It was better than working in Kresge's.

VG You didn't work at Kresge's, did you?

MA No, but I would have had to if I hadn't done the posters.

VG But you have had some basic jobs?

MA Oh yes, very basic. I was a waitress and also a cashier. I found out afterwards that they had hired me because I was inept. They wanted to see whether their confidential professional cashier had been fiddling the take, by hiring somebody so inept that they didn't know how to cheat them. So my memory of being a cashier is that of a line of irate lunch eaters, waiting for me to try and figure out the machine.

VG How long did that job last?

MA About one month.

VG Well, that's pretty good.

MA Yes. But I got hit with a Shriner's convention in the hotel. That was where I was the waitress and the cashier and running the soda fountain, too. And I think that is what did me in.

VG They haven't forgotten you yet, I'll bet.

The day Jack Webster came for his interview, I was in a tizzy. He had requested a bottle of single-malt scotch, just in case things got a little dull. There was at the time a strike in British Columbia and all the liquor stores were closed. A friend of mine who was returning from Toronto that very day was asked to pick up a bottle of Glenlivet so as to keep the dear boy happy. When Webster arrived at the studio he was astounded to discover that the single malt had been secured. "Never drink on the air, myself," said he. However, this time he made an exception. The clinking of ice-cubes throughout the interview gave it a rather melodic tone, to say nothing of the melody that streams from Webster himself. His delivery is machine-gun precise and laced with colourful turns of phrase. The man is a Scot, by God.

The interview started with his first music choice, the theme from the movie *The Sting*.

JW   I didn't want you to start with "The Entertainer."

VG   You didn't?

JW   No, but I love it dearly. I've seen the movie ten times and when I finally got a car—I'm not a status-symbol person—with a little cassette in it, I bought the music from *The Sting*. If I could do anything in my life again, I'd learn to play the piano and play Scott Joplin.

VG   I never thought the day would come when I would be interviewing you.

JW   Oh, you used to come and watch me when I was on the air. That is where you learned what skills you have.

VG   Oh, you are getting me all confused. What I meant to continue with is that poor old Scott Joplin, who never made much of a cent from that song, would have been surprised to discover that Marvin Hamlisch made a small fortune and it made him famous.

JW   Oh, don't get me discussing music. I'm not here to discuss music. I gave you a couple of suggestions for my favourite noises, but I don't want to talk about it.

VG   Well, you have to talk about your music. That is how we learn and understand the very nature of your soul.

JW   All right. I'll talk about music. When I was a boy in Scotland, in a good working-class family, on every holiday, like Hogmanay [New Year's eve], family birthdays, every occasion for a party, we all used to gather at my grandfather's house. My grandfather was an old ham, a

wonderful old ham. And in those days every child had
to do his turn. Do you know what a turn is?

VG His little party piece?

JW His little party piece.

VG What was yours?

JW Oh. My brother's party piece was much better. I hated
my brother for that reason.

> I had a little motor car.
> I paid an awful price for it,
> An awful price for me.
> It was not a big one, I'll allow
> But it was beautiful to look upon.
> Had I only purchased it to look upon,
> It would have been a great success indeed.

And that was his party piece.

VG And what was yours, pray?

JW My party piece was standing on a stool, with my wee
fat chubby knees showing from my short trousers, singing:

> Wi' a hundred pipers an' all, an' all
> A hundred pipers an' all, an' all
> Wi' a hundred pipers an' all, an' all
> We'll up an' give 'em a blow, a blow.

VG Well, it's a good thing you didn't take up singing. Were
you any good in school? Were you a clever boy?

JW For a quick botch job I had no equal. I was slippery,
very good at mental arithmetic. Tended to cheat on
occasion—little notes up the sleeve and this kind of
thing.

VG Did you ever get caught?

JW No, of course not. Good cheats never get caught.

VG I never did get caught. But I would write things on the
bottom of my running shoes and then that question,
the answer to which I had scribbled, would never come
up.

JW The very fact that you were prepared to cheat, even if
you didn't, put you on the top line for your examina-
tion. When I think back to my school days, there were
about sixty kids in the class and maybe twenty of them
would be refugees from somewhere else—Poland, Lith-
uania, Latvia, Russia. We had this brutal system of the

top of the class and the bottom of the class. If you were smart you were in the back row; if you were not so smart you were in the second row, and if you were a poor wee dolt, you were put in the front row. And the poor wee dolts in the front row never had a chance.

VG Were they abused, you mean?

JW No, they were ignored.

VG Your children have all turned out well.

JW Children, when exposed to a properly Presbyterian disciplinary fashion, adopt the mores set down by the good Lord as dictated in the James I version of the United Free Church of Scotland. I bet you didn't think I was religious and I don't suppose I am, but I wake at night sometimes hearing the schoolmaster say to me, "What is man's chief end?" I'm quite serious about this. And it comes to me, "Man's chief end is to glorify God and to enjoy Him forever more. Amen."

VG You would say that on command.

JW Oh, yes.

VG One of your first jobs was on the *Daily Graphic*, was it? You've referred to it as the world's worst newspaper.

JW The *Daily Sketch*—it became the *Graphic*. It was the plaything of Lady Kemsley and it was one of my first jobs after the war. I was a night news editor and the chief reporter, I think you would call it here, of Lady Kemsley's plaything.

VG If you'll pardon the expression.

JW Listen. Is this a grown-up programme?

VG It is.

JW True story. I was night news editor and a fellow called Jerry Cook was a picture editor. In those days we were very big on animals as well as society women. We had a centre spread—and we saw the page proof—of this magnificent Aberdeen Angus bull that was being exported to the United States at the end of 1946 for something like £50,000. Lady Kemsley walked through the newsroom. She saw the page proof of the side view of this magnificent animal, which was being sold for the purpose of breeding. She turned to Cook and said, "That is a rude picture. Kindly clean up the picture." And Cook said, "Ma'am, it's a bull, your ladyship. I can't clean up the picture." She said, "Clean up that picture." So he airbrushed the picture. Later the paper paid damages to the farmer because we had depicted a bull that was not a bull.

VG You have said that that paper was the worst, but you have also said that about the Vancouver *Province*. Which is it?

JW You can't compare scales of worseness between Vancouver and London. But I remember the good old days in Vancouver.

VG So do I.

JW No, you don't. You're not old enough.

VG Yes, I do.

JW How many papers were there?

VG The *News Herald*, the *Province*, the *Sun*, the short-lived *Times*—

JW Well, I am talking about the days when the *Sun* was in direct competition with the *Province*. Head-to-head news competition. Competition is the breath of life in news gathering, as it is in selling peanuts. Without competition there is no energy, there is no spur to do the thing. Then, of course, they carved up the town. Dear Roy Thomson [Lord Thomson of Fleet] came in and sold the *Sun* to the owners of the *Province*, and the *Sun* and the *Province* shared the market. The *Province* went morning and the *Sun* went afternoon and things have never been the same again. I don't see any great future for newspapers in this country, whatsoever.

VG Since your arrival in Vancouver from Britain you have lived here and seemingly have never been tempted to move to Toronto, except to do "Front Page Challenge."

JW Well, sometimes those offers were useful for bargaining purposes. An offer from CHUM or somebody in the east would come and I would say, "Hey, I don't want to have to go."

VG And then you would up the price.

JW Yes.

VG They really begged you, didn't they, offering almost anything?

JW Yes. But the smartest thing I ever did was not to go to the CBC.

VG Is that so. Well, I for one would be starving to death.

JW Well, I am sure you'd make a living somewhere or other if you lost your job. But for my particular line of bloody-minded independent action, I've got to be my own boss. I've just got to be.

VG You write your own rules?

JW Yes. And I am lucky that I've been able to and I realize that not everybody can write their own rules. Mind you, loud though I may be, and one shouldn't make public confessions, I am safe within the outer limits of the establishment.

VG You bet.

JW God. Somebody gave me a LL D. last year. I was really nervous about that because I didn't know whether to take it or tell them to keep it.

VG You took it?

JW And I am grateful for it.

VG So now you are Dr Webster.

JW If you please.

At this point it was time to play another piece of music, the Gatlin Brothers with "Midnight Choir."

JW I love this one. I just love it. It is highly irreverent and it's got a bad moral tone, the whole thing. It suits my twisted sense of humour.

VG You have had dinner with the queen.

JW I was the perfect gentleman. I outshone myself.

VG I understand that you waved to the assembled crowd, à la monarch.

JW Listen, I got a great hand when I went on board ship.

VG Was it the first time you had ever met the queen?

JW It was the first time I'd met Her Majesty. I had met Philip before, a number of years ago in Vancouver. I asked him the first question at the press conference and he looked at me—he seemed much taller in those days—and he said, "Oh, yes, I've been warned about you."

VG What was the question? Do you remember?

JW Something about royal money. There was a big fight at the time about royal money. It's got to be topical.

VG You do a television show daily now, but for years you did an open-line radio show. Why has that kind of show never really worked very well other than in Vancouver?

JW Well, it worked in Montreal with Pat Burns, but they haven't got the people in Toronto. They have never had anybody to do a good talk show. Never ever. But I have managed to survive in talk shows because I never forgot that my basic function was as a reporter. You've got to have a person on the air who knows what is going on in the province or is prepared to admit he doesn't know and find out on the air. I think talk shows have replaced newspapers as an information medium and most of it is quite sound. I won't take any trash. I still think that a bad talk show is better than no talk show.

VG The complaint being that people with precious little information are allowed to rattle on.

JW Not if you're running the right talk show. Just the other day, I had a call about a strike. A guy comes on and makes a perfectly abhorrent remark, saying the way to solve the problems in B.C. is with violence. WHAM, WHAM—gone. I don't need to hear it. Cut him off.

VG You have a seven-second delay.

JW I have one but you don't need a seven-second delay. You can almost tell by instinct if someone is going to be either libellous or obscene or stupid. The way you run a talk show is by tone of voice, and this is a non-sexist assessment. This is quite brutal. When I got complaints to the CRTC, as I used to all the time, from people who'd say, "Webster won't let me on the show," my response, and it was accepted, was that I am in the same position as somebody preparing an edited show for later rebroadcast. I must edit it as I go because my intention is to attract as many people as possible and not let some loud-mouthed hog take over.

VG You have brought a clip.

JW This is from CKNW. I hate to tell you how many years ago this was. This tape was recaptured from a very slow speed and we've tried to bring up the quality. It is entitled "Fifty-five Barber Green Road."

(Actually, Barber Green is Barber *Greene* Road, but neither Jack nor the caller knew that.)

Caller Is this Mr Webster?

JW Yes, Madam.

C I was told that you might help me find an address of the—I think you were interviewing Mr Charlie Hunter, were you not? The editor of Longman's Publishing Company?

JW I am at this very moment. Mr Curley Hunter.

C Oh, Curley Hunter.

JW They call him Curley Hunter because he's as bald as a coot.

C Send him my—oh, that's funny.

JW Well, aren't you listening to the radio, ma'am?

C I want to know—

JW Aren't you listening to the radio?

C Yes.

JW You are, are you?

C Yes. Well, my friend told me to call you because I wanted to get this number of Charley Hunter.

JW Curley Hunter, ma'am. He's as bald as a coot. Fifty-five Barber Green Road. Funnily enough, Barber Green Road. He hasn't been to a barber in years. Fifty-five Barber Green Road, Don Mills, Ontario.

C That's the address?

JW Yes, ma'am.

C How do you spell that?

JW Barber, as in hairdresser.

C Oh, Barber?

JW Yes, Barber. I can't say it the way you do, ma'am.

C Oh.

JW My glottal stops are too prominent.

C Oh, Barber?

JW Green Road.

C How do you spell that? Green?

JW Yes, as in pink. Green.

C G-R-double-E-N.

JW Yes, ma'am.

C Is that the road?

JW That's the road.

C That's the address.

JW Yes, madam.

C What a strange address.

JW Isn't it? He's a strange man.

C And what is Barber?

JW   That's the name of the road.

C   Oh, Barber Green Road?

JW   Yes, ma'am.

C   Oh. Oh, that's the road? Oh.

JW   Yes. Of course it is.

C   Oh, what a long name.

JW   Yes, isn't it?

C   And he's bald?

JW   Oh, bald as a coot.

C   Tell me again, how do you spell that name?

JW   Curley Hunter, Barber Green Road, Don Mills, Ontario.

C   Ontario?

JW   Don Mills.

C   What's Out Mills?

JW   Don—you know, when the sun comes up like thunder.

C   Yes. That's my name.

JW   That's Dawn. But son of Thunder, Don. D-O-N, as in Don Juan.

C   One?

JW   Don Mills. M-I-L-L-S as in flour.

C   Yes. Don Mills. Is that his name?

JW   No. That's the name of the town.

C   Oh, I'm awfully muddled, aren't I?

JW   You're delightful. You and I must do a comedy act on the stage sometime.

C   Oh, I have done that sometimes.

JW   You're pulling my leg, that's what you're doing.

C   Eh?

JW   You're pulling my leg.

C   No, I'm not.

JW   Okay. Let's start again.

C   Yes.

JW   Curley Hunter.

C   Charlie Hunter.

JW   Curley, Curley.

C   How do you spell that?

JW   C-U-R-L-E-Y. He's as bald as a coot.

C   Oh, I don't seem able to get that.

JW   Curley Hunter, fifty-five Barber Green Road, Don Mills, Ontario.

C   Oh my. Now I've got you.

JW That was more than twenty years ago.

VG It *is* a comedy routine. I can't help thinking that you don't sound much different today.

JW No, I don't, do I. But that was one of the treasured gems of one's broadcasting career. You can do all the magnificent things you like—come on in the morning, you're tough and you're reportorial and you're precise and all the rest of it. Then you walk down the street and people say, "When are you going to play 'Barber Green Road' again?" I must have played it fifty times. In fact we even did it on "Webster" [his T.V. show] at Christmas with little cartoons. It was very good indeed.

VG When I said you don't sound much different, you know I meant the accent.

JW Yes, well, there is no chopping it. I was too old when I came out here. I was twenty-eight, you see. Actually, when I go back to Scotland they treat me like a Yankee tourist.

VG Last summer I went to Glasgow and I went to the town of Uddingston to see my friend's sister. Her husband said to me, "Do you know a man in Canada, I think from Vancouver, who was on the television here? I think his name was Webster." Well, I just about fell on the floor. You had just done some T.V. show or other there.

JW That's true, that's true. There were three Webster boys, you see. Not just one Webster. Three. There was younger brother Drew [a London editor for United Newspapers] who is very la-de-dah and English and he's got his OBE. And then there was Sandy, my older brother. He is now departed. Departed in very good Webster style, as a matter of fact. He was also an editor. When he took over the *Sunday Mail* in Glasgow, he was a much rougher guy than I. I was quieter than Sandy. He took over the Sunday paper a number of years ago on condition that they get rid of everybody on the staff over thirty. He was then forty-five or forty-six, and he put the circulation up to just over eight hundred thousand, which is pretty good for the *Sunday Mail*. When he retired—the stinker—do you know what he did?

VG No.

JW After all the years of sneering at my radio work, he

started doing a radio talk show in Edinburgh.

VG Was he as good as you?

JW Not on your life was he as good as me.

VG Did you send him tapes so that he might know how to do it the proper way?

JW Oh, I did it with him a couple of times and tried to coach him, but he was still suffering from that U.K. thing.

VG Behave yourself on the radio?

JW Yes, the BBC syndrome.

VG There is a move to enliven Glasgow—

JW Best architecture in Britain, including Edinburgh.

VG I agree, but I was in Scotland for two weeks, and on not one tourist portfolio, on no train promotion—

JW —did it say Glasgow.

VG Right.

JW Annoys the hell out of me. It is just snobbery. You know, all these well-off people in Edinburgh—the cultural capital, so-called. But we have a saying about *them*. Edinburgh people, if they have no money, will always put on a show. So we in Glasgow say about all the fancy Edinburgh women, "They all wear fur coats but they've got nae drawers!" Is that too rude?

VG No.

JW Adult programme.

VG May I ask you about the television show?

JW Funnily enough it has been a great success, but let me tell you this. Television is twenty times harder than radio.

VG That is what I thought.

JW Because radio—you know this—you can do virtually by yourself. I know that you've got all kinds of people who prance around and call themselves executive producers and what-not, but you're the performer. You're there. You're alone. No matter what they give you. It lives and dies on you. But on television you must conform and you must have producers and you must have the graphics people. And you've got to be all dressed up. You've got to shave and you've got to be bright. You can't have more than two drinks at night. You can never get a night off when you're on the air the next day.

VG True enough. And the audience can see how rotten you look.

JW Oh, yes. And Pamela, my little make-up girl—

VG You can't say that any more, Jack.

JW Was that a sexist remark?

VG I think so.

JW Well, Pamela, my, well—she is my make-up person— she looks at me and says, "I'll need extra white underneath your eyes this morning."

VG Are you nice to your staff?

JW Well, we have an understanding. I tell them once a week that I'm sorry if I shouted at you. By and large I'm nice. I get a bit hairy at times, you know.

VG Hairy?

JW Hairy. Unbalanced. Coming up to nine o'clock in the morning and you're looking for some clips and you don't know what the count is going to be or you're not sure a bit has been edited yet. One gets a little hairy. But I have a good working understanding, yes.

VG Do as I say, not as I do?

JW There is something in that, but I think that I am liked by my own immediate staff. I've got one order for persons—not allowed to say "women," am I?

VG Yes, you can say "women."

JW If you're going to cry, cry in the washroom.

VG Oh dear, sometimes you make them cry?

JW I never try to. No, I don't. Never.

VG You do something on television that no one else does. You look around. Everybody on T.V. who is in a host position peers at the guest and pretends not to look at the countdown, but you look around. You shout at the camera operator.

JW That's right. And if I want to know something from Mark, who is sitting nearby, or Steve or Pat or Liz or Linda, on-camera I will say, "Hey, what was that?" and then they answer.

VG No one else does that.

JW You've got to be natural.

VG You are. Do you miss the radio?

JW I miss the lovely informality. I used to be able to come in in the morning, when I did the show from the

Georgia Hotel or in the other place in Gastown, and have my coffee at half past seven. At eight o'clock the police would drop in to see me. Lawyers would drop in and visit. I wore an old golf shirt sometimes. If guests didn't appear, I'd find some molehill and build it into a mountain by noon. But then, you've got so much more direct-tip information on radio. But you can still follow stories. You can still do interviews. I've done Trudeau as much on radio as I've done on television.

VG Do you like him?

JW Oh, you can't dislike the man as a performer. He is the one person for whom I've got to get up early in the morning, and my stomach's going around in circles and I'm working out every possible computation of what he is going to throw in my teeth. He is the toughest by far.

VG If you miss the radio, do you miss the paper?

JW Well I did walk into the *Sun* in its heyday. What a bunch of characters, the likes of which do not exist any more. Hal Straight was a magnificent newspaper editor. He always said to me, "If you know it, write it. I'll back you." Hymie Koshevoy, the man with the greatest collection of puns in the world—

VG *Treasure Jest of Golden Puns.*

JW Pierre Berton had just left. Thank God—I got his job. Jack Scott, the incomparable Jack Scott. Those were the days when reporters carried .45s on their hips. You know, I can think of a couple of reporters who carried .45s when they were covering the police beat. Crazy reporters who had sirens on their hoods. And we did something in those days that is not done now, we covered the courts. The only courts we cover now—and I'm talking about the news business in western Canada and across the country, really—the only things we cover now are the big stories. The Olson cases, the big murders, the big this, the big that. Whereas the police courts in a major city are one of the best reflections of the social problems of the town. Were I to be back in my heyday as a city editor again, I would cover those courts, because courts are where corruption shows its ugly head. If we don't keep an eye on the judges, nobody keeps an eye on the judges. I'm not saying that there is anything wrong with judges, but judges are like the rest of us. Let us operate behind closed doors and we won't be on our best behaviour.

VG Why is it that you have never been part of an administration?

JW Me? Ooooh—don't be stupid. I'm a maverick. An independent is of no consequence in the political scheme of things. You must understand that you must be a part of the group that accepts the policy and accepts the whip. Unless you accept the whip, you're useless. There is no place for mavericks. In other words, my political principles change according to the time of day and year that I am facing.

VG It is not as if you haven't been asked.

JW Two people have asked me to run very seriously. I don't know, I shouldn't say.

VG Oh, come—the Liberals for sure.

JW No, no.

VG They've never asked you?

JW Oh, yes, the Liberals have. So have the Tories. So have the Socreds. But on one occasion I said jokingly to a famous political party leader in British Columbia—if any British Columbians are famous across this fractured nation—when he asked I said, "Yeah, but give me a written guarantee you'll make me attorney general, then I'll run for you."

VG What did they do? Gag?

JW They gagged. That was that. But I have an abiding interest, as what we used to call a barrack-room lawyer.

VG One day you and I had occasion to share a cab and you quizzed the cab driver, as usual. You spoke to him in Arabic. You speak Arabic.

JW Mmmm. I'm very big in Arabic.

VG The war?

JW Yeah, learned it in the army. [He speaks in Arabic.] That means "How are you? If you are happy, I am twice blessed by God." I spent a long time in Israel and Palestine and Khartoum and Central Africa and the western desert.

VG You need two lives. You need another one hundred years.

JW I could think of three or four lives. But about language, I've always had a great ear. I'm ashamed of myself for not pursuing languages. A little bit of French, a little bit of Hungarian. [He speaks in Hungarian.]

VG What did you say?

JW I believe in a free Hungary.

VG But it all has a Scots accent.

JW No, no, no—*Scotch*. It's because of the gutterals.

VG Why do you say Scotch?

JW If Scotch was good enough for Robbie Burns, my patron saint, it's good enough for me.

VG Well, no one wants to get it wrong, you know.

JW Scotch is fine for the working class. Those with titles can be *Scottish* if they like. But I'm Scotch.

VG Are you going to write a book?

JW I am glad you've asked me that. When I read some of my colleagues' books, their anecdotal memoirs in which they retell their rather dull upbringings, and tell stories that they didn't have the guts enough to print when they were working in the media, it makes me pause and give second thought. It is very difficult to remember what happened yesterday and you can't tell the truth in a book. How can you tell the truth?

VG Isn't this just the country for writers? Have you ever had so many Canadian books come across on your desk as in the last couple of years?

JW Yes. And I just hate them.

VG You hate them all?

JW Yes, most of them. Except for the naturals like Don Cherry.

VG You two together are the funniest thing.

JW That's right. In his funny, old-fashioned, pimpish-type suits and the fancy collars. He is a great guy.

VG You're a great guy. Thank you very much.

JW Are we finished?

VG Yup.

Index of Names